Indian Rolling Stock in HO Scale
by Glyn Thomas BSc(Hons), MBA, MBCS, CITP

Edited by Julian Rainbow

Design and typesetting by .... Glyn Thomas
Published by....................................IngramSpark
Printed by ....IngramSpark

ISBN 979-8-218-03652-2

About the Author

Glyn Thomas was born in London, England to South African parents.

Glyn's family has long connections with British colonial railways - his great-grandfather, Henry Norman Thomas, worked for Babcock and Wilcox building the Manx Electric Railway on the Isle of Man. Henry eventually moved to South Africa to setup the Durban tramway system, and he became General Manager of Transport for Durban Corporation.

Growing up too late to see the end of mainline steam on railways at home in Britain, Glyn travelled extensively in the 1980s and 1990s visiting railways around the world that continued to use steam, either in accompanied groups or independently. He first visited India in 1982 with a Warwickshire Railway Society trip, and made subsequent independent visits in 1989 and 2010.

Glyn is a keen modeller with interests in railways around the world. In the 1990s he built an Indian-themed HO-scale layout, but needed to abandon it due to a job move to the USA. More recently, he has modelled US railroads. Photos of his layouts have appeared in Model Railroader, and he has had articles published in Continental Modeller, Model Railroad Craftsman, and NMRA magazine. He is a National Model Railroad Association's Master Model Railroader.

Steam Locomotives Book

Glyn's first book, *Indian Steam Locomotives in HO Scale,* was published by the British Overseas Railways Historical Trust in 2021 and is still available through them (website: borht.org.uk). British Overseas Railways Historical Trust has the following aims:

- To promote the study of the history of railways in the Commonwealth (excluding the UK).

- To promote the study of the British contribution to railways in other parts of the world.

- To locate and preserve any existing archive material and to make it available to researchers and historians.

- To establish a museum to tell the story of Britain's remarkable contribution in giving railways to the world, which will contain a representative collection of export locomotives and rolling stock.

- To create a library of relevant publications.

- To work with other groups with similar aims.

ROLLING STOCK

Estimates and Specifications supplied immediately upon receipt of request giving requisite particulars.

Burn & Co., Ltd.,

RAILWAY ENGINEERS AND CONTRACTORS,

BUILDERS OF

Railway Carriages, Wagons, Underframes and Bogies

MAKERS OF POINTS AND CROSSINGS, TROLLEYS, Etc.

HOWRAH, BENGAL.

Burn and Co. Ltd. advert from 1909 showing an early example of domestic coach construction

Contents

Contents

Introduction

Allahabad Station showing a variety of rolling stock; the foreground wagons are ABR 4-wheel vans [Julian Rainbow Collection]

This book is intended as a companion to "Indian Steam Locomotives in HO Scale", providing information on the equipment that those locomotives were likely to haul over their lifetime. The earlier volume covers steam locomotives built from 1900 onwards, several of which survived into the 1990s - this book covers coaches and wagons that ran during the same period. By the nature of its subject, this volume is more superficial than its predecessor because there were huge numbers of coaches and wagons in operation throughout the period in question (see tables in the following sections for numbers), and reference material is scarce. There is less material on the history and organization of Indian railways in this volume, because they were covered in the locomotive book.

By 1900, the major railway companies of the colonial era were in place. Most were owned by the Government of India, usually operated by remnants of the original private companies. Most of the remaining private guarantee companies were nationalised on a similar basis within the first 20 years of the 20th Century. A few railways, most notably Nizam's Guaranteed State Railway, were owned and operated by Princely States.

Unlike locomotives, there was large scale domestic fabrication of rolling stock at the railway company workshops and some private manufacturers during the colonial era using underframes and other parts shipped from Britain. It is likely that the larger railway workshops, which started to appear at the end of the 19th Century, were capable of producing coaches and wagons in their entirety but this did not happen in significant numbers during the colonial period.

Following Independence in 1947 ownership and operations of nearly all railways, including those of the Princely States, were taken over by the government. In 1951-52 the railways were organised into an initial version of the current Indian Railway zonal system.

The Indian Government has been steadfast in promoting a domestic railway manufacturing industry. In 1952, the Integral Coach Factory (ICF) was established in Chennai and dominated coach production through the remainder of the 20th Century. By 2015, ICF had built over 50,000 coaches for Indian Railways. For freight stock, the Bengal Nagpur Railway's Kharagpur workshop stepped up wagon production in the Independence era. In 1963, a new factory was opened at Raipur for the production of freight wagons. A number of private wagon manufacturers have also emerged in independent India.

In 2013, Indian Railways opened the Modern Coach Factory at Raebareli to build a new generation of coaches based on the Linke-Hoffmann-Busch (LHB) design that was introduced in 1995. The factory has capacity for 1,000 coaches per year, so it will have an increasing influence on the railway scene.

Coaches

Coaches at Kalka, October 22nd, 1994 [John Tolson, Transport Treasury, JMT13274]

It is an unfortunate aspect of the study of coaching stock that it is here that the inequalities of the colonial hierarchies are most apparent. The early promoters of Indian railways were unsure how popular passenger traffic was likely to be, and they were entirely unprepared for the almost immediate uptake of train travel among the general Indian population. The railways were sent scrambling for a means of accommodating large numbers of passengers at the lowest fares. As a result, while first class travel was luxurious, third class travel was very rudimentary. There was even a brief experiment with fourth class travel (without seats!), which was thankfully abandoned. 19th Century pilgrim trains were known to use converted goods vans.

In 1885, an "Inter" (intermediate) class was introduced between second and third class. During the colonial era, first class travel was used almost exclusively by rich or administratively powerful Europeans and second class was generally used by Europeans and Eurasians. Inter class was intended for richer domestic travellers. In 1955, luxury first class was eliminated, and the older second class became first, while intermediate became second class. Finally, in 1976, third class was eliminated and third-class coaches converted to second class.

Photographs show that the earliest Indian trains largely followed British practice, with four-wheel carriages - open for third class, and enclosed for second and first class. Relatively early on, sunshades made of wooden slats held proud of the tops of the windows were adopted to reduce coach interior temperatures in summer heat. It is possible that India was the first British colony to introduce this innovation, and it rapidly spread across the British Empire to other hot countries. In some cases, double layer roofs, open at the ends, were also used to provide a cooling airflow.

Bogie carriages started to appear for all classes at the turn of the 20th Century. Initially, these also were provided with sunshades. From about 1906, improvements in side insulation permitted designs without sunshades, and these externally resembled British panelled wood coaching stock of the same period.

The numbers of coaches on the major colonial era railways are shown in the table below.

Company	Gauge	Year				
		1900	1910	1920	1930	1940
ABR	MG	175	285	471	616	763
BBCIR	BG	556	677	933	833	977
	MG	1,689	1,511	1,578	1,612	1,449
	NG	0	51	122	66	74
BNR	All	569	1,095	1,491	1,430	1,390

Coaches

Company	Gauge	Year				
		1900	1910	1920	1930	1940
BNWR	All	795	1,068	1,079	1,492	1,503
EBR	BG	514	730	893	962	1,053
	MG	611	785	1,005	1,013	1,026
	NG	32	56	67	62	56
EIR	All	1,996	2,183	2,389	3,585	3,027
GIPR	BG	1,754	1,978	2,373	2,171	1,737
	Others	0	113	41	not recorded	50
MSMR	BG	1,143	705	883	945	773
	MG	950	1,157	1,195	993	826
NWR	BG	2,317	2,768	3,315	3,684	3,201
	Others	0	159	286	305	282
ORR*	All	802	880	1,109		
SIR	BG	0	306	364	358	436
	MG	981	1,171	1,479	1,356	1,435
	NG	0	21	35	23	34
Total	All	14,884	17,699	21,108	21,506	20,092

* Merged in to EIR in 1925

The vast majority of passengers on Indian railways travel as economically as possible, meaning third class until 1976 and second class since then. The following table shows passenger growth over the period covered, based on the Administration Report for Indian Railways and Indian Government statistics. In 2017, 8,116M passengers were carried.

Year	1900	1910	1920	1930	1939	1950	1960	1970	1980	1990	2000
Passengers	176M	~375M	559M	573M*	530M	1,284M	1,594M	2,431M	3,613M	3,858M	4,833M

* down from a peak of 634M in 1929

The Indian enthusiasm for standardization was applied to rolling stock in a similar way to locomotives. As with locomotives, there were major benefits of using interchangeable parts that were mainly imported from Britain. Furthermore, coaches and wagons were generally ordered in bulk by the Government of India, and then distributed between the railways according to need. In 1925, an Indian Railways Standard (IRS) was developed for coach bogies and underframes. This appears to have been more successful than the locomotive equivalent, and some of the resulting coaches survived into the modern age.

All-steel coach fabrication first made an appearance on electric stock provided for the Bombay suburban network from 1928 onwards. From 1935, the Great Indian Peninsula Railway (GIPR) introduced all-steel coaches for mainline trains. These early GIPR coaches were reputed to suffer from severe corrosion in the Indian climate and had shortened lifetimes as a result. However, experience with this stock informed post-Independence design.

Heat and humidity have been issues for train travellers since the start of Indian railways. Various forms of cooling have been attempted. In 1871, the GIPR experimented with water evaporation cooling apparatus for first class coaches. Sunshades were the most common 19th Century solution. First class compartments were fitted with punkas, a baffle to move the air operated manually by a servant. In the 20th Century, punkas were replaced by electric fans and insulation reduced the need for sunshades. Modern air-conditioning (AC) was first used in 1936 on a few GIPR trains. A 1938 paper by the GIPR made the case for expanding the use of air-conditioning so that windows could be sealed to reduce drag at higher speeds - it was predicted that the reduced drag would offset the power requirements of AC above 45mph. However, AC cars did not see widespread use before the introduction of the LHB designs in the 1990s. AC versions of some ICF cars were made available before the LHB designs were introduced.

Freight Stock

EIR HGS 2-8-0 no. 1521 (William Beardmore and Co., 5245/1920) with a freight train [Historical Railway Images, Flickr]

Nineteenth century goods wagons closely followed contemporary British practice with wooden bodies and iron underframe components. The iron components were imported, while bodies were usually built locally because domestic carpentry skills were readily available.

While railways round the world experimented with iron wagons, it was only the advent of mass-produced structural steel components in the 1890s that pushed the cost-benefit equation in favour of steel wagons. Even so, steel wagons were adopted earlier in India than in Britain.

The early private companies competed aggressively and it was initially administratively difficult to interchange wagons between them. This became an increasing issue as the continent-wide rail network expanded. The Indian Railways Conference Association (IRCA) was founded in 1903 and tasked with improving cross-railway coordination. While the IRCA addressed many inter-operation issues, it was most influential in developing agreements for forwarding wagons between railways and developing the necessary freight rates.

In 1921, the influence of the IRCA extended to the development of standardised railway wagon designs and the introduction of a cross-railway pooling scheme. In the ensuing years, freight yards became increasingly homogenised with predominantly IRCA standard covered vans.

The table below shows the growth of wagon fleets during the colonial era.

Company	Gauge	Year				
		1900	**1910**	**1920**	**1930**	**1940**
ABR	**MG**	1,161	2,826	4,104	4,772	5,130
BBCIR	**BG**	4,710	7,272	9,751	10,306	9,647
	MG	7,051	8,700	8,954	9,467	8,777
	NG	0	257	639	291	336
BNR	**All**	4,141	12,683	17,385	24,746	24,292
BNWR	**All**	4,663	7,516	8,352	11,364	12,624
EBR	**BG**	2,013	5,309	7,637	8,242	8,410
	MG	2,815	4,148	5,017	5,421	5,317
	NG	109	181	84	87	21
EIR	**All**	14,408	24,239	36,320	48,899	50,155
GIPR	**BG**	7,871	14,808	18,886	18,000	18,284
	Others	0	977	802	786	825

Company	Gauge	Year				
		1900	1910	1920	1930	1940
MSMR	BG	4,153	4,330	4,862	5,637	5,886
	MG	4,714	6,131	6,610	7,510	6,547
NWR	BG	11,351	20,392	29,415	29,620	29,446
	Others	0	977	802	786	825
ORR*	All	4,391	6,494	8,205		
SIR	BG	0	1,543	1,739	1,777	2,280
	MG	3,300	4,054	4,311	5,540	4,727
	NG	0	48	78	78	78
Total	All	76,851	132,168	173,320	192,727	192,946

* Merged into EIR in 1925

See also the table in the Freight Traffic section for a breakdown of types in 2000.

In a mirror of locomotive practice, Indian Railway Standard designs for freight stock were introduced in 1925, superseding IRCA designs, but in most cases with only minor changes. A national Central Standards Office (CSO) was founded in 1930.

Post-Independence Indian Railways initially adopted a covered van standard that closely resembled its IRCA and IRS predecessors. However, by the 1960s IR engaged American consultants who emphasised the efficiency benefits of larger bogie wagons, and these were to overtake 4-wheeled stock in the latter half-century.

With the formation of Indian Railways, most of the functions of the IRCA were no longer required. Although allocated to railway zones, broad-gauge stock joined a nationwide pool and settlements between railways were no longer required. IRCA still exists with a role in tracking disposition of metre-gauge wagons. Most of the IRCA's technical functions were initially assumed by the Railway Technical Research Centre (RTRC), founded in 1952. Subsequently, the CSO and RTRC were combined into the Research Designs and Standards Organization (RDSO), founded in 1957.

India has adopted a number of American railroad technologies in recent years. The entire railway system is switching from older British-designed vacuum brakes to air brakes. Modern stock is also fitted with America-style knuckle couplers to replace older screw link couplers and buffers.

Recent years has also seen the nature of freight traffic changing. In common with other major railway systems around the world, there has been an increase in the use of very long bulk trains to carry commodities such as coal and oil, equipped with uniform wagons, to facilitate automated loading and unloading. There has also been a massive increase in the use of inter-modal traffic using shipping container, which are replacing the covered van or boxcar for transport of single car loads.

Carriage and Wagon Builders

Colonial-Era British Builders

In the second half of the 19th Century, a number of carriage and wagon manufacturers were established in Britain. The major British railways also built carriages and wagons in their own workshops, so the independent builders looked to export markets and colonial railways in particular for expansion.

The early 20th Century saw a gradual concentration of the industry through a series of mergers and acquisitions, leading to only three major builders that survived to the end of the colonial era. Brief historical notes on these major builders are included below.

The largest of the survivors was Metropolitan-Cammell Carriage and Wagon Co. Ltd.. This company traces its origin to the Metropolitan Railway Carriage and Wagon Ltd., established in Birmingham in 1863. This company became the Metropolitan Amalgamated Railway Carriage and Wagon Co. Ltd. in 1902 by merging with:

- Ashbury Railway Carriage and Iron Co. Ltd. (Manchester, founded 1837)
- Brown, Marshalls and Co. Ltd. (Saltley, Birmingham, founded 1840)
- Lancaster Railway Carriage and Wagon Co. Ltd. (Lancaster, founded 1863)
- Oldbury Railway Carriage and Wagon Co. Ltd. (Bromsgrove, founded 1859)

In 1926, the company was renamed to Metropolitan Carriage and Wagon and Finance Co. Ltd. and in 1929 it merged with the railway business of Cammell Laird and Co. (originated as Laird and Co., Birkenhead, mainly a shipbuilding business, founded in 1824) to become Metropolitan-Cammell Carriage and Wagon Co. Ltd. The business was eventually sold to GEC-Alstom in 1989 and stopped building rolling stock in the UK in 2005.

Carriage and Wagon Builders

By merging with Cammell Laird, Metropolitan-Cammell acquired the former carriage and wagon building business of Leeds Forge, founded in 1874 as Fox Brothers and Refits, later Samson Fox Brothers. This company was incorporated as New Leeds Forge Co. Ltd. in 1889, following acquisition of Leeds Forge Co., and later reverted to the earlier name. Leeds Forge was notable as the main producer of Sheffield-Twinberrow rolling stock, based on the concepts of James Denis Twinberrow (1866-1932) who was an influential advocate of increasing the capacity of rolling stock, especially on narrow gauge railways. McKerrow and Co. were Leeds Forge's agents in the eastern colonies. In 1920, Leeds Forge acquired Bristol Wagon and Carriage Co. (Lawrence Hill, Bristol, founded 1889); unfortunately Bristol Wagon and Carriage Co.'s records were destroyed during the Blitz. Cammell Laird took a controlling interest of Leeds Forge in 1923.

A late addition to the Metropolitan Cammell stable was the Midland Railway Carriage and Wagon Co. Ltd., which was founded in 1853 at Landor Street, Birmingham and moved to Washwood Heath in 1912. It was acquired by Metro-Cammell in 1932.

Birmingham Railway Carriage and Wagon Co. remained an independent builder throughout its existence. It was established 1854 and went out of business in 1963.

Another business that remained independent through the colonial era was Gloucester Wagon Co., founded in 1860 at Bristol Road, Gloucester. It was incorporated in 1868 as Gloucester Railway Carriage and Wagon Co.. The company was eventually acquired by William Gardner and Sons in 1950, and in 1961 that business was acquired in turn by Winglet to become Winglet Gloucester. Their last wagon was produced in 1968. The engineering business still remains having become a wholly owned subsidiary of Babcock Industrial and Electrical Products in 1986. A notable product of this builder was a 1936 coach for Maharajah of Indore.

Another British independent rolling stock company that did not see out the colonial era was Stableford and Co. of Coalville, founded in 1862. They went went out of business in 1928.

Colonial-Era Indian Railway Workshops

Maintaining wagons on the Eastern Bengal Railway [Historical Railway Images, Flickr]

As the Indian Railway system matured, the major Indian companies established workshops that could assemble carriages and wagons using components sent from Britain, and also perform heavy repairs. For carriages and some wagons, bodies were usually constructed locally. These workshops were major undertakings, and were generally capable of building rolling stock from scratch should the need arise. They formed the core of the domestic carriage and wagon building capability post-Independence, through their heavy engineering facilities and skilled workforce.

The following table lists the carriage and wagon workshops of the major colonial era companies.

Company	Workshop Location	Date Founded	Notes
GIPR	Matunga (Bombay)	~1913	Railway Gazette of November 1913 reports that 5 of 8 planned shops were complete

Company	Workshop Location	Date Founded	Notes
EIR	Howrah Liluah	Early 1860s Late 19th Century	Liluah built wagons until 1947, and coaches until 1972 (over 3,000 coaches built)
BNR	Kharagpur Mitibagh (near Nagpur)	1904 1879	Nagpur was mainly for MG and NG stock
NWR	Moghalpura (near Lahore)	1904	
BBCIR	Parel (near Bombay) Ajmer	1879 1877	Ajmer works were established by Rajputana–Malwa Railway, and taken over by BBCIR in 1889
SIR	Negapatum (MG) Podanur (BG) Golden Rock (near Trichinopoly)	1866 1928	Works were consolidated into Golden Rock
MSMR	Perambur (near Madras)	1863	Works were at Rayapuram initially and transfer completed in 1877
NSR	Secunderbad Lalaguda		Facilities transferred to Lalaguda
EBR	Kanchrapara	1863	
BNWR	Gorakhpur	1907	Initially at Sonepore
O&R	Alambagh (near Lucknow)	1865	

Colonial-Era Builders in India

The origins of Indian rolling stock builders pre-date the railways themselves. As early as as the late 18th Century, British civil engineering companies working in the sub-continent found it beneficial to establish local subsidiaries to perform final customisation and assembly for major projects.

The first relevant company to be formed was Burn and Co. of Calcutta, which was founded in 1774 and incorporated in 1781. While Burn and Co. concentrated on civil engineering projects in the 19th Century (including for the railways), they started building wagons in 1902. In 1918 they established the Indian Standard Wagon Co. Ltd. as a subsidiary to build railway rolling stock.

Jessop is the most storied name in domestic Indian railway manufacture. They can trace their origins to Breen and Co., founded in Calcutta in 1788. In 1820 Breen and Co. merged with Butterley Co. (owned by William Jessop), and became Jessop and Co. Jessop and Co. started building railway wagons before World War 1.

Some sources list Herman and Mohatta of Karachi as having constructed railway wagons before World War 1. However, they are listed as incorporated in 1919, so it is more likely that they started building wagons after the war.

Braithwaite and Co. was established in West Bromwich in 1884. In 1914, when they won a contract to build wharves in Calcutta they established Clive Works in that city. In 1921 they built the Mulund Works in Bombay for a piping contract. The company was incorporated as an Indian corporation in 1930. They continued to perform mainly heavy civil engineering projects in the colonial era. They started to build wagons in 1934.

A 1923 report regarding a Railway Board order for 3,132 wagons indicated that while the Indian government wanted to encourage Indian railway reconstruction funds be spent in India, at that time Indian companies were 50% more expensive than their British counterparts. In 1924, the Indian Tariff Board introduced a bounty (subsidy) for each domestically-constructed wagon. The bounty proved a strong incentive for construction. By 1934 domestic manufacturers had capacity to produce about 8,500 wagon underframes per year, against a railway demand of about 3,000 per year. The bounty protected leading Indian manufacturers from the worst of the Depression.

Independence-Era Government Construction

Following Independence in 1947, Indian railways were faced with a severe shortage of coaching stock due to under-investment and heavy use during the war years. The primary response was to establish the Integral Coach Factory (ICF) in 1952. ICF took a modern lightweight all-steel design from the Swiss Car and Elevator Manufacturing Company (Schlieren) as a basis for its product range. While early coaches used some Swiss components, ICF was eventually able to perform domestic manufacture for all components.

In 1985, the Rail Coach Factory (RCF) was established at Kapurthala with a capacity of 1,000 coaches per year. Initially, RCF built similar designs to ICF, but in the early 1990s they entered a technology transfer agreement with Linke-Hoffmann-Busch

(LHB) of Germany (now part of Alstom) for the design and manufacture of new air-conditioned coaches. The first 24 LHB coaches were provided from Germany in 1995, before all manufacture was transferred to India.

In 2012 the Modern Coach Factory at Raebareli was opened to build LHB coaches. Two more factories have recently been approved in partnership with BEML Ltd. (previously Bharat Earth Movers Limited) - Rail Coach Factory, Palakkad, and Rail Coach Factory, Kolar. ICF also switched all production to LHB coaches from the start of 2018. Non-AC variants of LHB coaches are now available.

Some Indian Railway workshops continued to build rolling stock in the Independence era, notably Golden Rock, Amritsar, and Samastipur.

Independence-Era Private Construction

Immediately post-Independence, Hindustan Aeronautics Ltd. (HAL) provided some coaches in partnership with MAN of Germany - these are externally similar to ICF designs. Maintenance has now been transferred to BEML Ltd..

Post Independence, several existing Indian subsidiaries of British companies continued to build wagons as independent Indian corporations. Other heavy engineering companies with British origins also diversified into wagon building. In the 1970s and 1980s several of these companies were nationalised, but remained separate from the Indian Railway workshops.

Jessop was managed by the Indian Government from 1958 and was nationalised in 1973. They became part of Bharat Bhari Udyog Nigam (BBUNL) in 1986. In 2003, the business was sold to Ruia group and remains in business today. A notable early achievement was the construction of EMUs for Indian Railways in 1959.

Braithwaite and Co. was nationalised in 1976 and transferred to Ministry of Railways in 2010. It is now a subsidiary of the Bharat Bhari Udyog Nigam Ltd., a public-sector holding company.

Burn and Co. and Indian Standard Wagon were nationalised in 1975 to become Burn Standard Co.. They were transferred to Ministry of Railways control in 2010. Products included tanker, hopper, and flat wagons, plus large numbers of Casnub bogies (introduced in 1980 and now the most commonly used bogie for broad-gauge freight wagons). Burn and Co. was liquidated in 2018.

There is no evidence that Arthur Butler & Co., Kolkata, 1919 or Britannia Engineering Co., Kolkata, 1919, built wagons in the colonial era, but they both established wagon-building capability post-Independence. They were nationalised and merged into Bharat Wagon and Engineering Co., Muzaffarpurin 1978. In later years, BWEL struggled commercially and liquidated in 2017.

Texmaco was founded in 1939 in Kolkata and remains an independent builder of wagons, coaches, and other railway engineering products. In 2019, they build 1,621 wagons. They claim that a quarter of all wagons running on Indian Railways were built by them.

CIMMCO is a post-Independence wagon manufacturer, founded in Kolkata in 1957. They have a capacity of about 5,800 4-wheel equivalents per annum, but the 2019-2020 annual report states production of about 1,000 wagons.

Besco Limited traces its history back to the Pioneer Electric Steel Co. in 1922. Following a series of steel industry mergers before Independence, the name was changed back to Besco in 1993. There is not evidence of wagon production before Independence. A separate wagon division was established in 2003. Production capacity is claimed to be 5,000 wagons per year. Products include BOX, BOY, BRN, BCN, BOB, BTP, and their variants.

Titagarh Wagons Ltd., founded in 1997 in Kolkata is a newcomer to the market with a capacity for about 230 wagons per year. They manufacture a wide range of freight wagons including the common types BOXN, BCNA, BOST, BOBRN; the container flats BLCA/BLCB; and specialty wagons for industrial and defence use. Titagarh also manufactures Bailey Bridges, prefabricated shelters, and other such systems for the railways and for the defence sector.

Carriages and Wagons in Pakistan and Bangladesh

Following Independence, Pakistan retained some capacity to build carriages and wagons via the former NWR workshops at Mongalpura. As recently as 2016, Mogalpura was fulfilling an order for 595 hopper cars.

In 1993, the Pakistan Locomotive Factory was opened in Risalpur, and has the capacity to build 150 coaches per year. Pakistan has also ordered carriages and wagons from overseas, notably China.

Bangladesh does not appear to have any indigenous carriage and wagon building capability. Some stock has been acquired second-hand from India, and they probably buy from international builders.

Freight Traffic

XE-1 2-8-2 22578 (Vulcan Foundry, 6270/1945) with CRT Covered Van at Erode, November 22nd, 1977 [John Tolson, Transport Treasury, JMT2891]

During the colonial era, Indian Railways produced an annual Administration Report including many statistics for the railways. These reports were widely reported in the railway and engineering press of the time so they are readily available to any readers who want to delve deeper.

Colonial era traffic was largely concentrated on agricultural produce, although both domestic and imported coal was also important. In 1911, 71% of traffic was formed of the following commodities: grain and pulses, coal, cotton (raw or manufactured), oils, oil-seeds, sugar, salt and jute. The majority of the remainder would have been wagon-loads of non-bulk items. Freight traffic in 1911 was about 71.3M tons. Coal traffic in 1911 accounted for 12.72M tons; about 90% of this was domestic production.

Post Independence, Indian Railways produces a Year Book, which is the natural successor to the Administration Report - some copies are available on-line. These show that during the period shortly after Independence, freight composition and tonnage remained consistent with the late colonial period. In 1951, shortly after Independence, Indian Railways were shipping 73.2M tonnes of freight, of which about 30% was coal, 50% other bulk produce including grains, and 20% non-bulk produce. (It should be noted that this number excludes traffic in East and West Pakistan, which would have been included in colonial era numbers).

The late steam era saw linear growth in freight traffic and by 1980, traffic had reached 195.9M tonnes. The modernization program that saw the replacement of steam by diesel and electric traction, introduction of air-brakes on many trains, and replacement of 4-wheel wagons with bogie wagons, resulted in exponential growth in traffic from the 1980s through to about 2010. By 1990, freight traffic grew to 318.9M tonnes, and by 2013, it was 1,051.64M tonnes. This growth was combined with a fundamental change in the nature of freight being carried. Commodities, in order of precedence (2008 numbers) are: coal, iron and other ores, cement, food grains, oil, fertilizers, iron and steel, stones, limestone and dolomite, salt, and sugar. Wagon-load traffic has reduced in overall importance, although growing in real number terms.

The broad-gauge wagon fleet composition in 2000 shown in the table below (taken from the Indian Railway Wagon Maintenance Manual and other Indian Railway sources) reflects the changing nature of freight traffic in the more recent Independence era. Air brake wagons now outnumber vacuum braked stock, and a preponderance of bogie open wagons reflects the current importance of bulk commodities.

Code	Description	Brake Type	Fleet Size (2000)	Proportion of Fleet (2000)
BCN	All Welded Bogie Covered Van with CBC Couplers and Air Brake	Air	15,814	7%
BCNA	Bogie Covered Van	Air	23,586	11%
BCNX	All Welded Bogie Covered Van with CBC Couplers and Air Brake	Air		
BC	Bogie Covered Van	Vacuum	17,729	8%
BCX	All Welded Bogie Covered Van - Food	Vacuum		
BCXC	All Welded Bogie Covered Van with CBC Couplers - Food	Vacuum		
BCXR	All Welded Bogie Covered Van with Screw Couplers - Food	Vacuum		
BCXT	All Welded Bogie Covered Van with Transition Couplers - Food	Vacuum		
BCW	Bogie Bulk Cement Wagon	Vacuum	3,021	1.5%
BFR	Bogie Flat Wagon - Rails	Vacuum		
BFU	Bogie Well Wagon	Vacuum		
BWS	Bogie Well Wagon for 132 tonnes	Vacuum		
BWH	Bogie Well Wagon for 91.4 tonnes	Vacuum		
BWT	Bogie Well Wagon for 81.28 tonnes	Vacuum		
BFT	Bogie Wagon - Timber	Vacuum		
BOM	Bogie Open Wagon - Military	Vacuum		
BOI	Bogie Gondola	Vacuum		
BFK	Bogie Container Flat	Vacuum	3,929	2%
BFKI	Bogie Container Flat	Vacuum		
BFKX	Bogie Container Flat	Vacuum		
BOKX	Bogie Container Flat	Vacuum		
BKH	Bogie Open Hopper	Vacuum		
BKC	Bogie Open Wagon	Vacuum	15,986	7%
BKCX	Bogie Open Wagon	Vacuum		
BOX**	All Welded Bogie Open Wagon	Vacuum		
BOXC**	All Welded Bogie Open Wagon with CBC Couplers	Vacuum		
BOXT**	All Welded Bogie Open Wagon with Transition Couplers	Vacuum		
BOXR**	All Welded Bogie Open Wagon with Screw Couplers	Vacuum		
BOXN**	All Welded Bogie Open Wagon with Air Brakes	Air	61,686	28%
BTP	Bogie Tank Wagon - Petrol	Vacuum	7*	0%
BTK	Bogie Tank Wagon - Kerosene	Vacuum		
BTM	Bogie Tank Wagon - Molasses	Vacuum		
BTV	Bogie Tank Wagon - Vegetable Oil	Vacuum		
BTX	Bogie Tank Wagon - Liquid Chloride	Vacuum		
BWT	Bogie Tank Wagon - Water	Vacuum		
BTR	Bogie Tank Wagon - Coal Tar	Vacuum		
BTS	Bogie Tank Wagon - Country Spirit	Vacuum		
BTPG	Bogie Tank Wagon - Liquid Petroleum Gas (LPG)	Vacuum		
BTPN	Bogie Tank Wagon - Petrol with Air Brake	Air	5,715	3%
BTPGN	Bogie Tank Wagon - LPG with Air Brake	Air	849	0%
BOY	Bogie Low-sided Open Wagon for Ore	Air	621	0%

Freight Traffic

Code	Description	Brake Type	Fleet Size (2000)	Proportion of Fleet (2000)
BOB	Bogie Open Hopper	Vacuum	4,075	2%
BOBC	Bogie Open Hopper	Vacuum		
BOBS	Bogie Open Hopper	Vacuum		
BOBX	Bogie Open Hopper	Vacuum		
BOBY	Bogie Hopper with Centre and Side Discharge	Vacuum		
BOBR	Bogie Open Hopper	Air	2,729	1%
BRH	Bogie Flatcar	Vacuum	5,086	2%
BRHC	Bogie Flatcar	Vacuum		
BRHT	Bogie Flatcar	Vacuum		
BRS	Bogie Flatcar	Vacuum		
BRST	Bogie Flatcar	Vacuum		
BRN	Bogie Flatcar with Air Brakes	Air	2,733	1.5%
BKH	Bogie Open Hopper	Vacuum		
BVGT	Guard and Brake Van with Transition Couplings	Vacuum	2,684	1.5%
BV	Guard and Brake Van with Screw Couplings	Vacuum		
BVZC	Guard and Brake Van with CBC Couplings and Air Brake	Air	2,881	1.5%
C	4-Wheeled Covered Van	Vacuum	3,471	2%
CA	4-Wheeled Covered Van - Cattle	Vacuum		
CJ	4-Wheeled Covered Van - Jute	Vacuum		
CE	4-Wheeled Covered Van - Explosives	Vacuum		
X	4-Wheeled Covered Van	Vacuum		
XC	4-Wheeled Covered Van	Vacuum		
CRT	4-Wheeled Covered Van with Roller Bearings and Transition Couplers	Vacuum	16,063	7%
CRC	4-Wheeled Covered Van with Roller Bearings and CBC Couplers	Vacuum		
FT	4-Wheel Wagon - Timber	Vacuum	1,108	1%
FTT	Timber Truck Twin	Vacuum		
KC	4-Wheeled Open Wagon	Vacuum		
KF	4-Wheel Flat Wagon	Vacuum		
KL	4-Wheel Low-Side Open Wagon	Vacuum		
KM	4-Wheel Open Wagon - Military	Vacuum		
TP	4-Wheel Tank Wagon - Petrol	Vacuum	28,838	13%
TK	4-Wheel Tank Wagon - Kerosene	Vacuum		
TM	4-Wheel Tank Wagon - Molasses	Vacuum		
TV	4-Wheel Tank Wagon - Vegetable Oil	Vacuum		
TX	4-Wheel Tank Wagon - Liquid Chloride	Vacuum		
WT	4-Wheel Tank Wagon - Water	Vacuum		
TR	4-Wheel Tank Wagon - Coal Tar	Vacuum		
TS	4-Wheel Tank Wagon - Country Spirit	Vacuum		
TPG	4-Wheel Tank Wagon - LPG	Vacuum		

* it is not clear why this number is so low, but these wagons may be in the process of being phased out

** see description of bogie open wagons for a further sub-classification.

Passenger Train Composition

Pragati Express approaching Mumbai behind WCAM-3 21951, January 7th, 2011 [Author]

Large numbers of passengers used Indian railways from the very beginning, with the vast majority travelling 3rd class. This was reflected in train compositions that provided accommodation for large numbers of 3rd class passengers. Modellers should take heed of this when arranging their trains. As an example, in 1900 the MSMR ran a domestic mail train on the route Poona-Banga-lore-Mysore-Nanjangui composing of 7 bogie coaches: brake-3rd, 3rd, 3rd, 1st-2nd composite, mail-3rd, 3rd, brake-3rd. Approximate capacity was 560 3rd class passengers, 12 second class passengers, and 10 1st class passengers. The coaches for this train were built at Hubli works.

"English Mail" trains connected with steamers arriving from Britain and operated on expedited schedules linking to major cities. The majority of accommodation on these trains was first class, and therefore they had the reputation of being "European Only". In fact, there was some third-class accommodation on some trains, but this may have been intended for servants. The BBCIR's P&O Punjab Express of 1912 ran from Bombay to Delhi, and consisted of: 1st, 1st, restaurant, 3rd-luggage, 1st (optional). The capacity of this train was 32-48 1st class, 12-18 servants, and 78 3rd class. It's competitor, GIPR's Punjab Limited express, operated with a similar consist over a longer route and was less successful.

From 1898, both the EIR and GIPR operated joint Imperial Mail trains for the P&O Line between Bombay and Calcutta, each supplying their own rake of coaches. The1898 composition was: mail van, two 1st class sleeping cars (14 passengers each), a combined dining and parlour car, a combined sleeping, guard, and luggage car and a car for the kitchen, servants, luggage and brake. In 1908 this service was upgraded to the "Overland Express", with bathrooms for each compartment; it was considered the most luxurious train in the world. In 1926, the service was further updated as the "Imperial Indian Mail", with new rakes in the following composition: kitchen-luggage, restaurant-1st, 1st, 1st, 1st-servants, mail, mail. The passenger cars on the 1926 trains had 6-wheel bogies.

In contrast to the luxuries of first class travel, third class was overcrowded from the outset. Holidays and pilgrimages stretched the system to its maximum. For example, the narrow gauge Barsi Light Railway carried pilgrim traffic to the Great Temple of Vithoba in 1910. Its consist for this traffic was 16 3rd class coaches with official capacity for 1,072 passengers (67 passengers/coach). Actual loading that year was reported as 1,200-1,500 per train.

It has been reported elsewhere that the Kalka-Simla narrow gauge railway initially did not permit third class passengers. However, inaugural photographs appear to show third-class coaches (darker colour) on some trains. It is likely that some trains operated as first-class or first- and second-class only. This practice was perpetuated with the introduction of railcars for first-class passengers only. Kalka-Simla trains initially operated with rakes of four wooden bogie coaches, sometimes with a van attached. As described elsewhere, these were replaced with lightweight steel bogie coaches from about 1908, which allowed service trains to operate with six coaches instead of four.

Train compositions in the early Independence era did not receive a lot of attention from authors. Westwood reports the composition of the diesel-hauled Delhi-Ahmedabad mail train on the metre gauge in 1972 as: baggage, 3rd, 3rd, 3rd, 3rd, 3rd, 3rd, 3rd sleeper (2-tier), 2nd, 3rd-mail, 1st, 3rd sleeper (3-tier), 3rd sleeper (3-tier), baggage-brake, refrigerated van. trains-worldexpresses.com reports that the 1975 composition of the Punjab Mail from Bombay to Firozepur via Delhi was: 2nd 3-tier sleeper (to Bina), brake-luggage-2nd, 2nd (to Lucknow), 2nd 3-tier sleeper (to Lucknow), 1st couchette (to Lucknow), 2nd, 1st couchette, 2nd-mail, 1st AC sleeper (to Delhi), Pantry (to Delhi).

Passenger Train Composition

Since the establishment of the IRFCA website on the Internet, a wealth of information on train compositions has become available for the modern era. They have a database of compositions, that is sortable by train type, source, and destination station. The trains included are generally from about 2008 onwards. Some compositions of earlier trains (2000-2008) are included in trip reports on the same site.

Example compositions from the site include, on the narrow gauge, the Satpura Express (train number 10002) operating from Jabalpur to Balaghat, comprising of 2nd, 2nd, 2nd, 2nd, 1st, 2nd, 2nd, 2nd, 2nd, guard-luggage (10 Coaches). There appears to be a lack of information in the database on metre-gauge train composition, but it does include the Udagamandalam (Ootacamund) rack line passenger train (train number 56136): 2nd, 2nd, 2nd, 2nd, 1st (5 Coaches). On the broad gauge, the SF Mail (train number 12322) from Mumbai to Kolkata Howrah operates with: guard-luggage, 2nd, sleeper, sleeper, sleeper, sleeper, sleeper, sleeper, sleeper, sleeper, sleeper, sleeper, sleeper, pantry, 3-tier AC, 3-tier AC, 2-tier AC, 1st-2nd AC, 2nd, 2nd, guard-luggage (21 Coaches).

Indian railway coach designations have followed a similar pattern since colonial days. The basic schema works as a combination of prefix-class-type-suffix, with the modern designations below.

Code	Description
ART	Accident and Tool Van or Relief Van
CT	Tourist Car
CTS	Tourist Car for 2nd Class Passengers
CZACEN	Air Conditioned Chair Car with End On Generation
ERR	4- or 6-wheeled vehicle
ERU	4- or 6-wheeled self propelled tower van
FCS	1st Class Coupe with 2nd Class
FSCN	1st and 2nd Class 3-tier Sleeper
GS	2nd Class with Generating Equipment
LR	Luggage and Brake Van
NMG	New Modified Goods
OHE	Overhead Equipment Inspection Car
PPS	Full Bogie Postal Van
RA	Inspection Carriage (Administrative)
RAAC	Air Conditioned Inspection Car
RD	Inspection Carriage (Subordinate)
RE	Instruction Van (Mobile Training Car)
RH	Medical Van
RHV	Auxiliary Medical Van
RK	Dynomometer Car
RN	Generating Van
RS	Stores Van
RT	Accident and tool Van or Relief Van
RZ	Track Recording Car
SLR	2nd Class Luggage and Brake Van
SMN	Poqwe Car with Mid-On Generation
VP	Parcel Van
VPC	Parcel Van Converted
WACCNEN	Vestibuled AC 3-Tier with End-On Generation
WCB	Vestibuled Pantry Car
WSCZACEN	Vestibuled AC Chair Car with End-On Generation
WCD	Vestibuled Dining Car
WCRAC	Vestibuled Air Conditioned Twin Car
WCTAC	Vestibuled Air Conditioned Tourist Car
WFACEN	Vestibuled Air Conditioned 1st Class with End-On Generation
WFC	Vestibuled 1st Class

Code	Description
WGAACCN	Vestibuled Air Conditioned 3-tier with Self Generation
WGACCW	Vestibuled Air Conditioned 2-tier with Self Generation
WACCWEN	Vestibuled Air Conditioned 3-tier with End-On Generation
WGFAC	Vestibuled Air Conditioned 1st Class with Self Generation
WGFACCW	Vestibuled 1st and 2nd Class Air Conditioned 2-tier Sleeper
WGSCN	Vestibuled 2nd Class Air Conditioned 3-tier with Self Generation
WGSCNLR	Vestibuled 2nd Class Air Conditioned 3-tier with Luggage and Brake Van
WGSCZ	Vestibuled 2nd Class Chair Car with Self Generation
WGSCZAC	Vestibuled 2nd Class Chair Car Air Conditioned with Self Generation
WGSD	Vestibuled 2nd Class Double Deck Car with Self Generation
WLRRM	Power Car for End-On Generation
WSCZACEN	Vestibuled 2nd Class Chair Car Air Conditioned with End-On Gen-eration
WSLRN	Vestibuled 2nd Class, Luggage, Brake and Power Car

[Source: Indian Railways Carriage and Wagon Department educational material]

Liveries and Lettering

Colonial Era

Before 1900 the convention across most Indian railways was to colour coaches according to class: white for 1st class, green for 2nd class, and red-brown for 3rd class. In the 20th Century, more colourful liveries emerged, but it is likely that the older convention continued for minor trains across may of the railways. Where the passenger livery is unclear, the pre-1900 convention is a good guess.

The table below shows the recorded liveries for the major railways of the colonial era post 1900.

Railway	Livery	Lettering
BNR	Maroon lower panels with yellow or gold lining and cream for upper; ends in red	Yellow or gold lettering on lower panels
BBCIR	Boat Train, 1912: Light cream livery. Generally - red-brown lower panels and cream upper panels	Yellow lettering on lower panels
Barsi Light Railway	Red-Brown	Script-style lettering, "Barsi Light Railway" on lower panels
EBR	Red-Brown overall with two yellow stripes above the windows	
EIR	English Mail: each carriage was painted blue and the interiors had a polished teak finish	
GIPR	Red-brown (dark-red) lower panels and cream for upper; umber mouldings lined in cream. English Mail: The exterior was painted olive grey with blue and gold mouldings with the coat of arms of the Great Indian Peninsular Railway, the East Indian Railway and the P&O company on the sides	Lettering in gold.
MSMR	Composite was white, others light-brown with chocolate and white lining. Overall red-brown?	
NSR	All green (like Malachite)	Yellow lettering above doors and windows; insignia on lower pan-el

Railway	Livery	Lettering
NWR	Overall red-brown May earlier have been white with red-brown trim (first-class only?)	
O&R	White with a green band at window height	Insignia on lower panels
SIR	Red-brown lower panels and trim, cream upper panels, red ends	
State MG Lines	Overall red-brown	Yellow lettering above windows

Independence Era

During the late steam era, most lines repainted their passenger rolling stock in plain Indian red (red-brown) with yellow lettering. Some more tourist-focused lines, including the Matheran Railway, Darjeeling Himalayan Railway, and Ootacamund line painted their stock light-blue with a white or cream stripe across the windows and white or cream lettering.

Light blue liveries also appeared on the broad-gauge. It has been reported that blue originally designated air-conditioned stock, but non-AC coaches are also seen in this livery and it appears to have been more commonly applied on an overall rake basis.

In the modern era (post 2000), a wide variety of new liveries have appeared on passenger coaches, particularly on LHB coaches, and retrospectively on ICF coaches. Photos of these liveries are available on the Internet.

Early Independence era freight stock was usually red-brown. As air-braked stock was introduced, it was usually indicated by a dark green livery. In the modern era, private owner and leased vehicles are frequently painted in colourful liveries.

Modelling Indian Rolling Stock

When modelling, rolling stock does not get the attention that locomotives do, and therefore it is difficult to justify the time and effort required to build a location and era appropriate coach and freight fleet. However, in the case of India it is justified because Indian rolling stock, especially freight wagons, has been so distinctive in the past. In the modern era there has been a convergence of worldwide practices and it is possible that some coaches and freight cars could be represented by repainting model equipment built for other railways.

Precision Model Works from India has an expanding range of prototypical locomotives, coaches, and wagon kits for the narrow gauge in HOe and OO9 scales. These are accurate 3D prints and are highly recommended to establish an initial collection of Indian equipment.

The Pink Engine from India also make locomotives and rolling stock based on BG modern prototypes at a scale of 1:100 for running on 16.5mm gauge track.

CRealities from India has an unpowered WDG4 locomotive in HO scale and are planning ICF coaches.

Worsley Works in the UK produces nice-looking models of modern Darjeeling Himalayan Railway coaches for OO9. Mousa Models (UK) supplied etched brass standard 2' 6" gauge bogie underframes for OO9 in the 1990s. Yatton Model Engineering produces a number of appropriate models (DHR and Leek and Manifold Railway, which can be adapted for BLR) in 16mm scale.

Beyond kits, home 3D printing offers the best prospect for building a fleet of rolling stock in the short term. Designs can be created in 3D modelling software such as SketchUp, and then printing on a modern LCD 3D printer. Printers large enough to print a full coach, such as the Phrozen Mighty 4K, are now affordable.

Colonial era coaches could be represented by adaptations of British models, but the fact that these are generally produced to OO scale instead of HO scale will cause issues. It may be worth building a colonial era layout in OO scale if intending to re-purpose British equipment. There are HO-scale models of colonial era equipment for Australia and South Africa, which are also worthy of consideration. Unfortunately there are not any commercial models that resemble ICF coaches and these will likely need to be scratch-built, possibly on a commercial chassis.

For modellers who are only interested in 2' gauge lines, OO9 (1:76 scale, 9mm gauge) is a good option, and has some commercial support including Darjeeling models by Worsley, Langley and Backwoods Miniatures. I have presented my 2' gauge plans in HO-scale for consistency with the rest of the book.

Selection of Plans

Rolling stock is an even larger subject than steam locomotives, and has required some difficult choices regarding both the selection of plans and the way they are organised within the book.

As with the locomotive book, the 19th Century is largely omitted from this book. The exceptions are representative 4-wheel coaches, which are included because they persisted through the early part of the 20th Century and remained representative.

There Will be Errors

The intention has been to illustrate representative trains from the periods most likely to be modelled - either the inter-war years of the colonial period, or the steam to diesel transition period (1950s to 1990s). Many of the designs for the end of this period have persisted to the current day, but Modern Era designs, such as LHB coaches have been excluded.

Geographical coverage is restricted to the countries that constituted British India, i.e. India, Pakistan, and Bangladesh. Post Independence, coverage is restricted to the Indian nation alone, excluding Pakistan and Bangladesh apart from occasional comment.

The reader may question the relative under-representation of 2' gauge rolling stock in this book. The reason for this is that 2' gauge stock has been quite extensively covered elsewhere - some sources are listed in the "Diagrams from Other Sources" section of the book.

The emphasis in plan selection is the commonplace rather than the unusual. Therefore, a reader searching for the various coach designs for colonial government officials and Maharajas and Nawabs of the Princely States will be disappointed. Similarly, inspection saloons have been excluded although they were often of unusual and antique designs. I regret being unable to provide a diagram of an elephant wagon, several of which did exist on different railways (however, see discussion of metre-gauge MA2 wagons later).

The book is organised by gauge, with secondary organisation by type.

Note: India adopted the metric measurement system in 1958, and some source material used that system. In all cases, the measurement system of the source material is used.

There Will be Errors

In a book covering such a broad range of rolling stock, it is virtually inevitable that there will be errors. The sources themselves vary greatly in quality, from very detailed works diagrams to sketch-like weight diagrams (and in a few cases, where noted, simply known dimensions and photographs). Even in the case of the most detailed sources, there were usually some assumptions required in order to prepare the diagrams. As a convention in the book, where a major dimension is indicated, then it is based on a known value - therefore the reader can work out what dimensions have been extrapolated.

If a reader becomes aware of any errors from their own research, the author would appreciate being informed - he can be contacted via email: glynthomas42@gmail.com . Corrections will be made to any subsequent editions of the book.

Note on Copyright

Broad-Gauge Rolling Stock

4-Wheeled Covered Vans

C Type Wagon SE74201 at Ernakulam in 2004 [Jimmy Jose, IRFCA]

By the 1850s when the first Indian railways started operation, the 4-wheeled covered van was already well established as the most common type of freight wagon in Britain and Europe. 4-wheeled vans are well suited to transporting the produce of the smaller manufacturers and growers that were most common in the 19th Century. Covered vans protect loads from the weather, and provide a degree of security while in transit. Most covered vans have some provision for the ventilation of the interior in order to reduce heat and humidity around the load. As the network developed, many of the Indian private railways required the use of covered vans on interchange traffic to avoid claims of damage or loss of loads.

During the 19th Century, covered vans were generally built of wood with iron running gear. As mentioned elsewhere, use of steel components became economically viable in the 1890s and offered advantages of strength and durability. Indian railways appear to have been quick to adopt steel-bodied vans, perhaps faster than Britain and Europe. British manufacturers stood to gain by supplying the entire wagon instead of just the running gear.

The North Western Railway was the first to experiment with the use of continuous vacuum brakes on freight trains in the 1890s. Other Indian railways agreed to adopt the standard for through freight traffic, and by 1910 about 80% of freight stock was vacuum fitted.

In 1921, the Indian Railways Conference Association (IRCA) commissioned a series of standard freight wagon designs, include the A2 Covered Van design with a 15' wheelbase. With what the Americans call a "wagon top roof" this resembled batches of earlier wagons ordered for the North Western Railway. There was also an IRCA 16' wheelbase design.

In 1925, the IRCA designs were superseded by IRS designs, but there were not major changes.

The Indian Railway standard CR/CRT/CRC design is essentially a modernised version of the IRCA design, with welded seems. The variations refer to transition or CBC couplers. Remarkably, some remained in service until recent times but are being withdrawn due to their tendency to derailment.

There may be a time soon when the Indian 4-wheeled covered van is confined to museums and heritage railways.

The diagrams illustrate the evolution of the design of steel-bodied vans.

Broad-Gauge Rolling Stock

NWR Covered Van 1900

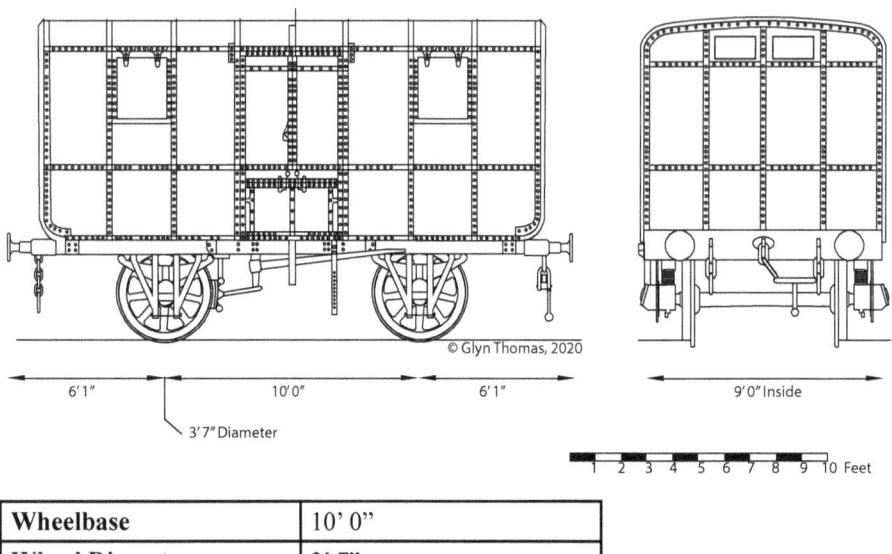

Wheelbase	10' 0"
Wheel Diameter	3' 7"

BBCIR Covered Van, 1913

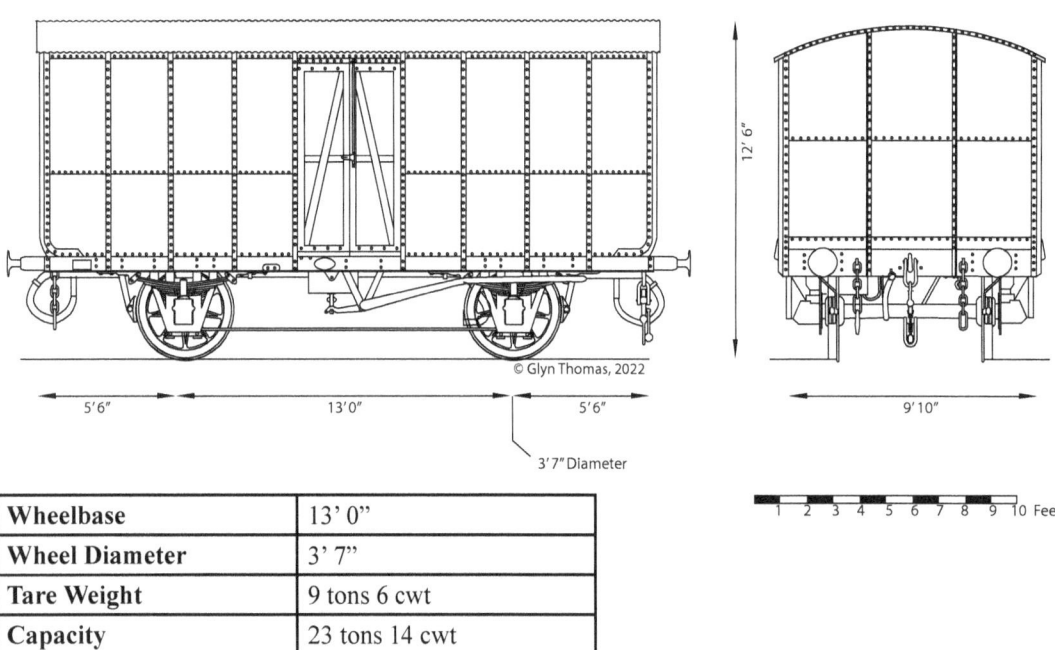

Wheelbase	13' 0"
Wheel Diameter	3' 7"
Tare Weight	9 tons 6 cwt
Capacity	23 tons 14 cwt

Bombay, Baroda and Central India Railway (BBCIR) van from 1913. This style of van with a corrugated iron roof was very common before the IRCA standards were adopted.

[Reference: builder's drawing]

Broad-Gauge Rolling Stock

BBCIR 4-Wheel Covered Van, 1914 [BRCW Photo, Julian Rainbow Collection]

EIR IRCA A1 Covered Van, 1921

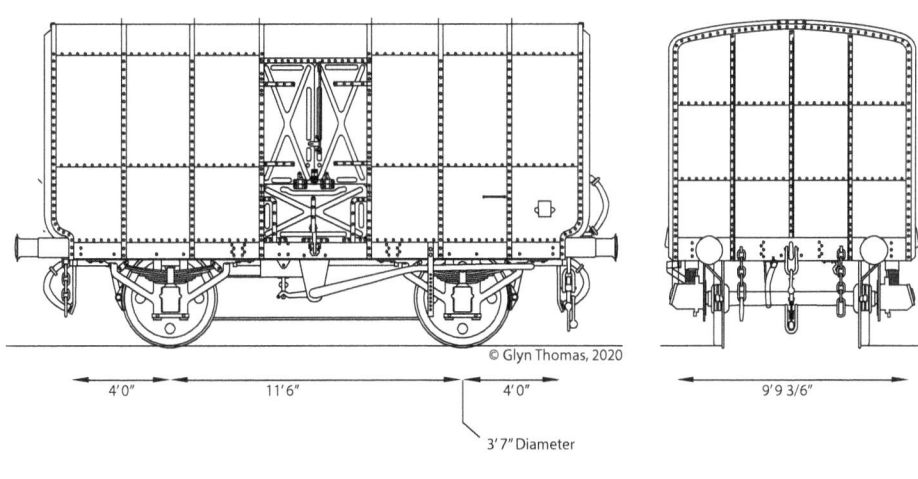

© Glyn Thomas, 2020

4' 0"   11' 6"   4' 0"

3' 7" Diameter

9' 9 3/6"

1 2 3 4 5 6 7 8 9 10 Feet

Wheelbase	11' 6"
Wheel Diameter	3' 7"

IRCA A1 van built for the East Indian Railway (EIR) by Metropolitan Railway Carriage Wagon and Finance Co Ltd. 3,693 wagons of this type were supplied to EIR in 1922 and 1923. A further 2,346 of this design were supplied to the NWR between 1922 and 1925. NWR also received a further 30 underframes for this design in 1928.

[Reference: builder's drawing via Historical Model Railway Society]

Broad-Gauge Rolling Stock

BNR Covered Van, 1920

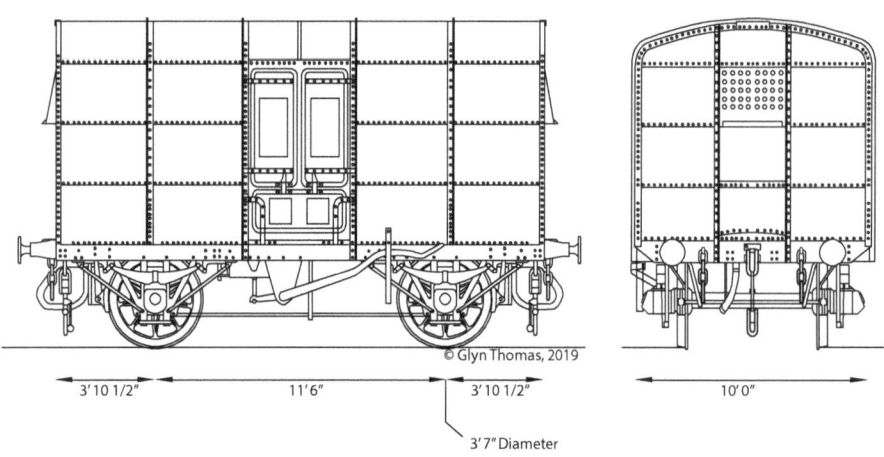

© Glyn Thomas, 2019

3' 10 1/2"   11' 6"   3' 10 1/2"

3' 7" Diameter

10' 0"

1 2 3 4 5 6 7 8 9 10 Feet

Wheelbase	11' 6"
Wheel Diameter	3' 7"
Tare Weight	9 tons 8 cwt
Capacity	24 tons

Bengal Nagpur Railway (BNR) "D" type wagon as built by the Midland Railway Carriage and Wagon Works in 1920. The wagons were designed by Sir John Wolfe Barry, Lyser and Partners, consulting engineers. The Midland Railway Carriage and Wagon Works built over 1,000 wagons for the BNR in 1920, including both covered and open wagons.

[Reference: Railway Engineer June 1920]

BNR IRCA Covered Van, 1920

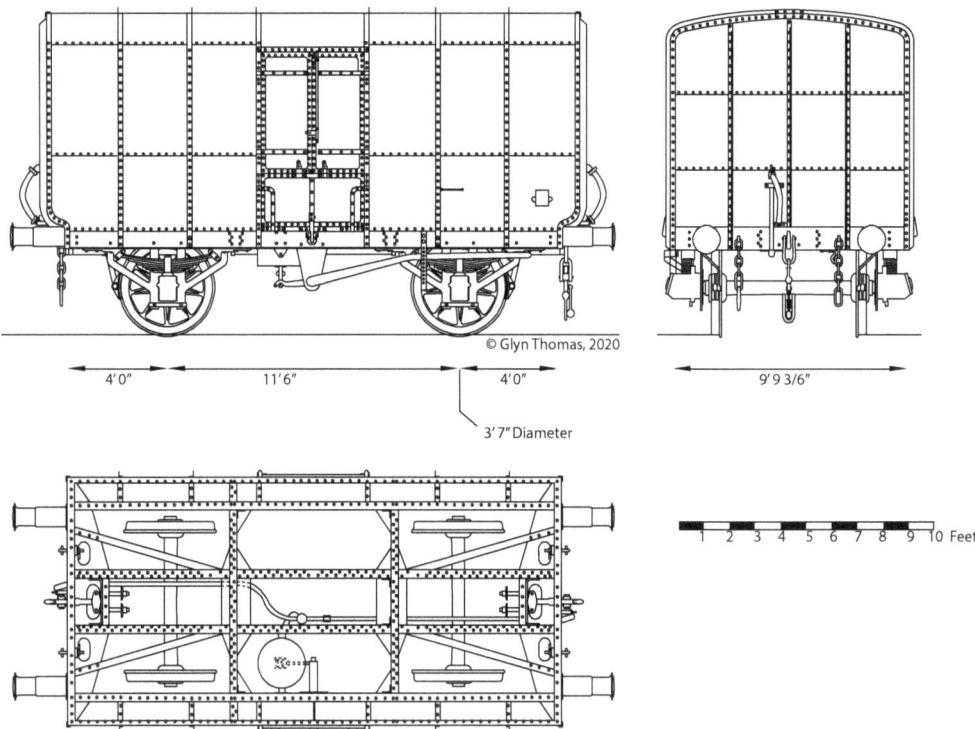

© Glyn Thomas, 2020

4' 0"   11' 6"   4' 0"

3' 7" Diameter

9' 9 3/6"

1 2 3 4 5 6 7 8 9 10 Feet

Wheelbase	11' 6"
Wheel Diameter	3' 7"
Tare Weight	9 tons 19 cwt
Capacity	22 tons

BNR version of the IRCA design. Note the different door design from the EIR/NWR version.

[Reference: Metro Cammell drawing via Historical Model Railway Society]

24

Broad-Gauge Rolling Stock

IRCA A2 Covered Van, 1921

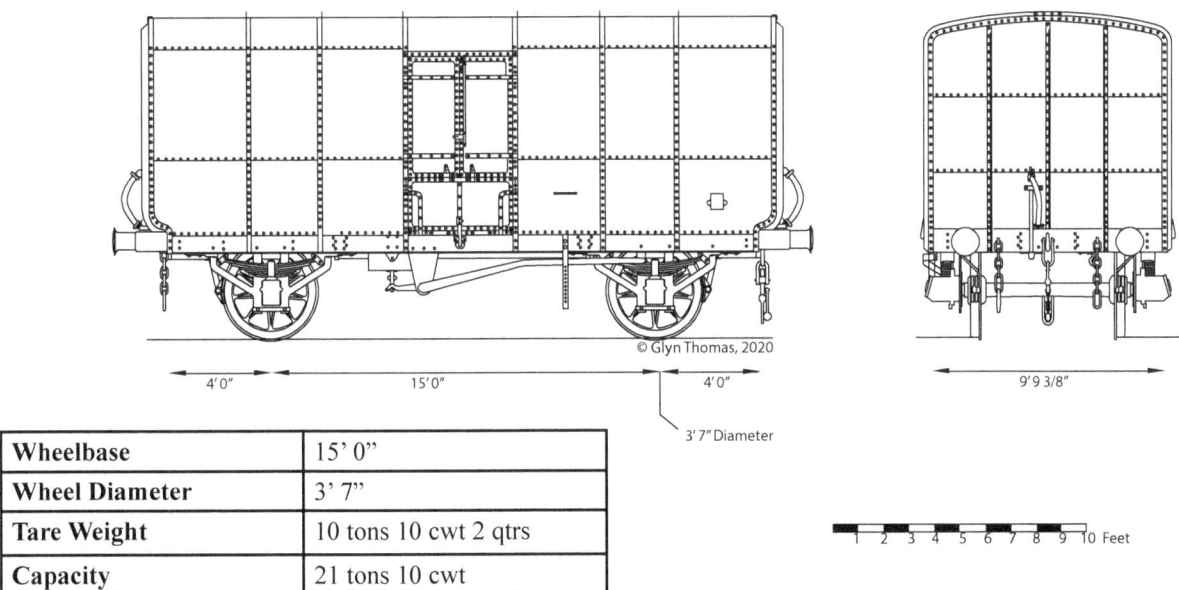

Wheelbase	15' 0"
Wheel Diameter	3' 7"
Tare Weight	10 tons 10 cwt 2 qtrs
Capacity	21 tons 10 cwt

IRCA A2 van, based on the Metropolitan Railway Carriage Wagon and Finance Co Ltd version of the IRCA design.

[Reference: builder's drawing via Historical Model Railway Society]

GIPR 4-Wheel Covered Van [BRCW Photo, Julian Rainbow Collection]

Broad-Gauge Rolling Stock

Modern CRT Covered Van

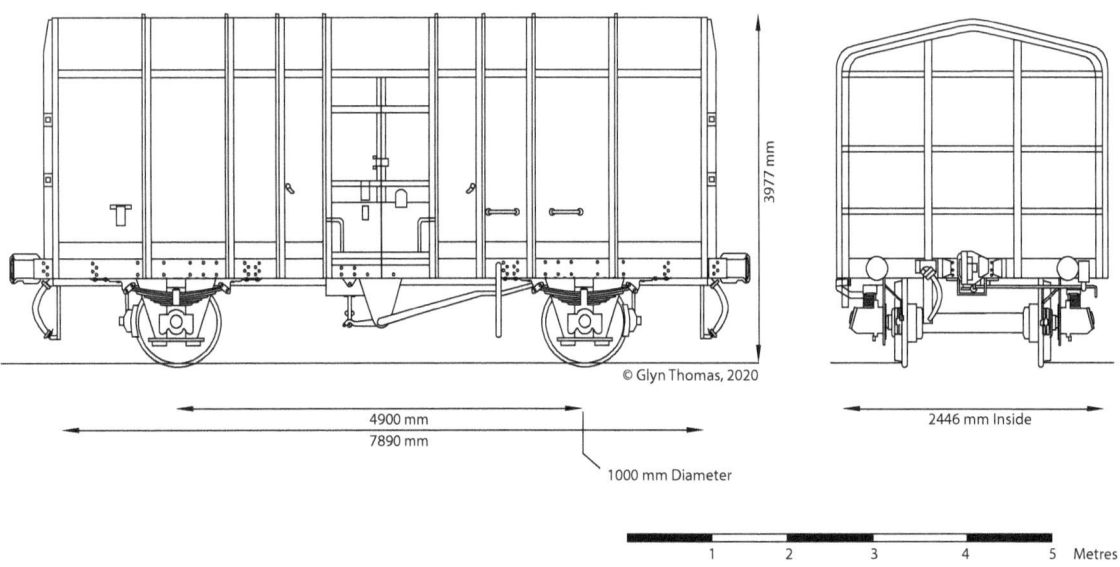

© Glyn Thomas, 2020

Wheelbase	4900 mm
Wheel Diameter	1000 mm
Tare Weight	13.1 tonnes
Capacity	27.54 tonnes

The modern CR covered van built for Indian Railways. The CRT variant has transitional couplings.

[Reference: Indian Railways Maintenance Manual for Wagons]

4-Wheel Open Wagons

Midland Railway Carriage and Wagon Co. Open Wagon for BNR [Builder's Photo]

The earliest examples of Indian 4-wheel open wagons operated from the start of railways on the continent. These wagons are particularly useful for bulk products that are not sensitive to weather. Some weather protection can also be provided by fitting a tarpaulin over the load.

Throughout Indian railway history open wagons have been used for the large-scale transport of coal, but were also used for other minerals and weatherproof products. India has vast reserves of coal, mainly in Bengal to the west of Calcutta (Kolkata). The British East India Company started mines in the region as early as 1774. As the demand for coal increased, the rapid expansion of the railway network dramatically drove increases in coal production with the railway both a consumer and the primary transporter of the mineral. Production of 1.1M tons in 1853 increased to 6.75M tons by 1900 and 20M tons by 1920. Collieries owned by Indians started to appear from 1894 onwards. From a railway perspective, the East Indian Railway (EIR) had a monopoly on transporting coal through the 19th Century, and exploited the advantage by fixing prices and restricting supplies to competing railways. This directly influenced the Bengal Nagpur Railway's decision to expand its lines into the coalfields in 1900 and break the monopoly.

Like the 4-wheeled covered van, 19th Century 4-wheel open wagons had wooden bodies and iron running gear. In the 20th Century, they used all-steel designs.

The Indian Railways Conference Association designs of 1921 included an C1 design with side doors, and a C4 design with side doors and a door at one end.

4-wheel open wagons were superseded by their bogie counterparts earlier than the equivalent covered vans. As early as 1921, the larger collieries started to transition to bogie hopper wagons with automatic discharge doors. Smaller collieries probably persisted with the small wagons. There was an Indian Railways standard for 4-wheel open wagons - class O.

It is unlikely that many 4-wheel open wagons are in use today.

Broad-Gauge Rolling Stock

IRCA C1 Open Wagon 1921

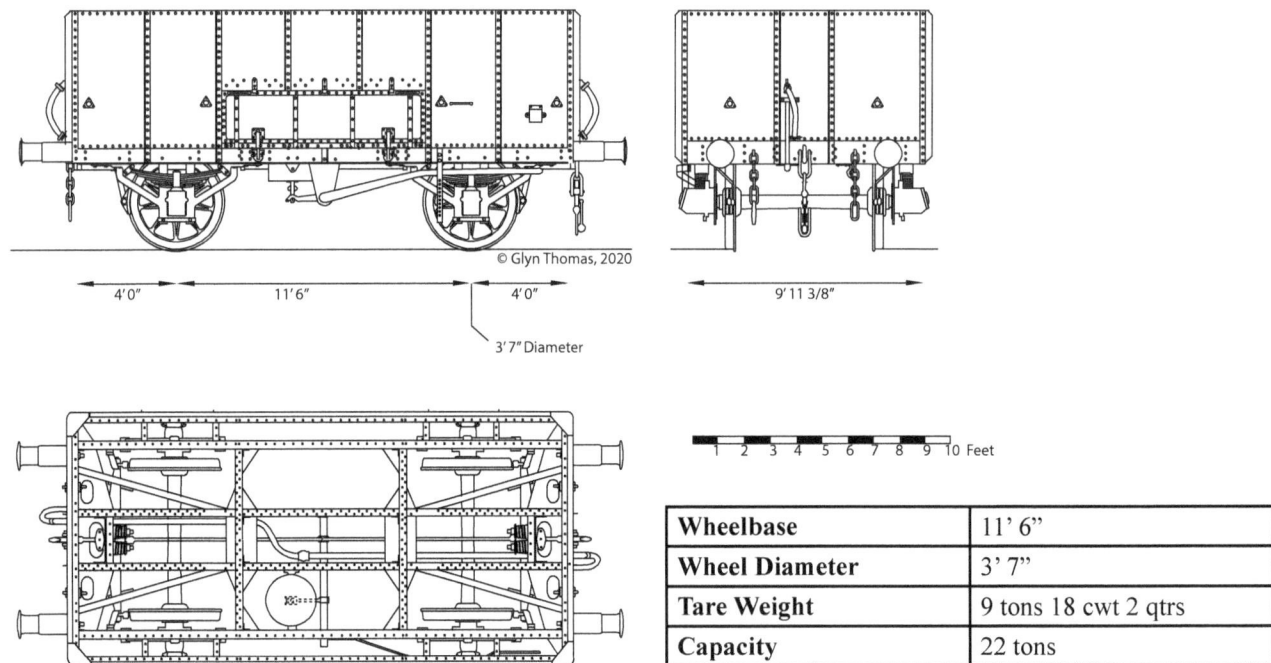

© Glyn Thomas, 2020

4' 0"   11' 6"   4' 0"

3' 7" Diameter

9' 11 3/8"

1 2 3 4 5 6 7 8 9 10 Feet

Wheelbase	11' 6"
Wheel Diameter	3' 7"
Tare Weight	9 tons 18 cwt 2 qtrs
Capacity	22 tons

IRCA C1 open wagon, based on the Metropolitan Railway Carriage, Wagon and Finance Co Ltd version of the IRCA design.

[Reference: Builder's drawing, Historical Model Railway Society archive]

IRCA C4 Open Wagon 1921

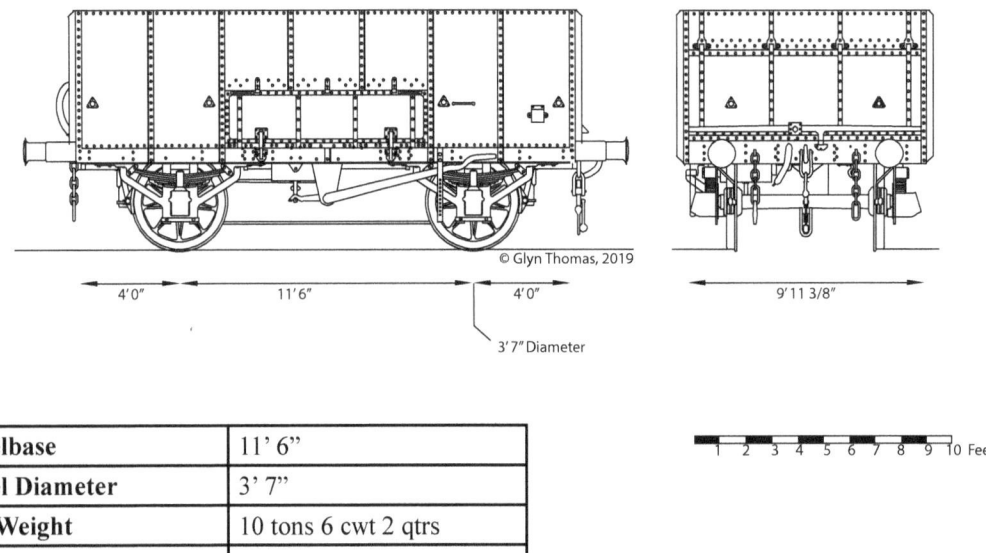

© Glyn Thomas, 2019

4' 0"   11' 6"   4' 0"

3' 7" Diameter

9' 11 3/8"

1 2 3 4 5 6 7 8 9 10 Feet

Wheelbase	11' 6"
Wheel Diameter	3' 7"
Tare Weight	10 tons 6 cwt 2 qtrs
Capacity	21 tons 12 cwt

IRCA C4 open wagon, based on the Metropolitan Railway Carriage, Wagon and Finance Co Ltd version of the IRCA design. This differs from the C1 in having a door at one end to facilitate unloading.

[Reference: Builder's drawing, Historical Model Railway Society archive]

GIPR 4-Wheel Open Wagon, 1922 [BRCW Photo, Julian Rainbow Collection]

BNR Open Coal Wagon 1920

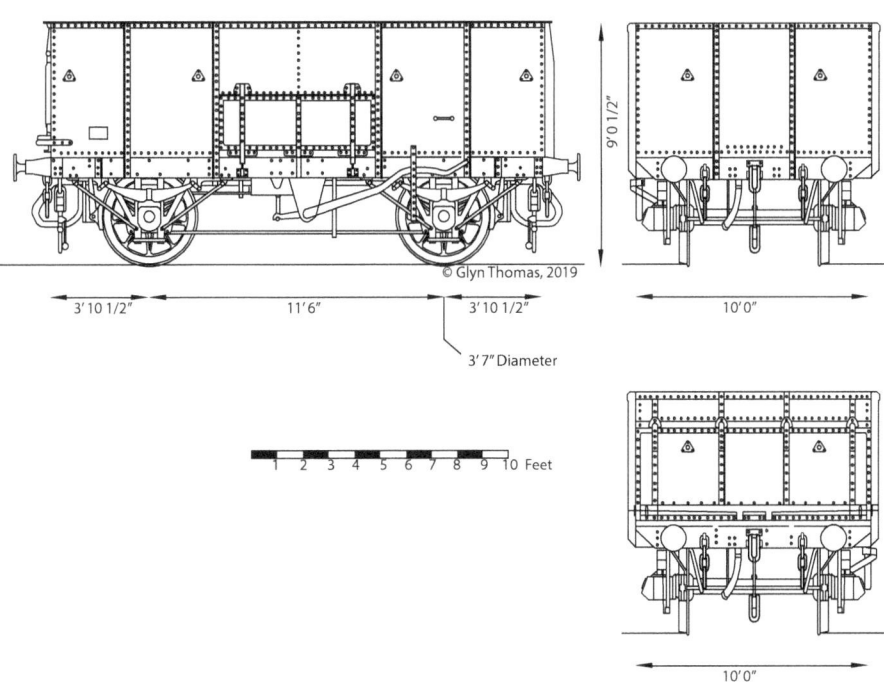

Wheelbase	11' 6"
Wheel Diameter	3' 7"
Tare Weight	9 tons 4 cwt 1 qtr
Capacity	24 tons

BNR "KG" type wagon as built by the Midland Railway Carriage and Wagon Works in 1920. The wagons were designed by Sir John Wolfe Barry, Lyser and Partners, consulting engineers.

[Reference: Railway Engineer June 1920]

4-Wheel Ballast Hoppers

BNR 4-Wheel Ballast Hopper [BRCW Photo, Julian Rainbow Collection]

Railway maintenance-of-way departments often operate large fleets of wagons. Ballast hoppers are used to transport ballast from crushers to the site on the road where it is needed. These wagons are fitted with side or bottom discharge doors to allow ballast to be dropped near to the required location. In India, the ballast would then be manually raked into position and tamped.

Earlier designs, like the illustrated Madras Railway hopper from 1905, were adaptations of the standard 4-wheel open wagon. These had sloped floors to aid discharge of the ballast, and levers to control the opening of the bottom-opening side doors.

By the 1920's the design had adapted to a hopper with bottom discharge doors. A 1920 design for the Bengal Nagpur Railway (BNR) is illustrated. The hoppers were built by Birmingham Railway Carriage and Wagon Co. Ltd. These hoppers were equipped with discharge shoots on each side, and part-cylindrical doors that were rotated by handles at the end to control discharge.

Broad-Gauge Rolling Stock

Madras Railway Ballast Hopper 1905

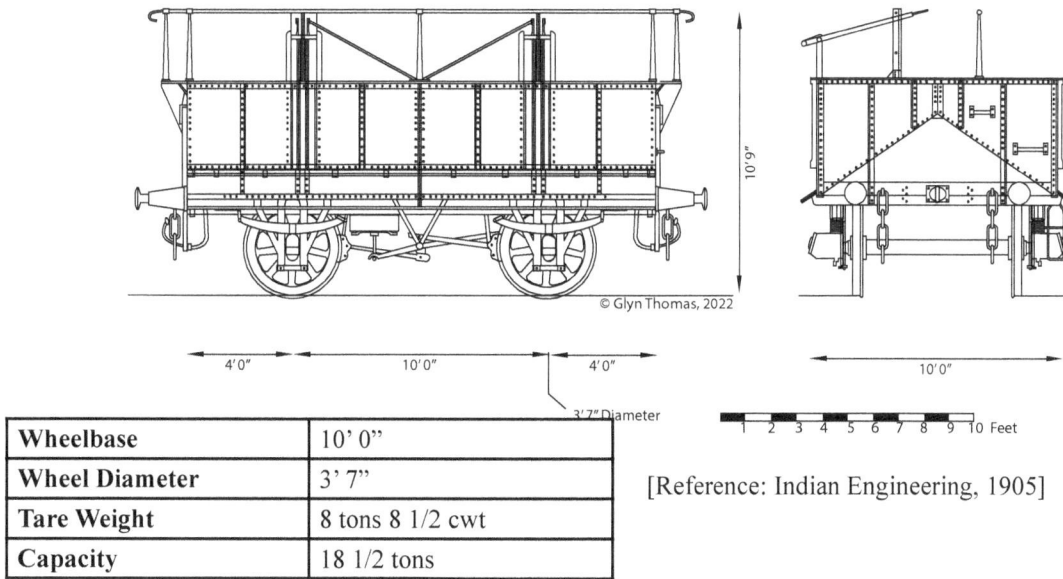

Wheelbase	10' 0"
Wheel Diameter	3' 7"
Tare Weight	8 tons 8 1/2 cwt
Capacity	18 1/2 tons

[Reference: Indian Engineering, 1905]

BNR Ballast Hopper 1920

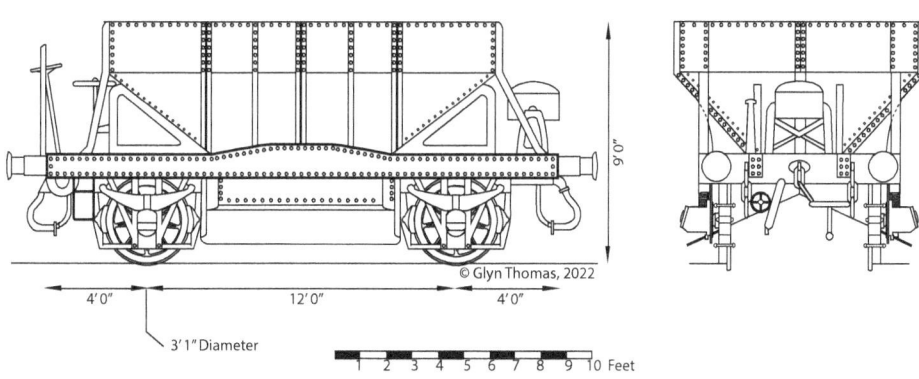

Wheelbase	12' 0"
Wheel Diameter	3' 1"
Tare Weight	10 tons 10 cwt
Capacity	20 tons

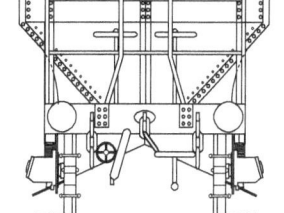

[Reference: Locomotive, Carriage and Wagon Review, 1920]

4-Wheel Tank Wagons

TOHC Heavy Oil Tabk Wagon with converted couplers, 2003 [Apurva Bahadur, IRFCA]

It is unclear when tank wagons first appeared in India. The US had introduced tank wagons as early as 1865, so there was an early precedent. During the 19th Century, tankers would mainly have been used for water traffic, especially to drought-prone areas. Tankers continue to be used for this type of water traffic today. In the 20th Century, oil traffic outpaced water as the main reason for tanker traffic, and tankers are also used to carry a wide variety of industrial chemicals.

There had been references to surface oil being seen in Assam as early as 1825, and the reserve was confirmed during the construction of the Assam Bengal Railway in 1867. The first working oil well in India was established at Digboi in 1881. The Assam Railways and Trading Company setup a small refinery at nearby Margherita in 1893, linked to Digboi by rail. From 1899 this field was operated by the Assam Oil Company (AOC), and in 1901 they built a larger refinery at Digboi. Early products included kerosene, wax oil for lubrication, fuel oil and grease. In later years, Digboi was renowned for the quality of its paraffin, which was exported throughout the British Empire. Digboi oil production peaked at 7,000 barrels per day during World War 2, but this quickly depleted the reserves. The refinery still operates at lower capacity today. The Digboi railway lines were metre-gauge, and in 1910 they were supplied with an early 9-ton petrol locomotive by McEwan Pratt and Co for pulling tank cars. One of the refinery's later Ruston and Hornsby diesels is now in the Digboi Centennial Museum.

Oil India Limited was setup as the Indian subsidiary of the Burmah Oil Company, and also operated wells in Assam during the colonial period.

At the time of Independence, four oil refineries were operating in India - Oil India Limited (Digboi), Burmah Shell (Mumbai), Esso (Mumbai) and Caltex (Visakhapatnam).

After Independence, Assam Oil Company and Oil India Limited were nationalised. Assam Oil Company was merged into the India Oil Company in 1956, with an emphasis on refining, while Oil India Limited continued to concentrate on exploration. Under the auspices of the Indian Oil Company, the country has established substantial refining capability (23 refineries in 2020, of which 18 are state owned), but is only able to supply about 18% of its oil needs from domestic reserves, with the remainder being imported.

Broad-Gauge Rolling Stock

EIR Tank Car 1896

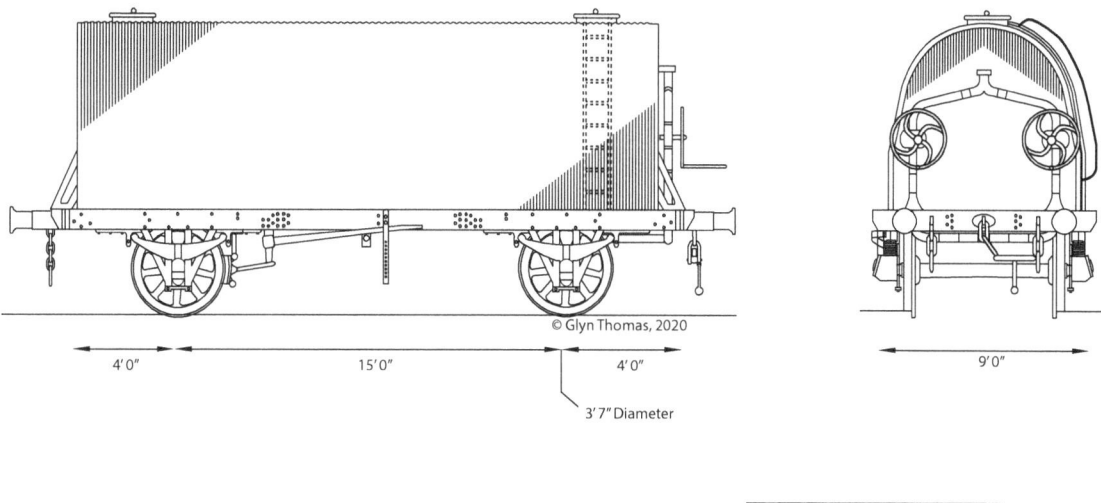

Wheelbase	15' 0"
Wheel Diameter	3' 7"
Tare Weight	
Capacity	3,750 gallons

In 1896, East Indian Railway ordered 38 tank wagons for mineral oil use from the Leeds Forge Co. Ltd. These used welded seams, and were fitted with two rotary pumps for unloading. Using these pumps, a wagon could be unloaded in 90 minutes. They were clad with a corrugated iron cover, but underneath looked like a conventional tank wagon. Since the Assam Bengal Railway was metre-gauge, Digboi oil would have been transshipped to EIR wagons for domestic distribution, or they would be used for imported oil.

[Reference: Railway Engineer, January 1896]

BNR Tank Car 1904

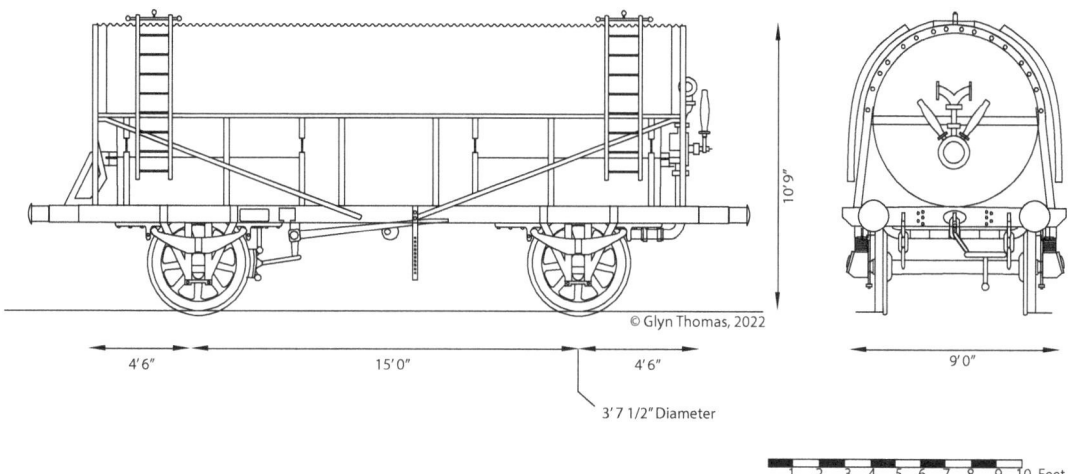

Wheelbase	15' 0"
Wheel Diameter	3' 7"
Tare Weight	14 tons
Capacity	40 tons, 5,000 gallons

[Reference: Indian Engineering, 1904]

Broad-Gauge Rolling Stock

IRCA Tank Car 1921

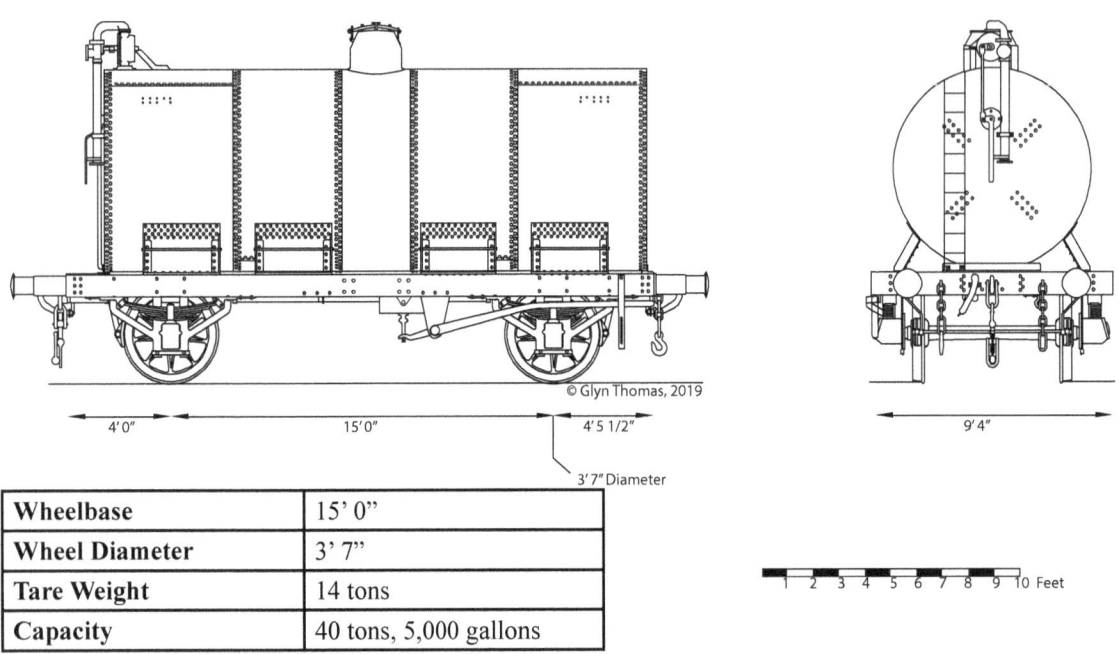

Wheelbase	15' 0"
Wheel Diameter	3' 7"
Tare Weight	14 tons
Capacity	40 tons, 5,000 gallons

The 1921 IRCA design, using riveted seams and a single manual pump for discharge. These were built by the Metropolitan Cammell Carriage and Wagon Co. Ltd.

[Reference: builder's drawing via Historical Model Railway Society]

Modern Tank Car

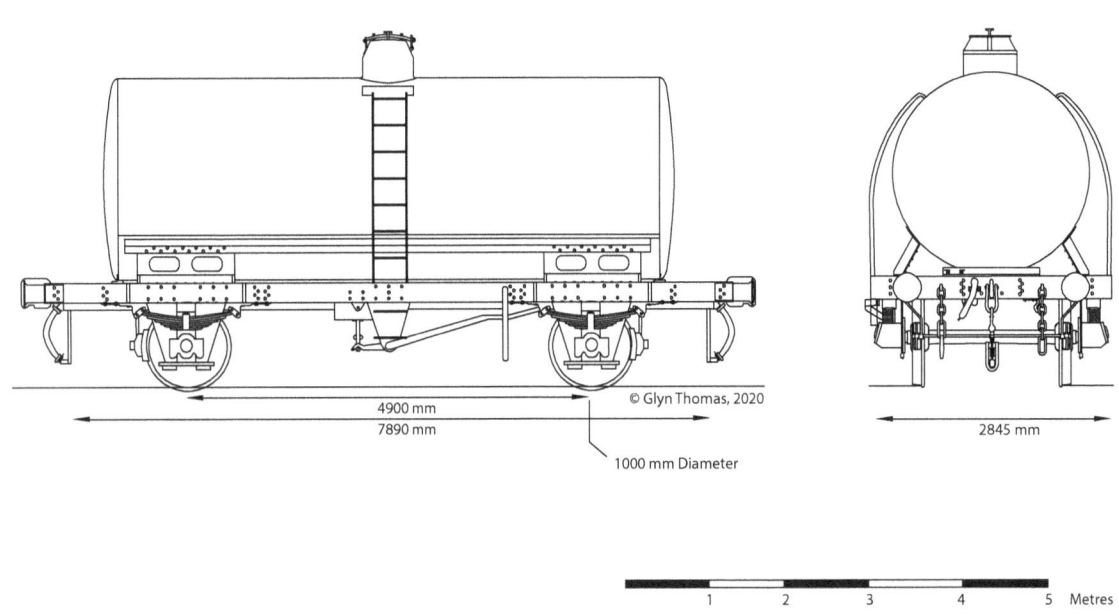

This diagram shows the modern 4-wheel tank wagon design.

[Reference: photographs]

Bogie Covered Vans

NWR IRCA Bogie Covered Van by Birmingham Railway Carriage and Wagon Works, 1922-3 [Builder's Photo, Julian Rainbow Collection]

Bogie covered vans, "boxcars" in American terminology, were introduced in Americas during the 1840s and quickly took hold of the majority of freight traffic there. On lightweight, rough, track they ride better and distribute the load more evenly than 4-wheel covered vans. It was much later before they became common in Britain and Europe, where the track was generally built to a higher standard so the shortcomings of the 4-wheel van were less obvious.

India followed British practice and the permanent way on broad gauge lines was constructed to a high standard, so 4-wheel vans predominated through the 19th Century and early part of the 20th Century. The Indian Railway Conference Association (IRCA) designs of 1921 included a range of bogie vehicles sharing a common underframe design. A bogie covered van was included. This was probably intended to increase capacity instead of solving ride issues and was essentially equivalent of two 4-wheel vans joined on a common frame. Photographic evidence suggests that these were not widely used during the colonial period.

Indian Railways introduced the hugely successful BCN covered van design, which rapidly displace 4-wheeled covered vans of CR design and its predecessors. Visually, there is a clear similarity to its IRCA predecessor. Variations on the BCN design have dominated post-Independence Indian Railways and continue to be built today.

From a traffic point of view, bogie covered vans and their 4-wheel predecessors were probably mainly used for agricultural products, likely shipped in sacks or barrels.

The most important Indian agricultural product is textiles. West Bengal is a major producer of jute. Rajasthan, Maharashtra and Gujarat are major centres for growing cotton. Before the establishment of domestic mills, raw agricultural products were exported to Britain for processing. As domestic mills developed, jute was generally shipped to mills in the area around Calcutta (Kolkata) and cotton was originally shipped to mills around Bombay (Mumbai) and Ahmadabad. Indian businessmen were important in establishing mills in western India - C. N. Davar in Bombay, and Ranchhodlal Chhotalal in Ahmadabad. In more recent years textile manufacture has become more widely distributed across the country.

India is one of the world's largest producers of sugar. Sugar cane is grown in Uttar Pradesh, Maharashtra, Karnataka, Gujarat, Tamil Nadu, and Andhra Pradesh. The industry was largely kick-started by the introduction of tariff protection in the early 1930s, which led to an increase of sugar mills from 30 to 135 between 1930-1931. Most of these early mills were privately owned by Indian businessmen and centred in Bihar and United Provinces. (The industry has continued to grow and there are 453 mills operating in 2020.) For processing, cane is usually brought from fields to the mills in open wagons via private tramways, or by road. Processed sugar and related products are forwarded by covered van on the regular railways.

India has ideal conditions to produce salt, and control of production and trade fuelled the early expansion of the British East India Company. In the 19th Century, a 230-mile customs fence was erected in Bengal to facilitate taxation, and taxes were set at a level to depress local production in favour of British imports. By the end of the 19th Century, salt taxes were reduced and Indian production rose to about 1M tons per year, but taxation remained a source of conflict. Salt taxes were opposed by early Independence leaders, Gandi's Dandi March of 1930 was partially to protest salt taxes. With government encouragement since Independence, Indian salt production rose from 1.9M tons in 1947 to 22.2M tons in 2012. India is now one of the largest salt producers in the world and is a major exporter. The largest producing areas are Gujarat (76%), Tamil Nadu (12%) and Rajasthan (8%) with the remainder from other regions. 7% of salt traffic moves by rail in covered vans. These are usually marshalled in rakes of 40 vans and given preferential treatment by the railways.

GIPR Bogie Covered Van, 1914 [BRCW Photo, Julian Rainbow Collection]

BCN Covered Van at the Goods Intermodal Transshipment yard, Pune, 2003 [Apurva Bahadu, IRFCA]

GIPR Bogie Covered Van 1910

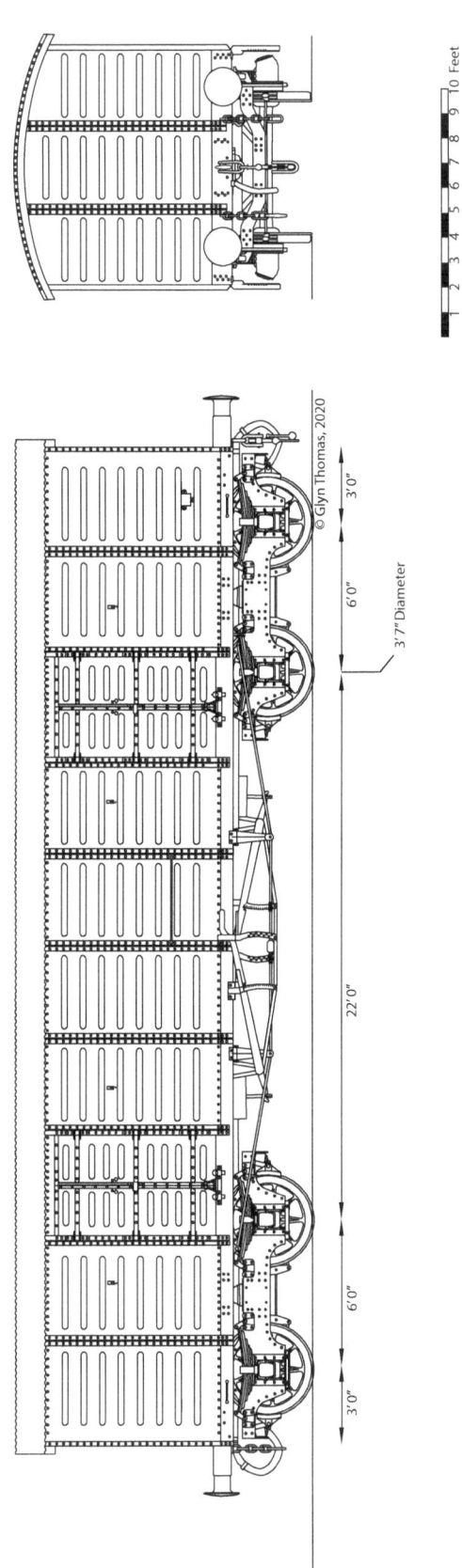

© Glyn Thomas, 2020

3'0"

6'0"

3'7" Diameter

22'0"

6'0"

3'0"

Bogie Wheelbase	6' 0"
Bogie Centres	28' 0"
Wheel Diameter	3' 7"
Tare Weight	20 tons 19 cwt 1 qtr
Capacity	40 tons

The GIPR was an early adopter of bogie wagons for broad gauge traffic in order to handle increased loads into the port of Bombay. An initial order for prototypes of a covered van and an open wagon was made to BRCW in 1910. Following the success of these prototypes, there were subsequent orders of both types. The prototype van was numbered 19002. The van was designed for cotton traffic, but was probably used for other commodities as well.

The van shown has pressed ribs in the steel sides and ends to increase strength without increasing bracing.

At least one of these vans has survived as an exhibit in the Howrah Railway Museum. It is similar in most details, although additional riveting on the underframe may indicate strengthening during service.

[Reference: Photographs and dimensions from Indian Industries and Power, 1913]

IRCA Bogie Covered Van 1921

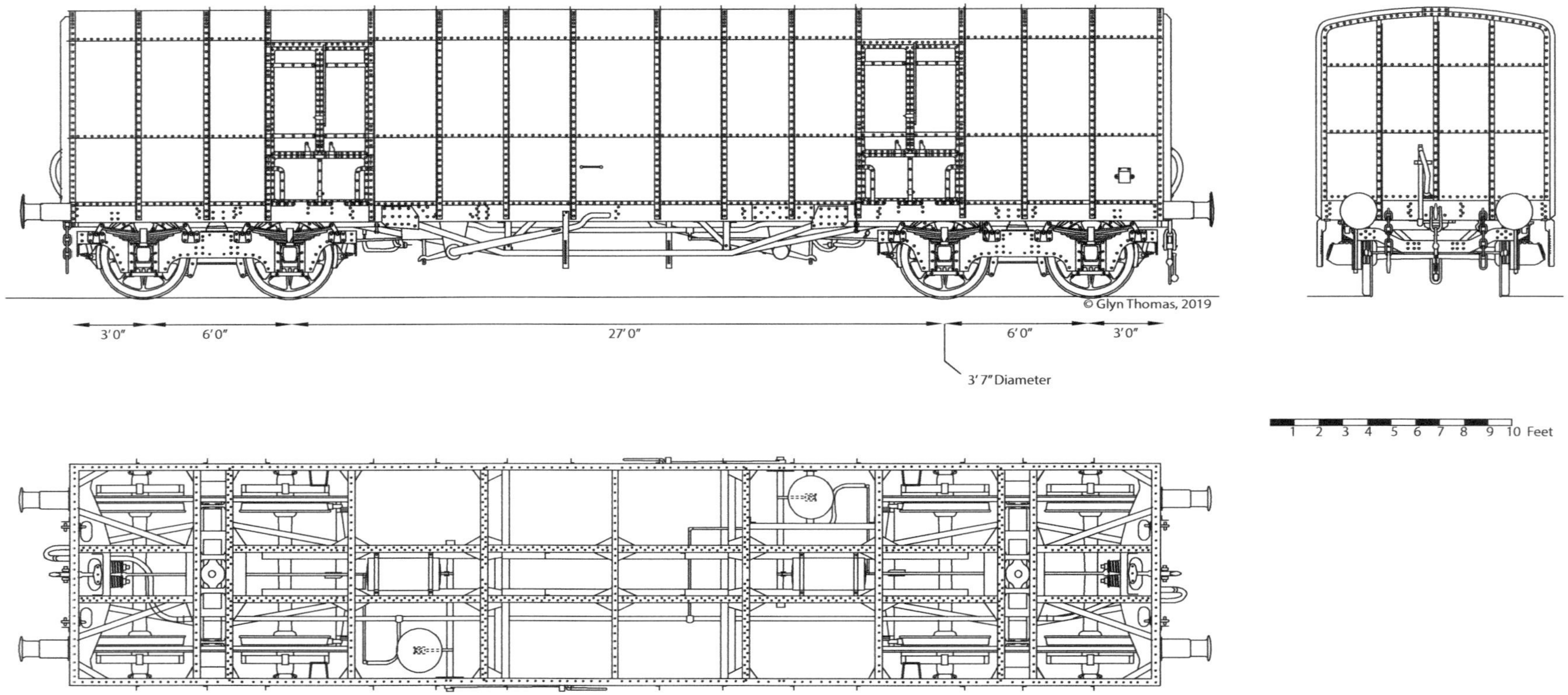

© Glyn Thomas, 2019

3' 0"

6' 0"

3' 7" Diameter

27' 0"

6' 0"

3' 0"

10 Feet
1 2 3 4 5 6 7 8 9

Bogie Wheelbase	6' 0"
Bogie Centres	33' 0"
Wheel Diameter	3' 7"
Tare Weight	22 tons 12 cwt 1 qtr
Capacity	41 tons 8 cwt

IRCA bogie van design, based on the original engineer's specification.

[Reference: Metro Cammell drawings via Historical Model Railway Society]

BCN Bogie Covered Van

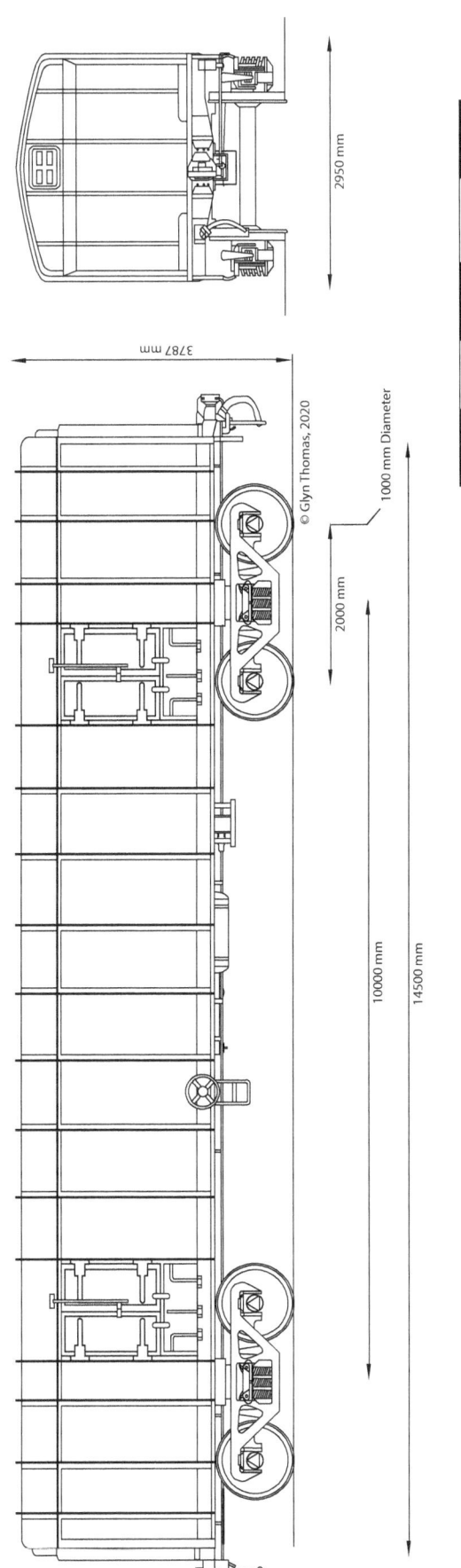

© Glyn Thomas, 2020

2950 mm

3787 mm

1000 mm Diameter

2000 mm

10000 mm

14500 mm

Bogie Wheelbase	2,000 mm
Bogie Centres	10,000 mm
Wheel Diameter	1,000mm
Tare Weight	27.2 tonnes
Capacity	54.08

Modern Indian Railways BCN design.

[Reference: Maintenance Manual for Wagons]

1   2   3   4   5   Metres

Bogie Open Wagons

BOXC was the forerunner of the BOXN [Jimmy Jose, 2006, IRFCA]

The bogie open wagon was an obvious 20th Century adaptation of the 4-wheel open wagon, aimed at increasing capacity without increasing axle load.

Over time, bogie wagons took over the coal traffic in the coalfields. They were also used for iron ore traffic in Bengal.

The Indian Railway BOX high-sided bogie open wagon was introduced in 1989 and built in large numbers. There have been numerous variations on this design, which continue to be built until today, as shown in the following table (courtesy of IRFCA).

Type	Description
BOX	Original design
BOXT	Transition couplers
BOXR	Screw couplers
BOXC	CBC couplers
BOXN	Pneumatic brakes
BOXN-HA	High axle load version
BOXN-HS	High axle load and high speed
BOXN-HL	Variation of HS design
BOXN-CR	Corrosion resistant version
BOXN-LW	Low tare-weight version with steel body
BOXN-AL	Low tare-weight version with aluminum body
BOXN-EL	Enhanced-loading version
BOXN-25M	25-ton axle load version
BOXC	Side discharge with sliding roof

GIPR Bogie Open Wagon

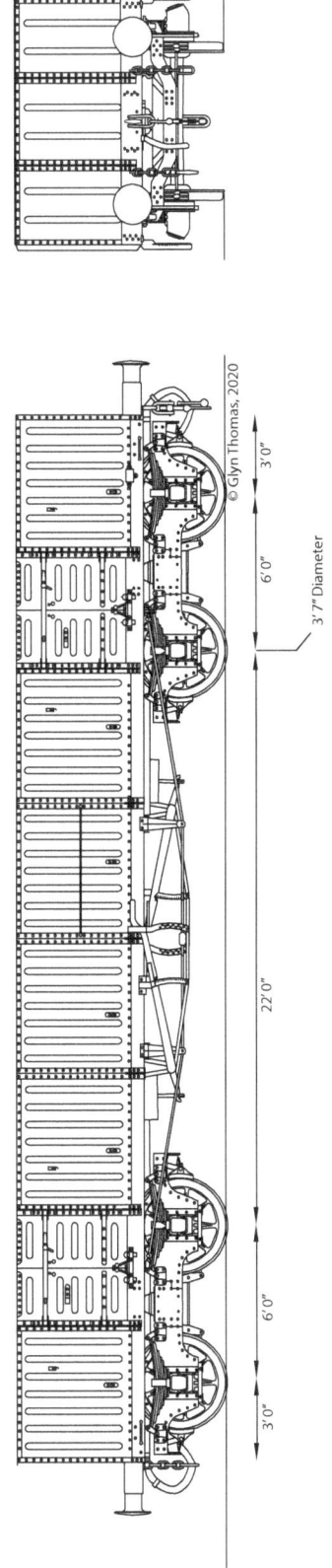

© Glyn Thomas, 2020

3'7" Diameter

Bogie Wheelbase	6' 0"
Bogie Centres	28' 0"
Wheel Diameter	3' 7"
Tare Weight	18 tons 19 cwt 3 qtr
Capacity	40 tons

Birmingham Railway Carriage and Wagon (BRCW) built the prototype of these bogie open wagons for GIPR in 1910. They were rapidly adopted and were used for a long time on the railway. There is photographic evidence of one still in use in 1963. An early numbering example is 39037. The 1963 example was numbered 39204. Early loads include manganese, ore, coal, and grain.

[Reference: BRCW Photographs and Dimensions from Indian Industries and Power]

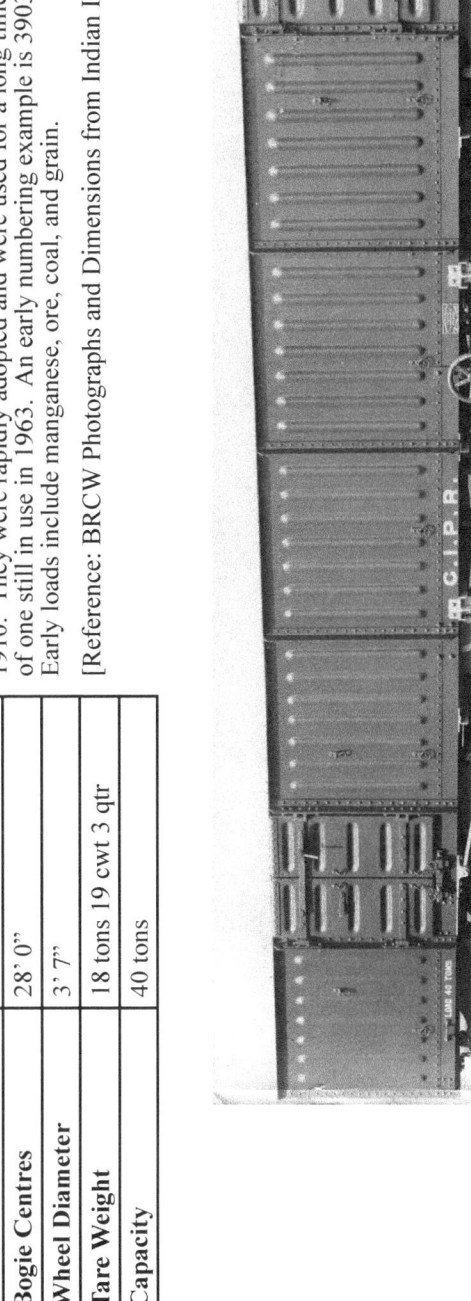

GIPR Bogie Open Wagon, 1912 [BRCW Photo, Julian Rainbow Collection]

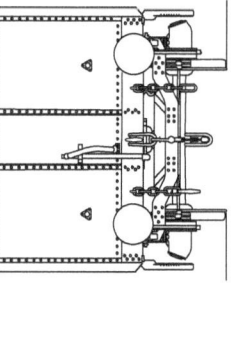

© Glyn Thomas, 2019

3'0"

6'0"

3'7" Diameter

27'0"

6'0"

3'0"

The IRCA standard design of 1921 uses the equivalent of two 4-wheel open wagon bodies on the IRCA standard underframe.

[Reference: Metro Cammell drawing via Historical Model Railway Society]

Bogie Wheelbase	6' 0"
Bogie Centres	33' 0"
Wheel Diameter	3' 7"
Tare Weight	23 tons
Capacity	41 tons

1 2 3 4 5 6 7 8 9 10 Feet

BOXN Bogie Open Wagon

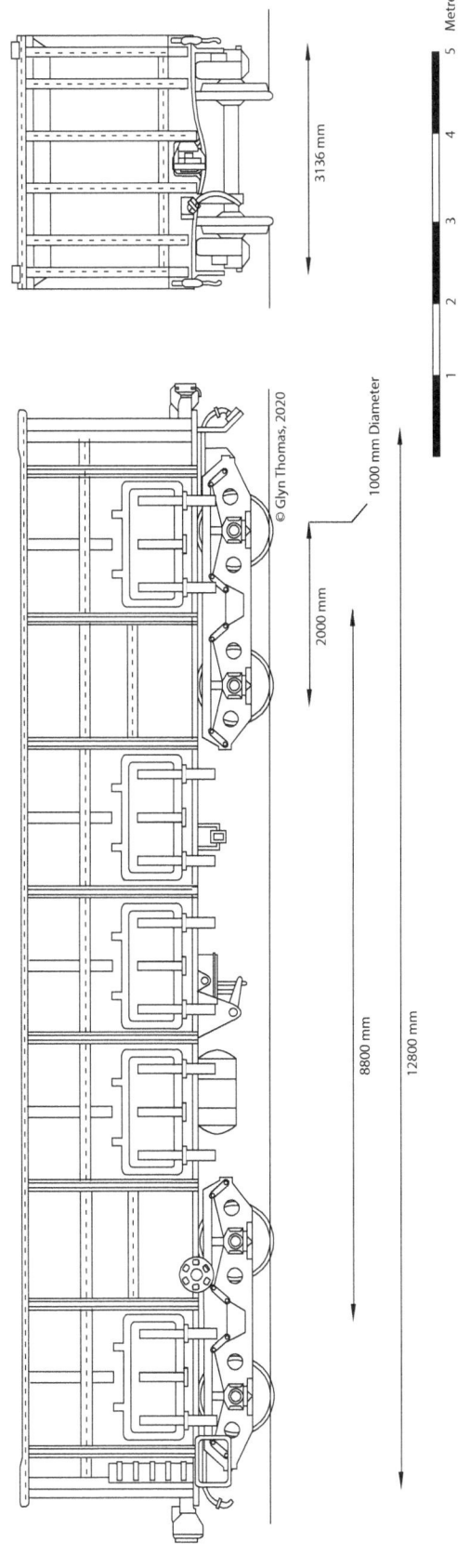

© Glyn Thomas, 2020

3136 mm

1000 mm Diameter

2000 mm

8800 mm

12800 mm

0 1 2 3 4 5 Metres

Bogie Wheelbase	2,000 mm
Bogie Centres	8,800 mm
Wheel Diameter	1,000mm
Tare Weight	22.47 tonnes
Capacity	58.81 tonnes

In recent years, bogie open wagons of BOX and it's variants have overtaken covered vans as the most numerous wagons on Indian railways. The illustration is based on the BOXN design fitted with UIC G70 bogies. [Reference: Maintenance Manual for Wagons]

Bogie Flat Wagons

IRCA Bogie Flat Wagon for the GIPR by Birmingham Railway Carriage and Wagon Works, 1921 [BRCW Photo, Julian Rainbow Collection]

Bogie flat wagons are useful for carrying loads that are best loaded from the side and may include unusual shaped objects that can be tethered. Railways often use them to carry rail; industries may them for steel components or heavy machinery; with the stakes up, they can be loaded with logs or timber. In the past, it was common to see narrow gauge rolling stock carried on these by Indian Railways.

The initial Indian Railways design was designated BRH. In 1994, this was superseded by the BRN design. There are two known variants of the design: BRNA was a prototype from 1992, and BRNA-HS is a high-speed version.

Typical Indian truck on a BRN flatcar at Mumbai Madgaon, June 3rd, 2002 [Lalam, IRFCA]

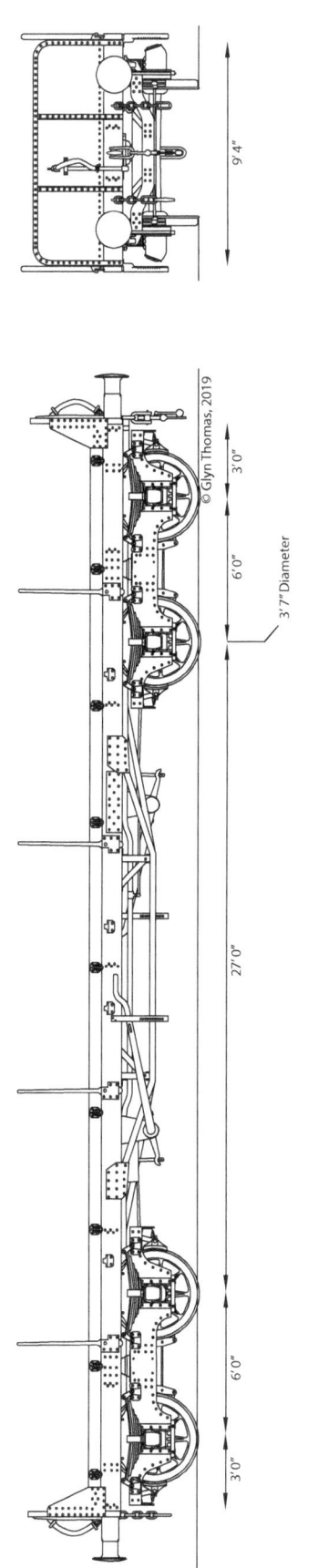

IRCA Flatcar 1921

The IRCA 1921 standard included a design based on the standard bogie underframe.

[Reference: Metro Cammell drawing via Historical Model Railway Society]

Bogie Wheelbase	6' 0"
Bogie Centres	33' 0"
Wheel Diameter	3' 7"
Tare Weight	20 tons 17 cwt 1 qtr
Capacity	43 tons

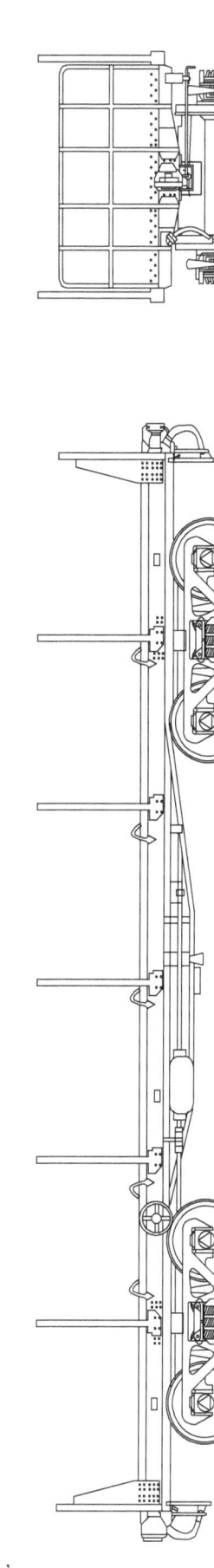

BRN Flatcar

A BRN wagon with air brakes and CASNUB 22W bogies.

[Reference: Maintenance Manual for Wagons]

Bogie Wheelbase	2,000 mm
Bogie Centres	9,144 mm
Wheel Diameter	1,000mm
Tare Weight	22.47 tonnes
Capacity	58.81 tonnes

BNR Bogie Ore Hopper

BNR Bogie Hopper Wagon[The Locomotive, 1930, Author's Collection]

These large bogie iron ore hoppers were built by the Metropolitan Cammell Carriage Wagon and Finance Company in 1930 for use on the Bengal Nagpur Railway. They were designed by the railway's consulting engineers, Sir John Wolfe Barry and Partners, to carry ore from the mines to the iron and steel works. They discharged the ore through bottom doors on either side.

Iron and steel was an early success for Indian industry. The necessary raw materials (iron ore, coal, and water) were available domestically, but the British financial and engineering markets did not consider that it was feasible to produce high-quality iron and steel in India. Tata Iron and Steel Company (TISCO) was established in 1907 by an Indian industrialist, Jamsedji N. Tata, to build an integrated iron and steel plant at Sakchi (Jamshedpur). Although supported by the Indian government from the outset, the company did not receive direct economic support until 1924, when it was granted tariff protection in recognition of its value during World War 1. During the 1930s depression, TISCO was successful in driving down their production costs, and they ended the decade operating the largest plant in the British Empire. TISCO's plant was served by a 40-mile BNR branch to the iron ore fields at Gorumahisani. Coal came over the existing BNR network from Jharia, hauled by Beyer-Garratt locomotives in the final years of steam. Tata Steel continues to be one of the largest steel producers in the world and is partially owned by Tata Group.

In 1918, a second integrated plant was setup at Burnpur promoted by Burn and Company, and operated by the Indian Iron and Steel Company. In 1936, this merged with a smaller operation at Kulti that had opened as Bengal Iron Works in 1881, which became the Bengal Iron and Steel Company in 1892, managed by Martin and Company. This second plant received iron and magnesium via a BNR branch to Dangoaposi and Gua.

Soon after Independence, three new integrated iron and steel plants were built, at Bhilai, Rourkela, and Durgapur, and managed by Hindustan Steel Limited of Ranchi. Bhilai receives iron ore via a railway line from Bhilai to Dalli-Rajhara (this traffic was also hauled by Beyer-Garratt locomotives in the final years of steam). Rourkela receives ore from a line to Kiriburu.

In 1967, an integrated steel plant was built at Bokaro. New lines were required from Muri to Chandrapura and Ranchi to ship the raw materials for this plant.

In the 1980s a further plant was developed at Visakhapatnam, now operated as Vizag Steel. The Koraput-Rayagada rail line was built to serve this plant and other industries in the area.

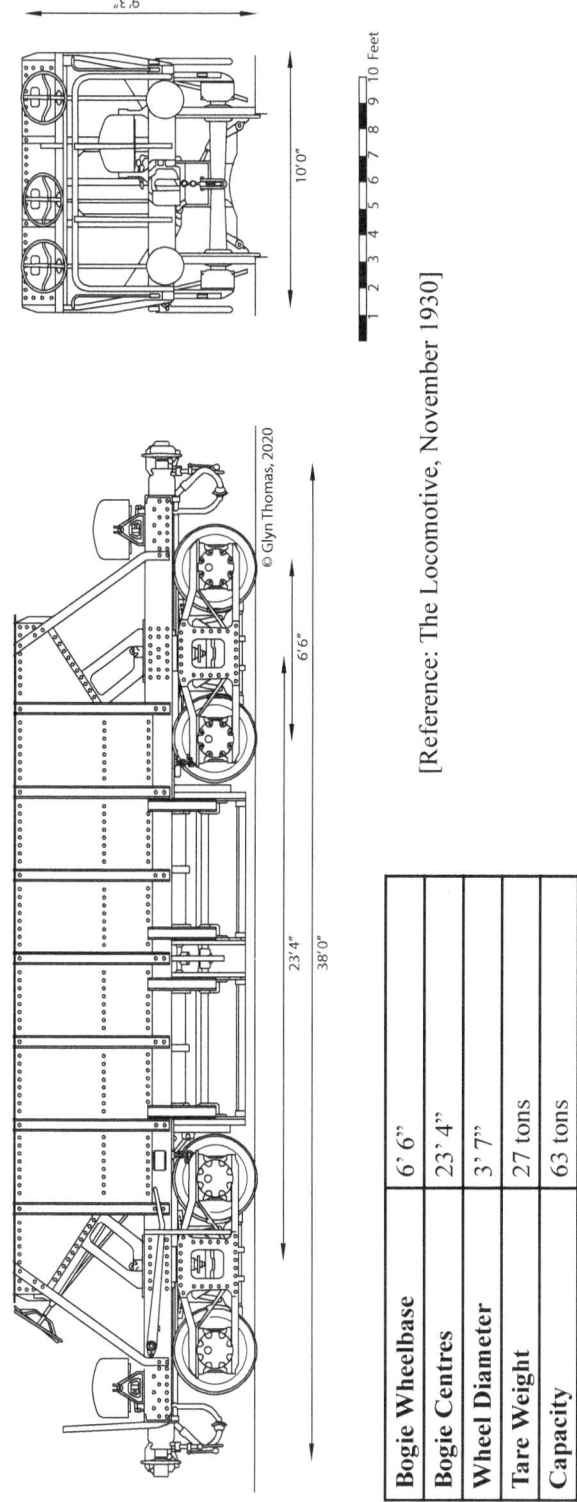

© Glyn Thomas, 2020

[Reference: The Locomotive, November 1930]

Bogie Wheelbase	6' 6"
Bogie Centres	23' 4"
Wheel Diameter	3' 7"
Tare Weight	27 tons
Capacity	63 tons

Bogie Oil Tanker

BTPN Petrol Tank Wagon [The Train Explorer, Pexels]

The Indian Railway Conference Association (IRCA) designs of 1921 included a bogie oil tanker to use the standard underframe, with a capacity approximately double the 4-wheel version.

Bogie tank wagons have become much more common on the railways in the post-Independence era, and now carry a wide variety of chemical products.

BTPN Petrol Tank Wagon

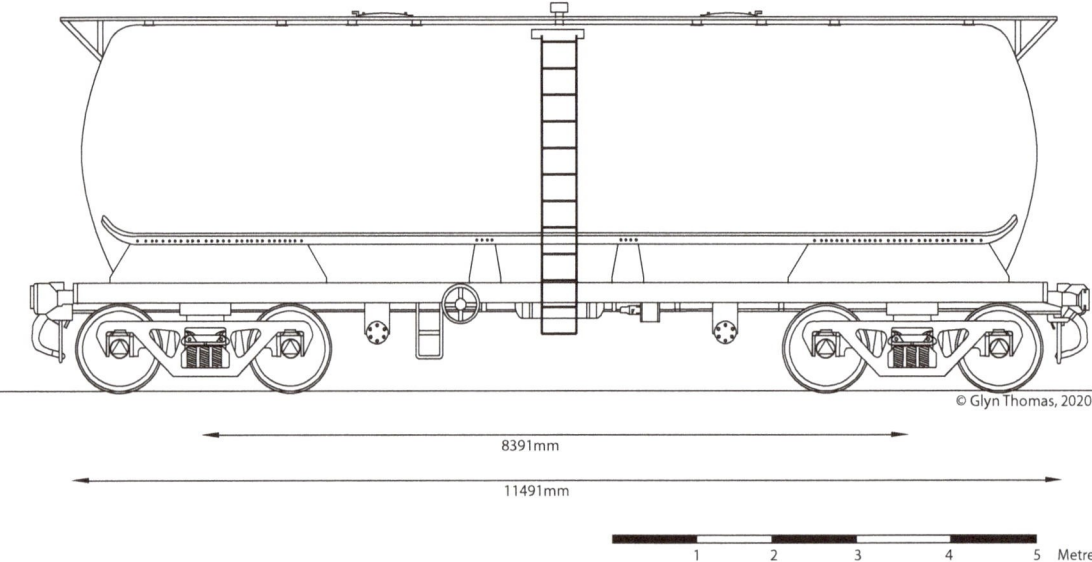

8391mm

11491mm

1 2 3 4 5 Metres

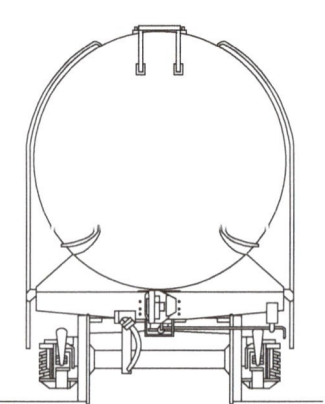

Bogie Wheelbase	2,000 mm
Bogie Centres	8,391 mm
Wheel Diameter	1,000 mm
Tare Weight	27 tonnes
Capacity	54.28 tonnes

[Reference: backdated from Touax Texmaco Railcar Leasing Ltd diagram for a BTFLN wagon]

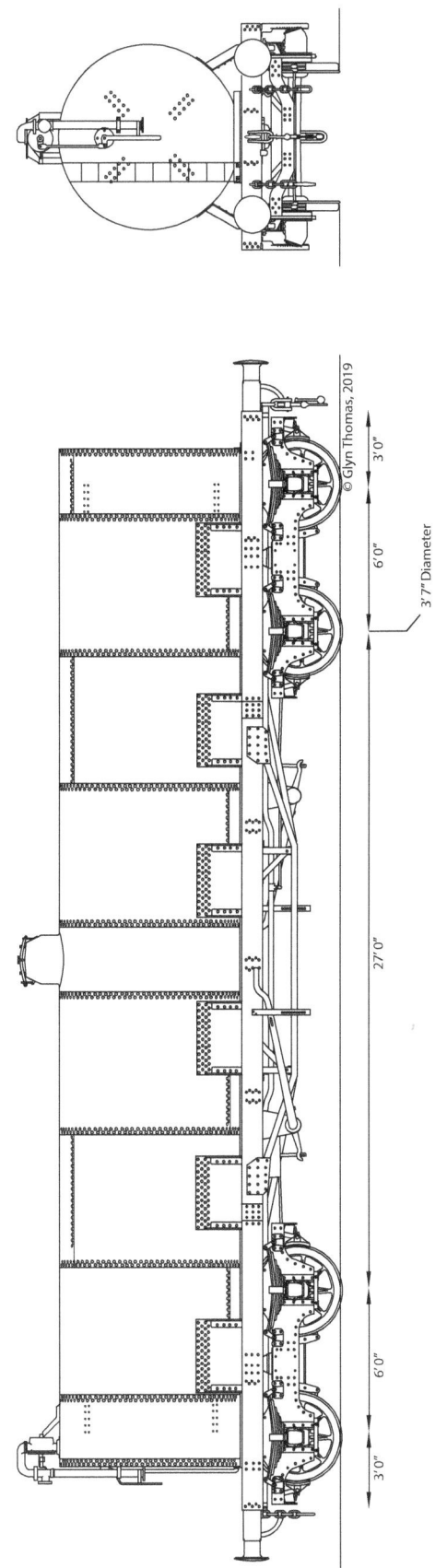

IRCA Bogie Tank Wagon, 1921

© Glyn Thomas, 2019

3'7" Diameter

3'0"

6'0"

27'0"

6'0"

3'0"

1 2 3 4 5 6 7 8 9 10 Feet

[Reference: Metro Cammell drawings via the Historical Model Railway Society archives]

Bogie Wheelbase	6' 0"
Bogie Centres	27' 0"
Wheel Diameter	3' 7"
Tare Weight	28 tons 18 cwt 2 qtr
Capacity	40 tons, 10,000 gallons

Brake Vans

Brake Van 72212 somewhere between Hubli Junction and Alnavar Junction [Ramdev Gowda, IRFCA]

Brake vans originated during the period when wagons were hand-braked. A Guard rode in the van and assisted the driver by adjusting the brakes according to speed and gradient. Brake vans continued to be used after the introduction of vacuum brakes to adjust the brakes and detect if couplers parted in the train. They also proved useful as a riding platform for the train crew when in motion.

During the early part of the 20th century there was considerable variation in designs between the individual railway companies. These vans often resembled their British contemporaries, including the provision of lookouts set out from the sides to permit viewing of the train in motion.

By the 1930s designs started to resemble the final Indian Railway standard BVG or BVGT 4-wheeled brake van. The BVGT uses a transition coupler.

In recent years, brake vans have largely disappeared from freight trains due to the roll-out of air brakes, improved couplers, and block trains.

Broad-Gauge Rolling Stock

NSR MVC Brake Van

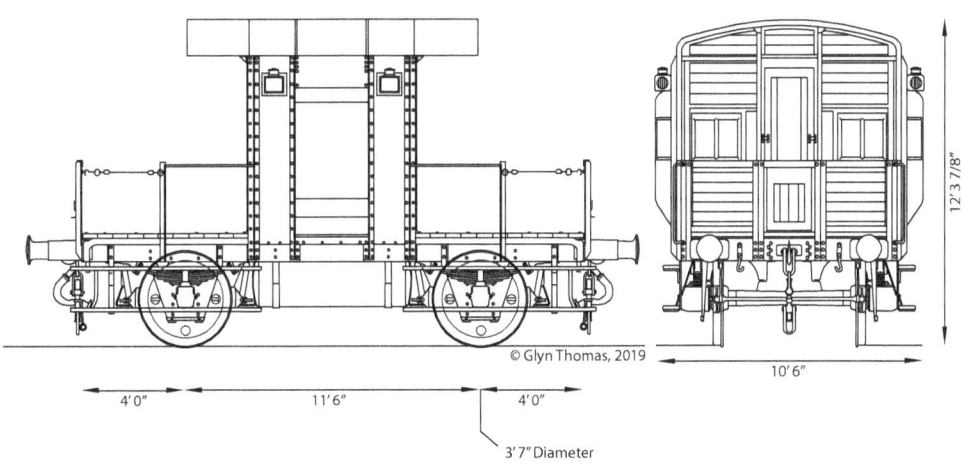

Wheelbase	11' 6"
Wheel Diameter	3' 7"
Tare Weight	10 tons 16 cwt
Capacity	10 tons 11 cwt

Nissam's State Railway (NSR) MVC design of 1939. These were very similar to the later Indian Railways BVG design, but still had wooden ends instead of steel.

[Reference: Metro Cammell Metro Cammell diagram via Historical Model Railway Society]

GIPR Brake Van

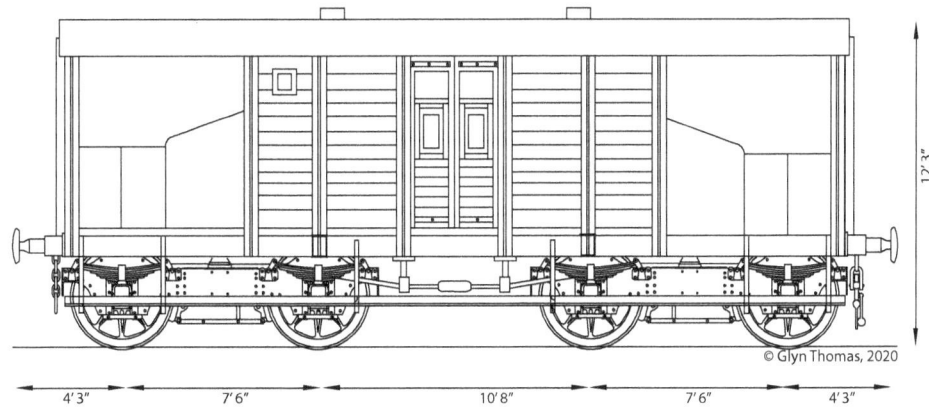

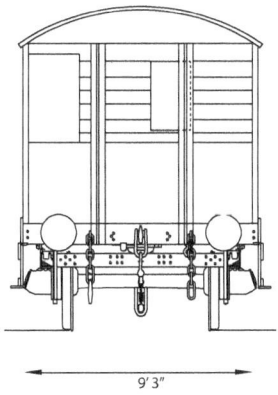

Bogie Wheelbase	7' 6"
Bogie Centres	18' 2"
Wheel Diameter	3' 7"
Tare Weight	40 tons

GIPR design for a 40 ton brake van from 1917. These were used for braking on 1,500 ton trains. At the time these were built, about two-thirds of freight wagons were fitted with vacuum brakes. The house on the van included accommodation for traveling railway officials and transport of small livestock such as sheep and goats.

[Reference: The Locomotive, June 1917]

Eastern Bengal Railway 4-Wheel Coaches

NWR First Class 4-Wheel Coach no. 135 is similar to the coaches illustrated [Historical Railway Images, Flickr]

During the 19th Century, coaches on Indian Railways were almost exclusively built to 4-wheel designs. Early examples still resembled horse-drawn road coaches. There were also early experiments with double-deck coaches, with third-class seating in the open on the top deck and first class below (supposedly to provide a form of human heat insulation!)

By the 1870s the early experiments had been superseded by similar designs across most Indian railways, consisting of an iron or steel (after 1885) 4-wheel underframe and a wooden coach body. Separate coaches were provided for each class of passenger, and the coaches were fitted with sunshades to provide heat protection. First class coaches were furnished with plush chairs and often had lavatory facilities. Second class coaches had less comfortable seating but may still have toilet facilities. Third class was fitted with benches.

The examples drawn here were built by the Eastern Bengal Railway (EBR) at their Kanchrapara workshop in 1898. While slightly early for the time period of the book, they demonstrate that these early designs were still being built right up to the start of the 20th Century. With the expected lifetime of wooden coaches being 35 years, 4-wheel style coaches continued to dominate the railway scene, especially on secondary trains, through the early part of the 20th Century. The diagrams show the third-class coach as used on short-haul journeys, and a 1st-2nd class composite. On journeys over 50 miles, the third-class coaches also had toilets.

Broad-Gauge Rolling Stock

EBR 1st-2nd Composite

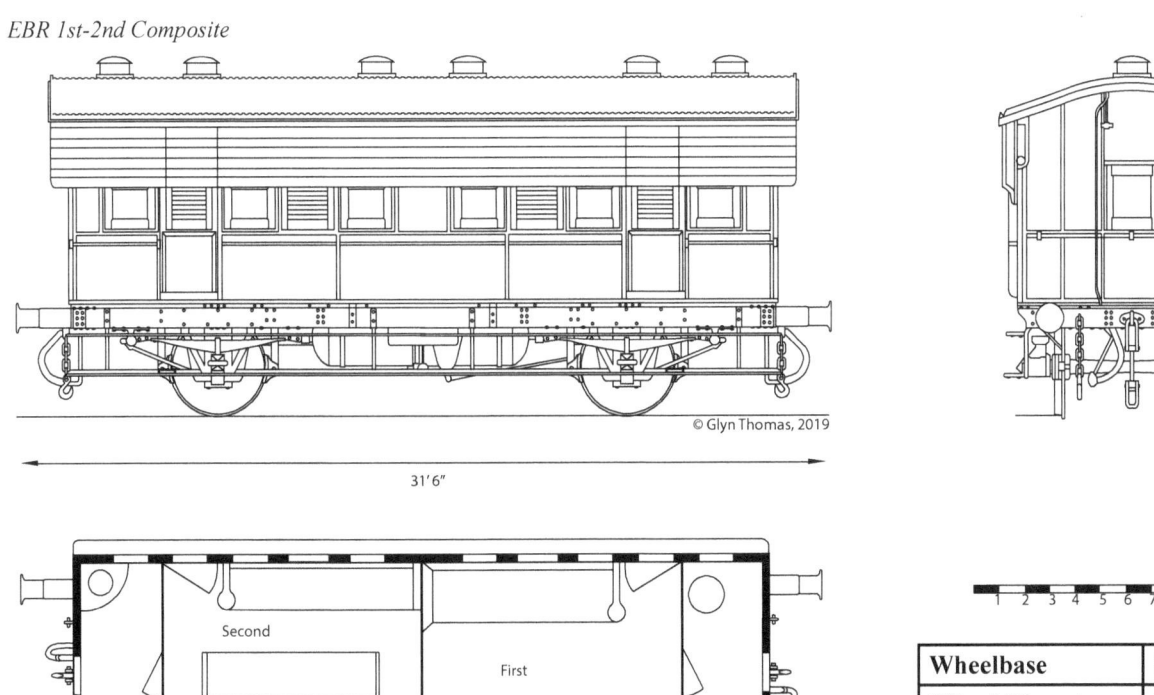

© Glyn Thomas, 2019

31' 6"

Second

First

1 2 3 4 5 6 7 8 9 10 Feet

Wheelbase	31' 6"
Wheel Diameter	3' 7"

EBR 3rd Coach

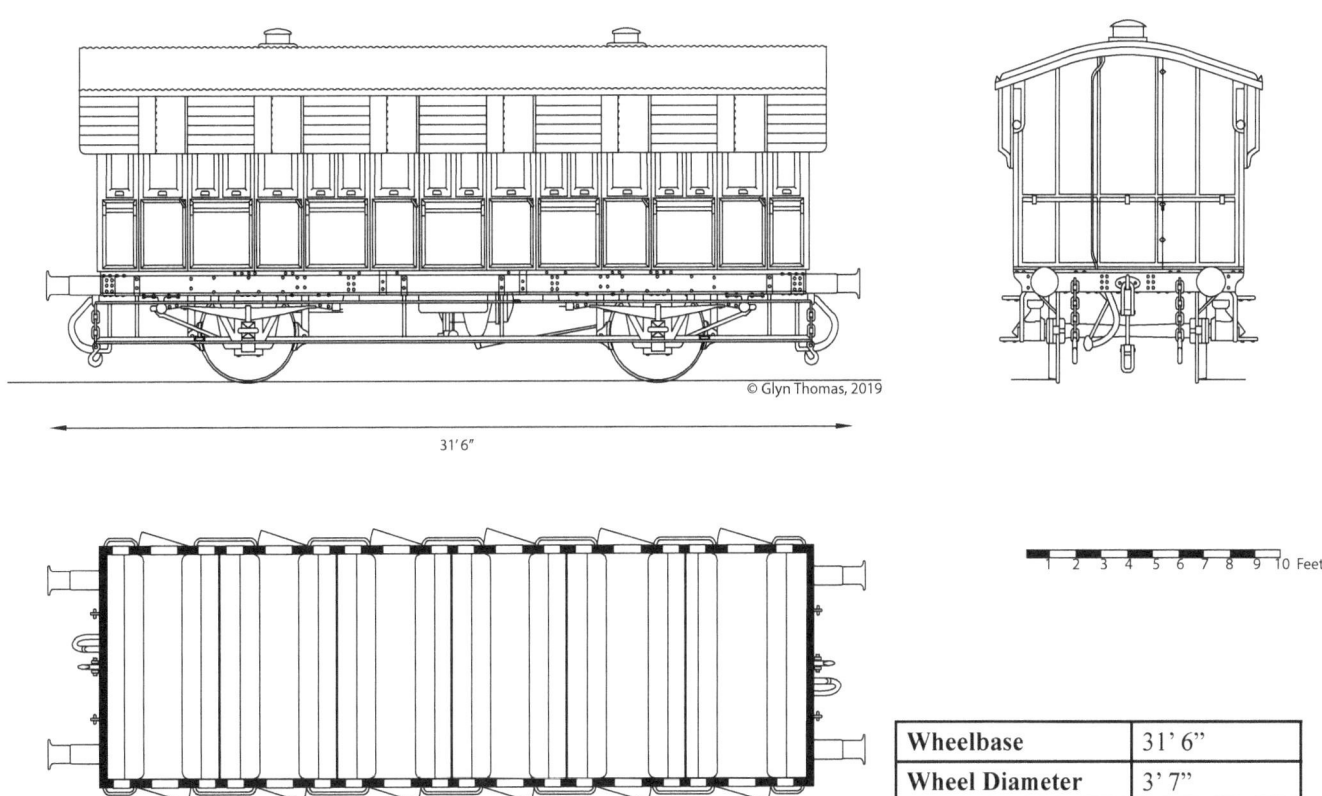

© Glyn Thomas, 2019

31' 6"

1 2 3 4 5 6 7 8 9 10 Feet

Wheelbase	31' 6"
Wheel Diameter	3' 7"

[Reference: Railway Engineer, 1898]

GIPR-Madras Railway Mail Bogie Coaches

GIPR First Class Coach no. 1890 is similar to the coaches illustrated here [Historical Railway Images, Flickr]

Before telephone and Internet, mail was the primary form of long distance communication and was essential to the effective operation of both government and business, especially in a country as large as India. Even before the railways, mail was conveyed by cart along the military roads, but the railways reduced communication delays from weeks to days, while also improving security. Carrying mail was second only to carrying troops in importance to Indian railways.

Dalhousie's vision for Indian railways included trunk routes between all the major colonial era cities. Mail trains plied the new routes as soon as they were developed. English Mail trains that connected with steamers to England carried first and second class passengers operated on the fastest possible schedules that line conditions permitted. Other mail trains operated on slower schedules to maximise interconnections, and carried all classes of passenger. In most cases, the routes were managed by more than one company, and interoperating agreements were made to expedite the mail. Trains were either jointly owned, or the railways would each own rakes and just interchange locomotives at the division points.

In later years, traveling post offices were attached to trains with the capability of picking up and dropping mail at speed, further expediting mail between stops en route.

The conveyance of all classes of passenger on regular mail trains probably contributed to the cohesiveness of the Indian population and help foster the idea of India as a nation.

The carriages drawn here were owned jointly by the Great Indian Peninsula Railway (GIPR) and the Madras Railway (MR) for mail trains between Bombay and Madras. These were built in 1901 at GIPR's workshop at Parel. From a design perspective the carriages are transitional, with longer bogie underframes, but still using the sunshades for heat reduction. The composite coach was fitted with grass blinds that were periodically wetted by an automatic apparatus to aid cooling.

GIPR-MR Mail 1st Class Coach

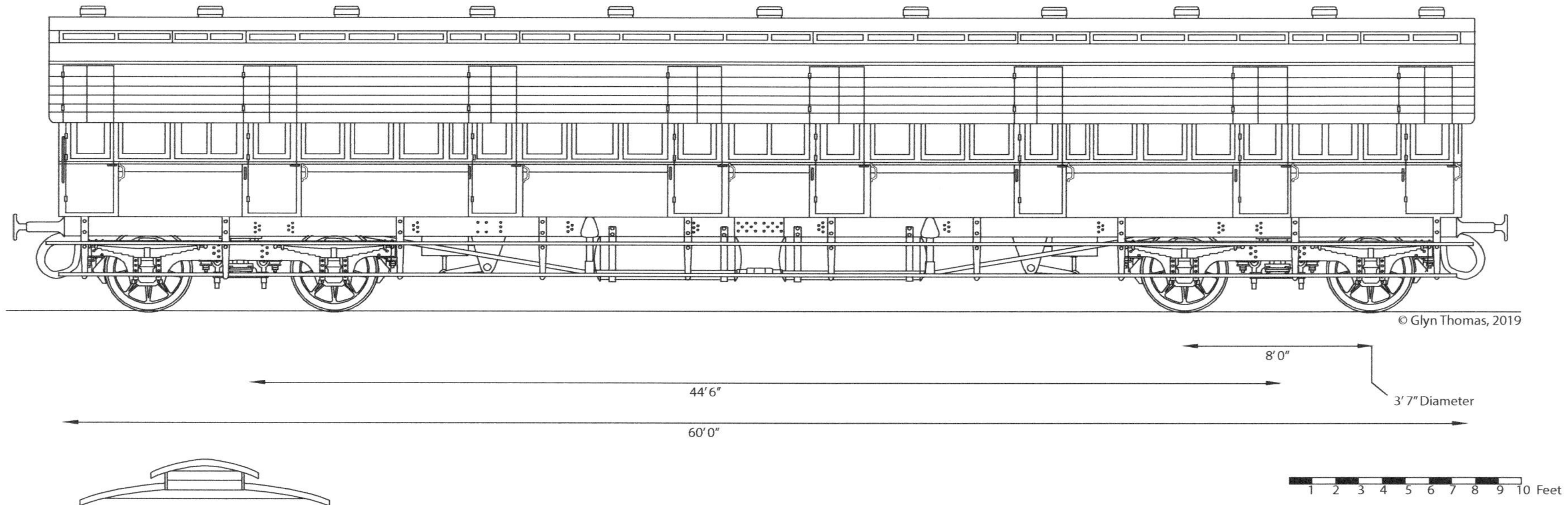

© Glyn Thomas, 2019

3' 7" Diameter

8' 0"

44' 6"

60' 0"

1 2 3 4 5 6 7 8 9 10 Feet

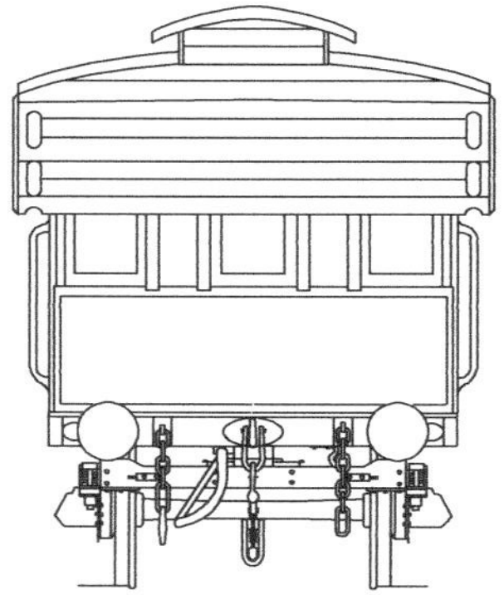

Note the rudimentary third class servant's compartments linked to the first class compartments in the plan below.

[Reference: Railway Engineer, April 1901]

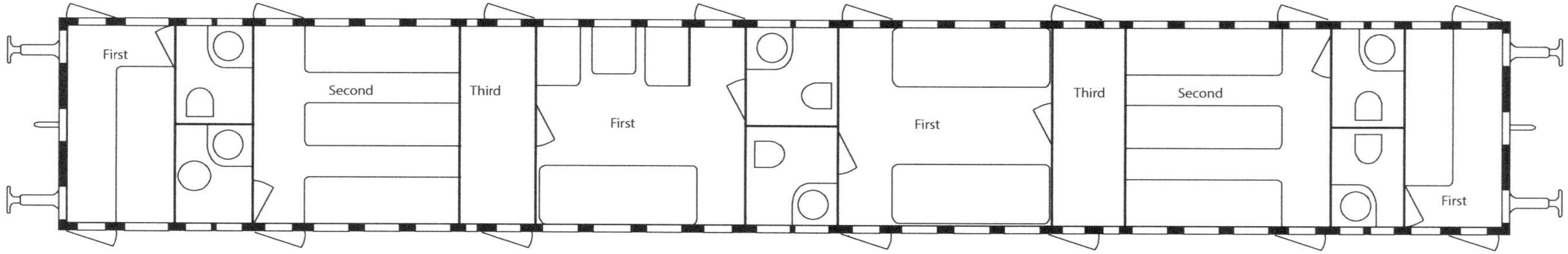

Bogie Wheelbase	8' 0"
Bogie Centres	44' 6"
Wheel Diameter	3' 7"
Capacity	10 first class, 12 second class, 10 third class (servants)

First

Second

Third

First

First

Third

Second

First

© Glyn Thomas, 2019

3'7" Diameter

8' 0"

44' 6"

60' 0"

1 2 3 4 5 6 7 8 9 10 Feet

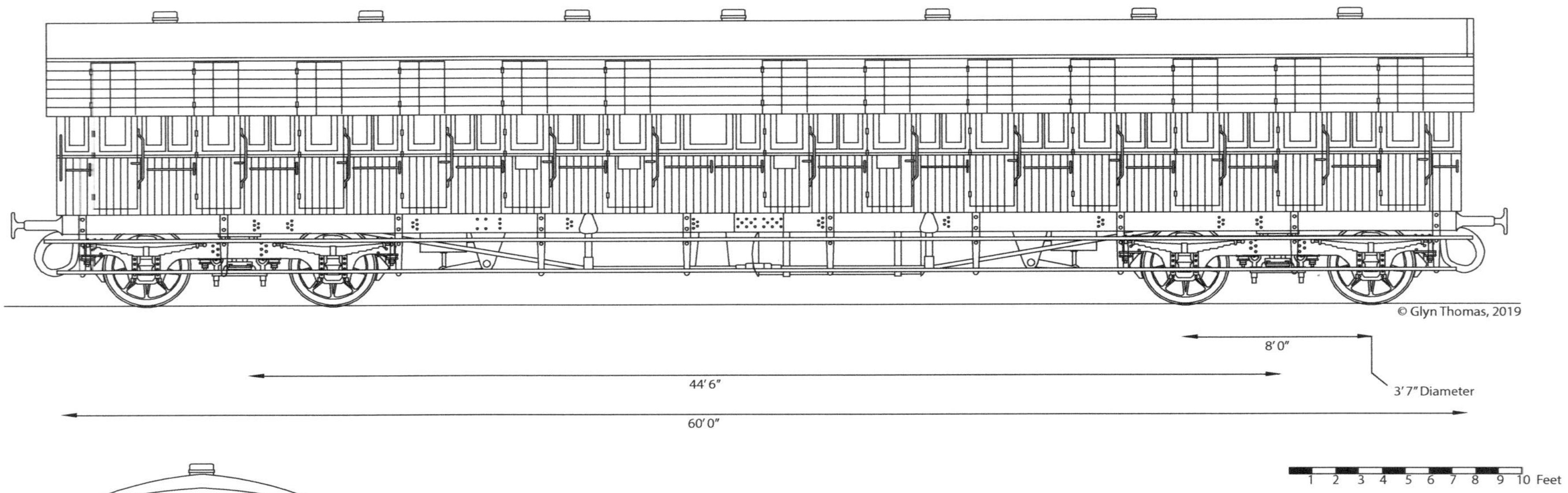

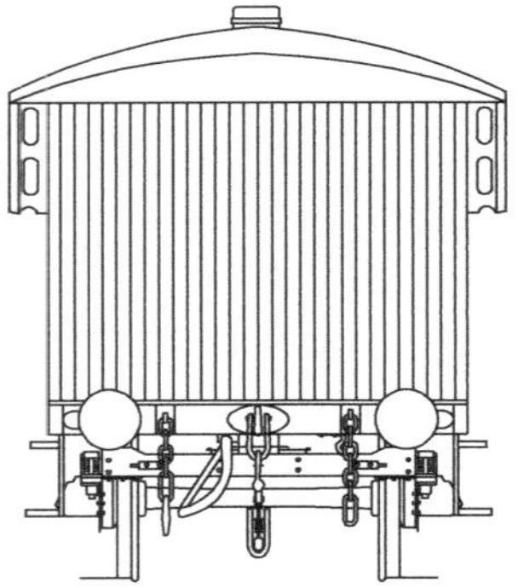

Bogie Wheel-base	8' 0"
Bogie Centres	44' 6"
Wheel Diameter	3' 7"
Capacity	126 passengers

[Reference: Railway Engineer, April 1901]

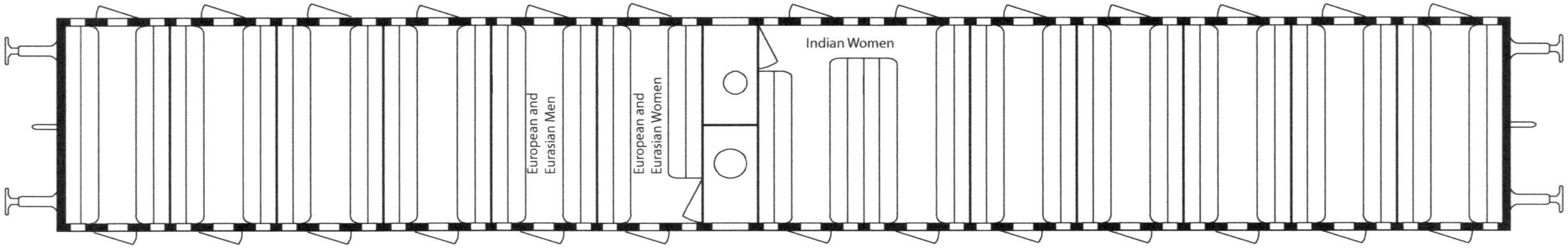

Indian Women

European and Eurasian Women

European and Eurasian Men

GIPR-MR Mail 3rd Class Coach

EIR Third Class Coaches

CBT class 0-8-0T number 1488, built by Borsig (5131/1903) and rebuilt from CB no. 705 by Jamalpur works in the early 1920s, heads a Jherriah branch train at Dhanbad in the 1920s. [Chris Walker Collection, cjweir034]

The East Indian Railway served the region around Calcutta (Kolkata). By the early 20th Century and encouraged by the railways, Calcutta had developed extensive suburbs, and the largest commuter rail network in India to serve them. Howrah station became one of the busiest stations in India. In common with other commuter networks, the EIR developed high-capacity coaches to bring as commuters into and out of the city during peak periods. While these coaches are rated for 104 seated passengers, it's likely that peak loadings were much higher.

The Calcutta suburban network was relatively late to convert to electric traction, starting in 1957, so some post-War photographers were able to capture photos of steam commuter services.

EIR composite first-second-inter class coach similar in design to the third-class types illustrated here [Chris Walker Collection, cjweir036]

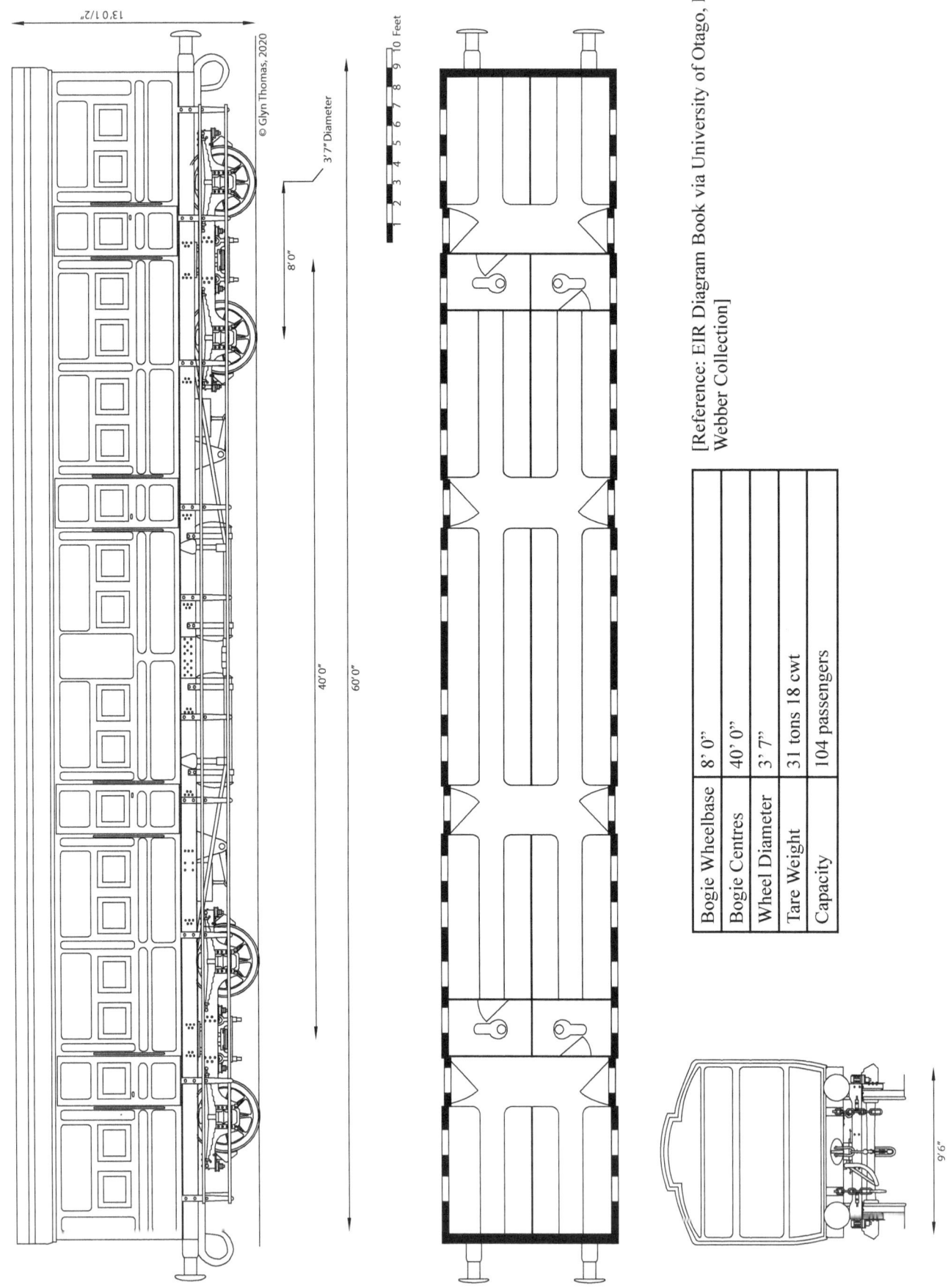

© Glyn Thomas, 2020

13' 0 1/2"

3' 7" Diameter

8' 0"

40' 0"

60' 0"

9' 6"

1 2 3 4 5 6 7 8 9 10 Feet

[Reference: EIR Diagram Book via University of Otago, Ernie Webber Collection]

Bogie Wheelbase	8' 0"
Bogie Centres	40' 0"
Wheel Diameter	3' 7"
Tare Weight	31 tons 18 cwt
Capacity	104 passengers

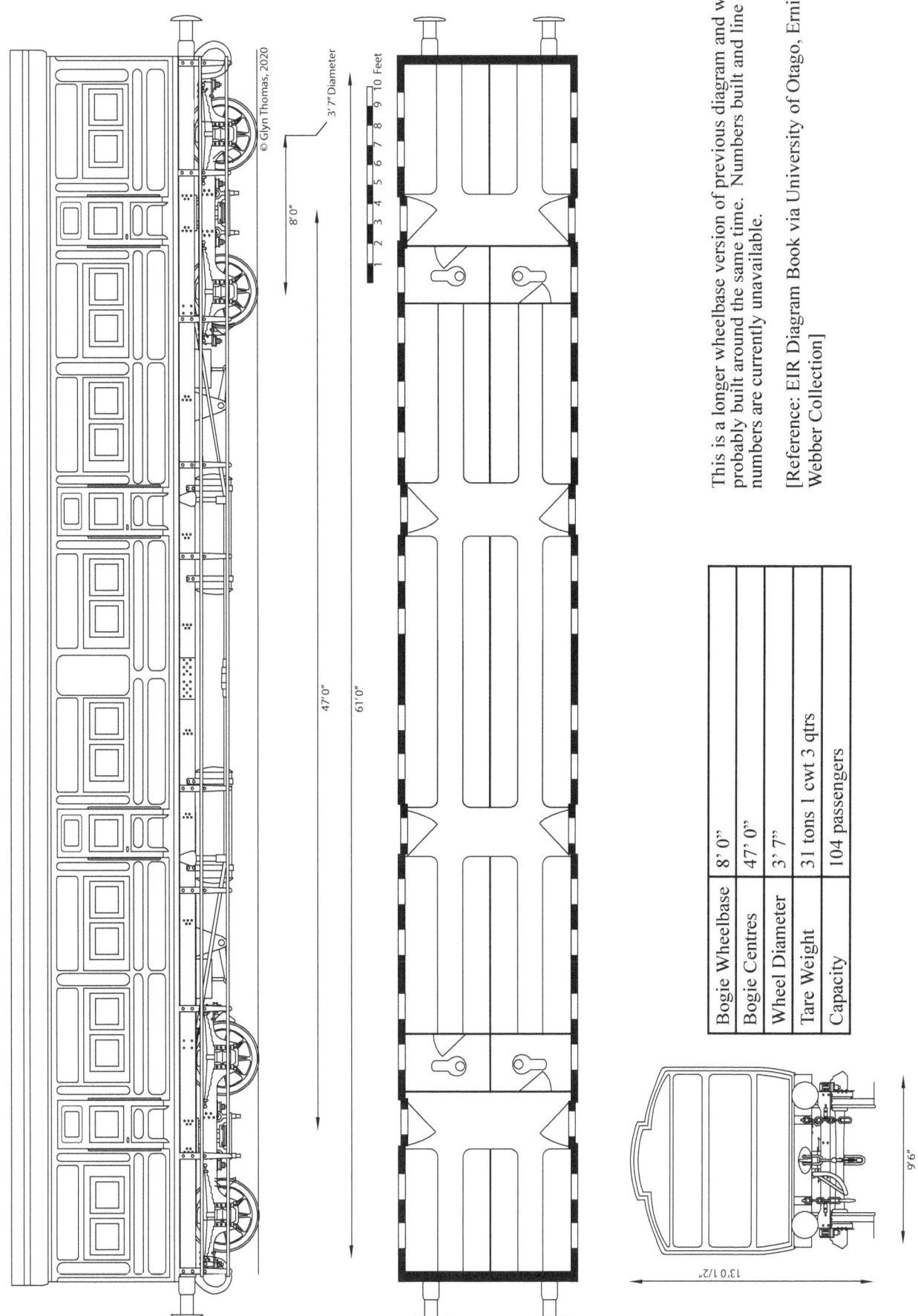

© Glyn Thomas, 2020

3' 7" Diameter

8' 0"

47' 0"

61' 0"

1 2 3 4 5 6 7 8 9 10 Feet

13' 0 1/2"

9' 6"

This is a longer wheelbase version of previous diagram and was probably built around the same time. Numbers built and line numbers are currently unavailable.

[Reference: EIR Diagram Book via University of Otago, Ernie Webber Collection]

Bogie Wheelbase	8' 0"
Bogie Centres	47' 0"
Wheel Diameter	3' 7"
Tare Weight	31 tons 1 cwt 3 qtrs
Capacity	104 passengers

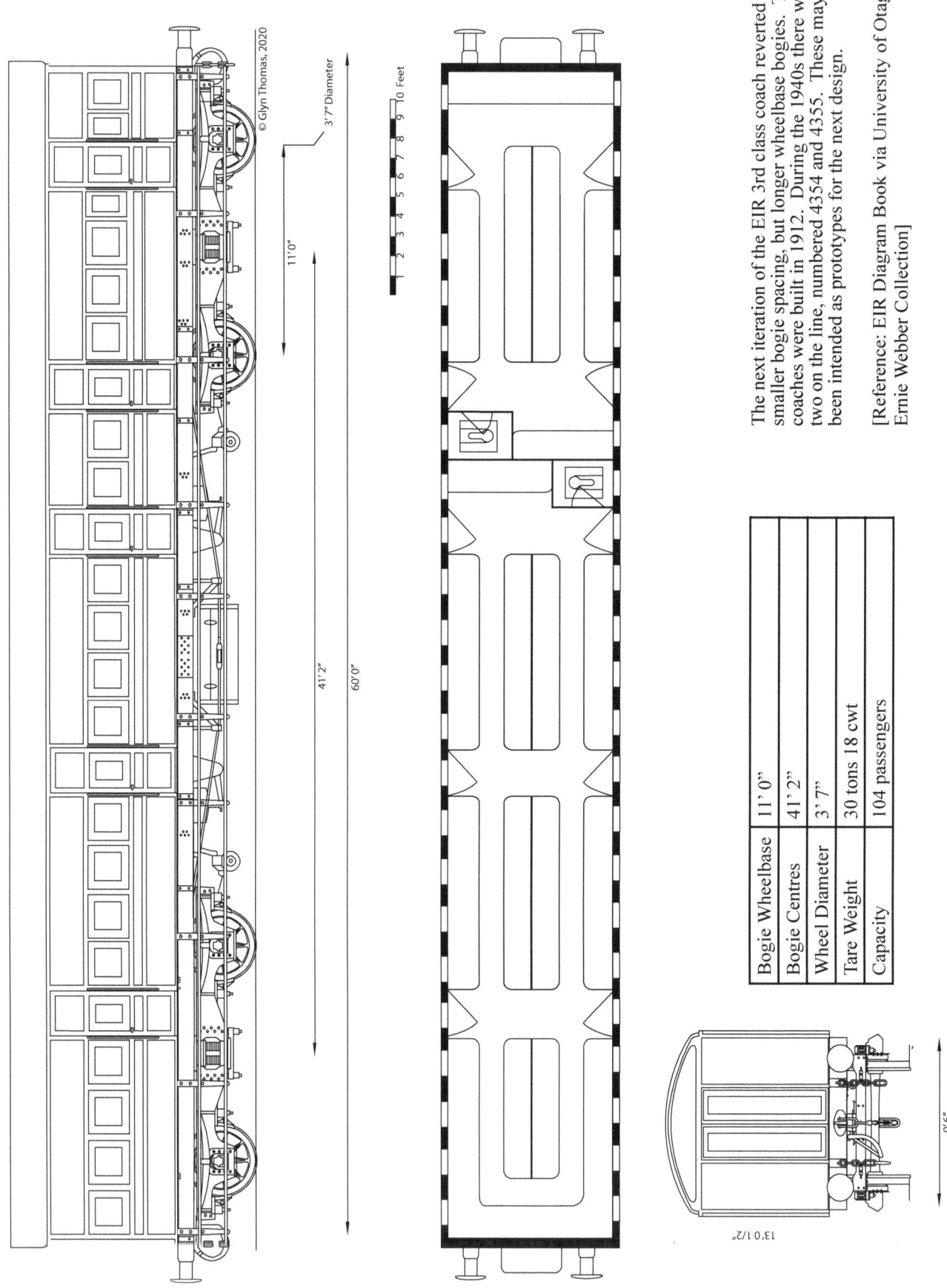

© Glyn Thomas, 2020

3' 7" Diameter

11' 0"

41' 2"

60' 0"

1 2 3 4 5 6 7 8 9 10 Feet

9' 6"

13' 0 1/2"

Bogie Wheelbase	11' 0"
Bogie Centres	41' 2"
Wheel Diameter	3' 7"
Tare Weight	30 tons 18 cwt
Capacity	104 passengers

The next iteration of the EIR 3rd class coach reverted to a smaller bogie spacing, but longer wheelbase bogies. These coaches were built in 1912. During the 1940s there were two on the line, numbered 4354 and 4355. These may have been intended as prototypes for the next design.

[Reference: EIR Diagram Book via University of Otago, Ernie Webber Collection]

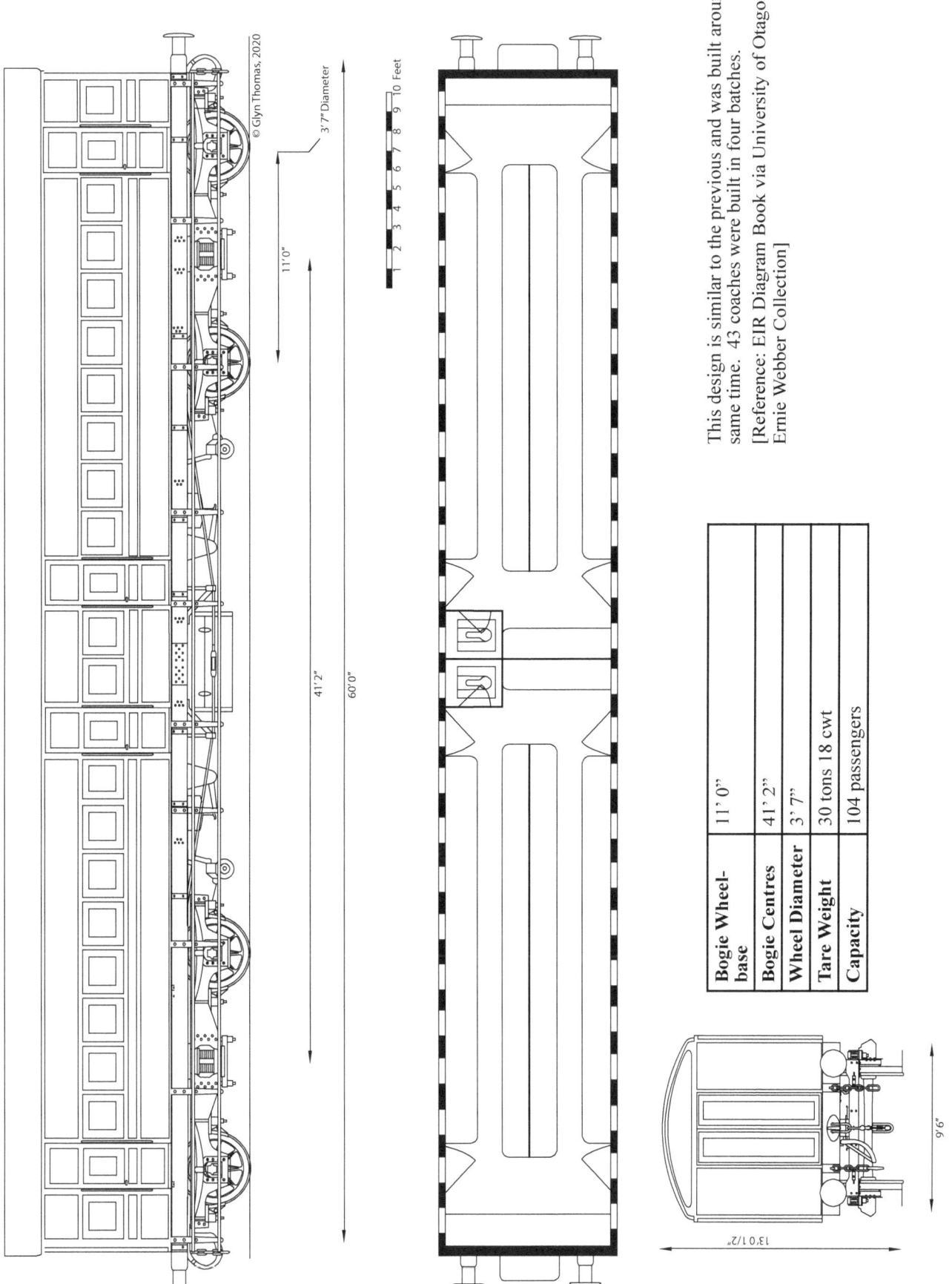

© Glyn Thomas, 2020

3'7" Diameter

11'0"

41'2"

60'0"

1 2 3 4 5 6 7 8 9 10 Feet

9'6"

13'01/2"

This design is similar to the previous and was built around the same time. 43 coaches were built in four batches.

[Reference: EIR Diagram Book via University of Otago, Ernie Webber Collection]

Bogie Wheel-base	11' 0"
Bogie Centres	41' 2"
Wheel Diameter	3' 7"
Tare Weight	30 tons 18 cwt
Capacity	104 passengers

GIPR Race Special

GIPR E1 4-4-2 933 at Nagpur [Kelland Collection, Bournemouth Railway Trust, 47195]

The British colonial powers carried their own ideas of civilised culture to the colonies that were established. Horse racing had long been considered to be a gentleman's sport and fitted well with Indian traditions of breeding fine horses. European-style horse racing was introduced at Akra near Calcutta as early as 1769, but were banned there in 1798. Probably as a consequence, the first official horse races in the Bombay area started in 1798. The Bombay Turf Club was founded in 1802, and became the Royal Western India Turf Club. Their Pune Race Track was established on army land near Pune in 1830.

Calcutta relented on their ban in 1847, when the Royal Calcutta Turf Club was formed and became the pre-eminent horse racing venue for the remainder of the 19th Century, but by the early 20th Century, Bombay and Pune were ascendant.

In 1905, the Great Indian Peninsula Railway (GIPR) pandered to the popularity of the sport with dedicated luxury trains to ply between Bombay and Pune on race days. These ran to an express schedule designed to get race-goers there and back within the day, with enough time to enjoy the races. These were all first class, and included a dining car so that patrons could eat in the evening while returning.

From a design point of view, it is interesting to contrast these coaches with the GIPR-MR coaches designed only four years earlier. The Carriage and Wagon Superintendent, A. M. Bell, recently arrived from the Great Eastern Railway in England introduced current British practices. The older sunshades are gone, with improved asbestos insulation. Coaches are fitted with electric lights and fans, and have vestibules, which would have greatly facilitated operation of the dining car. With the exception of the clerestory, which disappeared in later designs, these coaches are similar to most produced from this time until the start of the steel coach era.

A typical train composition in 1905 was Brake-1st, 1st, Parlor, Restaurant, 1st, Baggage. These trains would have been hauled by passenger 4-6-0 locomotive.

In 1930, the weekend Pune race day trains became the "Deccan Queen" named train with new coaching stock. By that time, electrification had reached Pune and these trains were hauled by either WCP1 or WCP2 electric locomotives. This was expanded into a daily service soon afterwards. In 1955, third class carriages were added.

The Deccan Queen is still one of Indian Railway's most prestigious expresses and now runs to 17 ICF coaches with electric traction.

GIPR Race Special Baggage

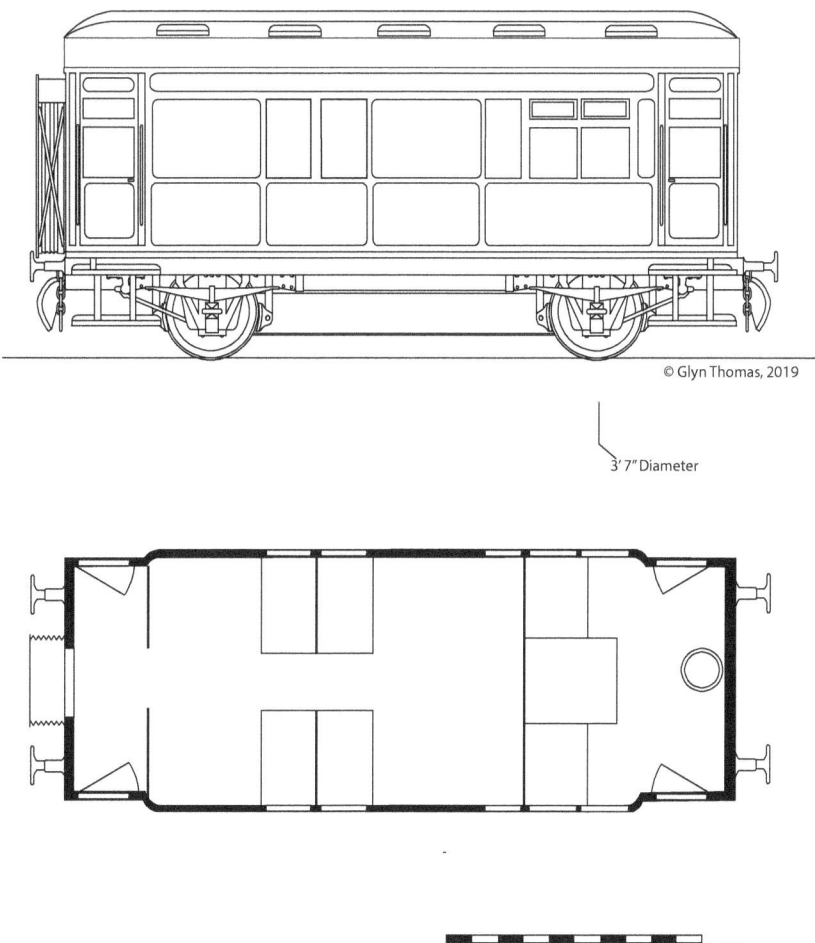

© Glyn Thomas, 2019

3' 7" Diameter

1 2 3 4 5 6 7 8 9 10 Feet

[Reference: Railway Engineer, October 1905]

© Glyn Thomas, 2019

3' 7" Diameter

10' 0"

40' 0"

62' 0"

1 2 3 4 5 6 7 8 9 10 Feet

Shower

Shower

Shower

Shower

Bath

Servants' WCs

[Reference: Railway Engineer, October 1905]

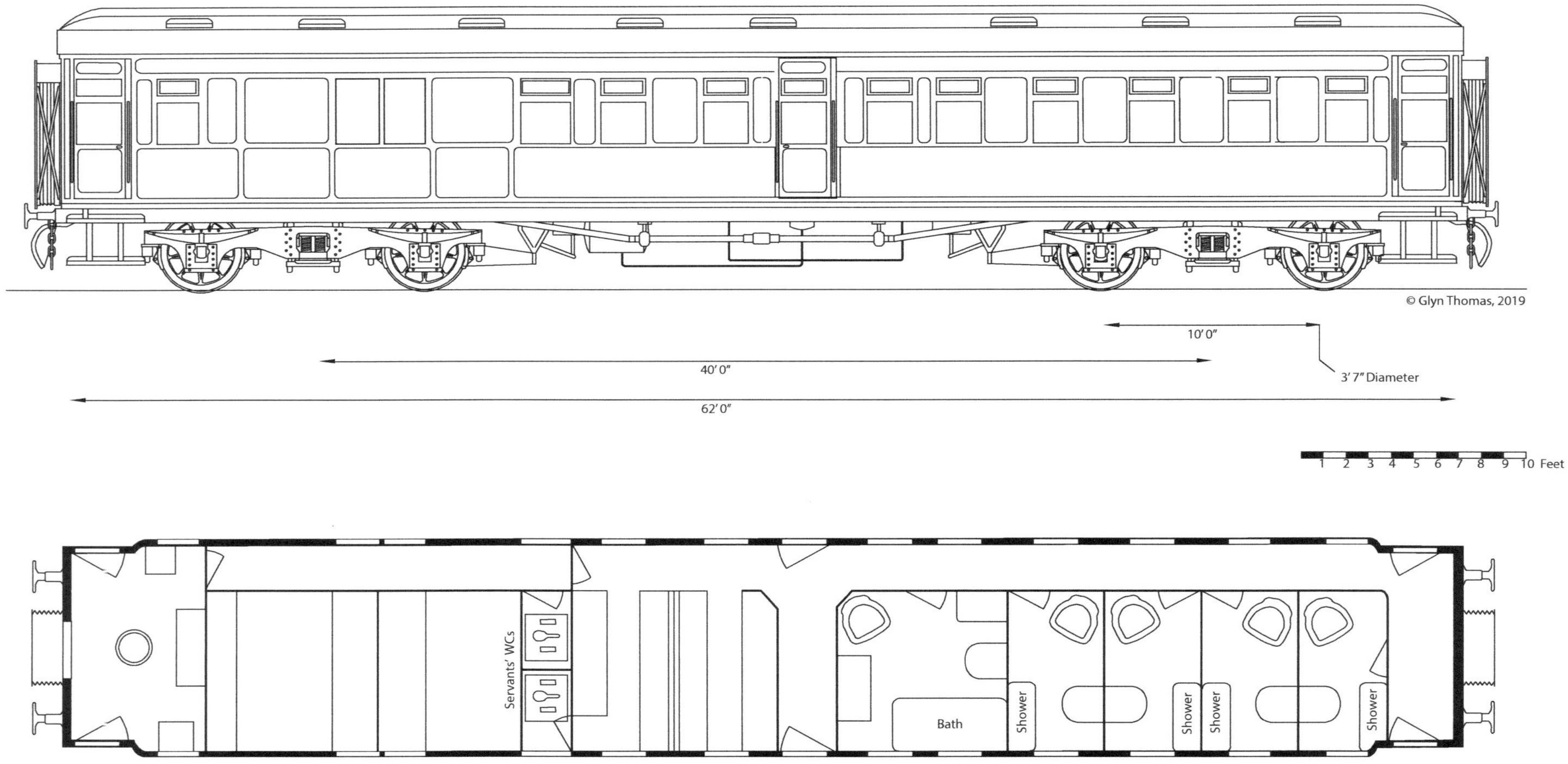

Bogie Wheel-base	10' 0"
Bogie Centres	40'
Wheel Diameter	3' 7"

GIPR Race Specia. 1st-Brake

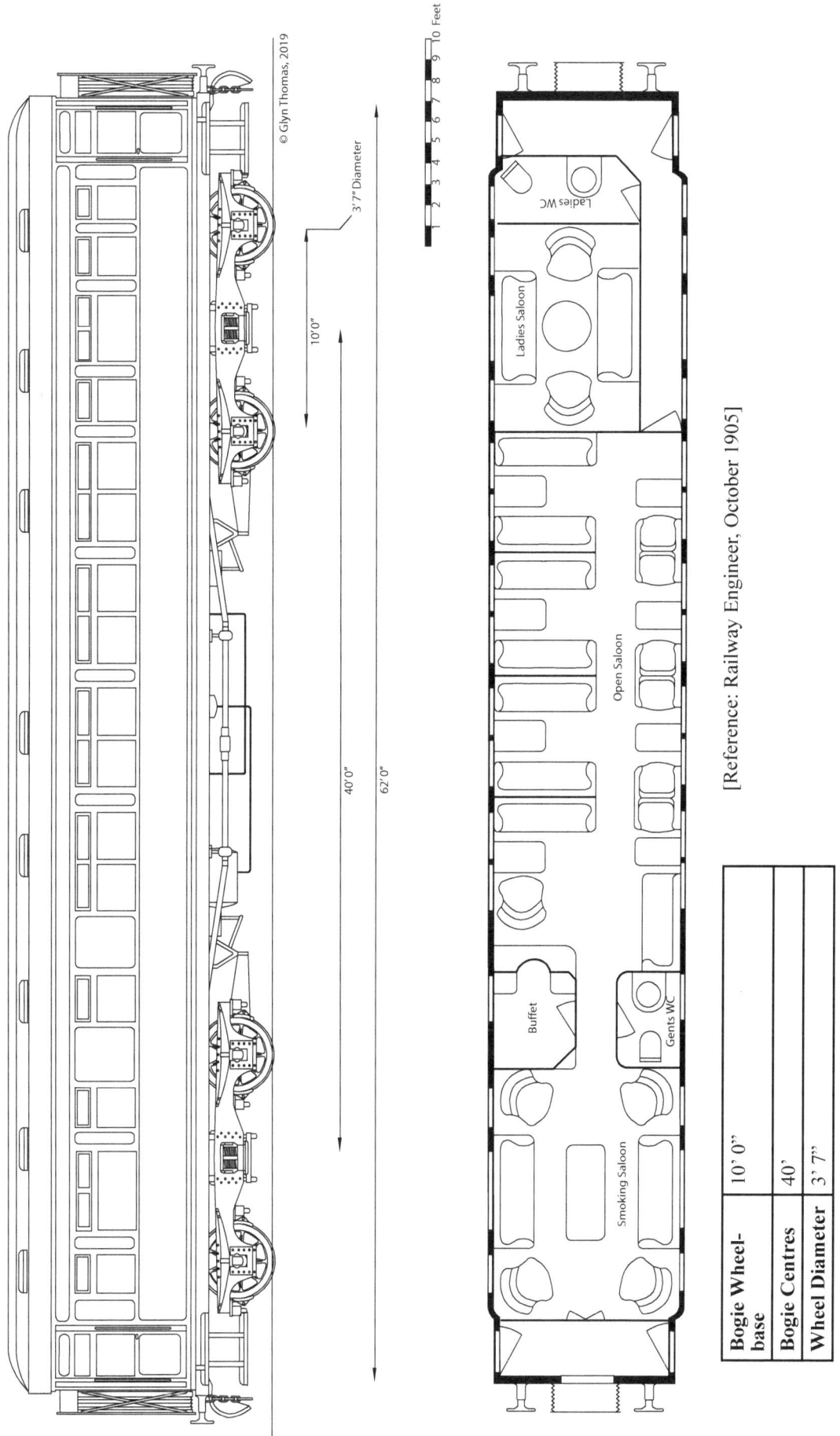

© Glyn Thomas, 2019

3' 7" Diameter

10'0"

40' 0"

62' 0"

1 2 3 4 5 6 7 8 9 10 Feet

Ladies WC

Ladies Saloon

Open Saloon

Buffet

Gents WC

Smoking Saloon

[Reference: Railway Engineer, October 1905]

Bogie Wheel-base	10' 0"
Bogie Centres	40'
Wheel Diameter	3' 7"

GIPR Race Special 1st Class Parlor

GIPR Race Special Restaurant

© Glyn Thomas, 2019
40′ 0″
62′ 0″
3′ 7″ Diameter
1 2 3 4 5 6 7 8 9 10 Feet
Pantry
Kitchen

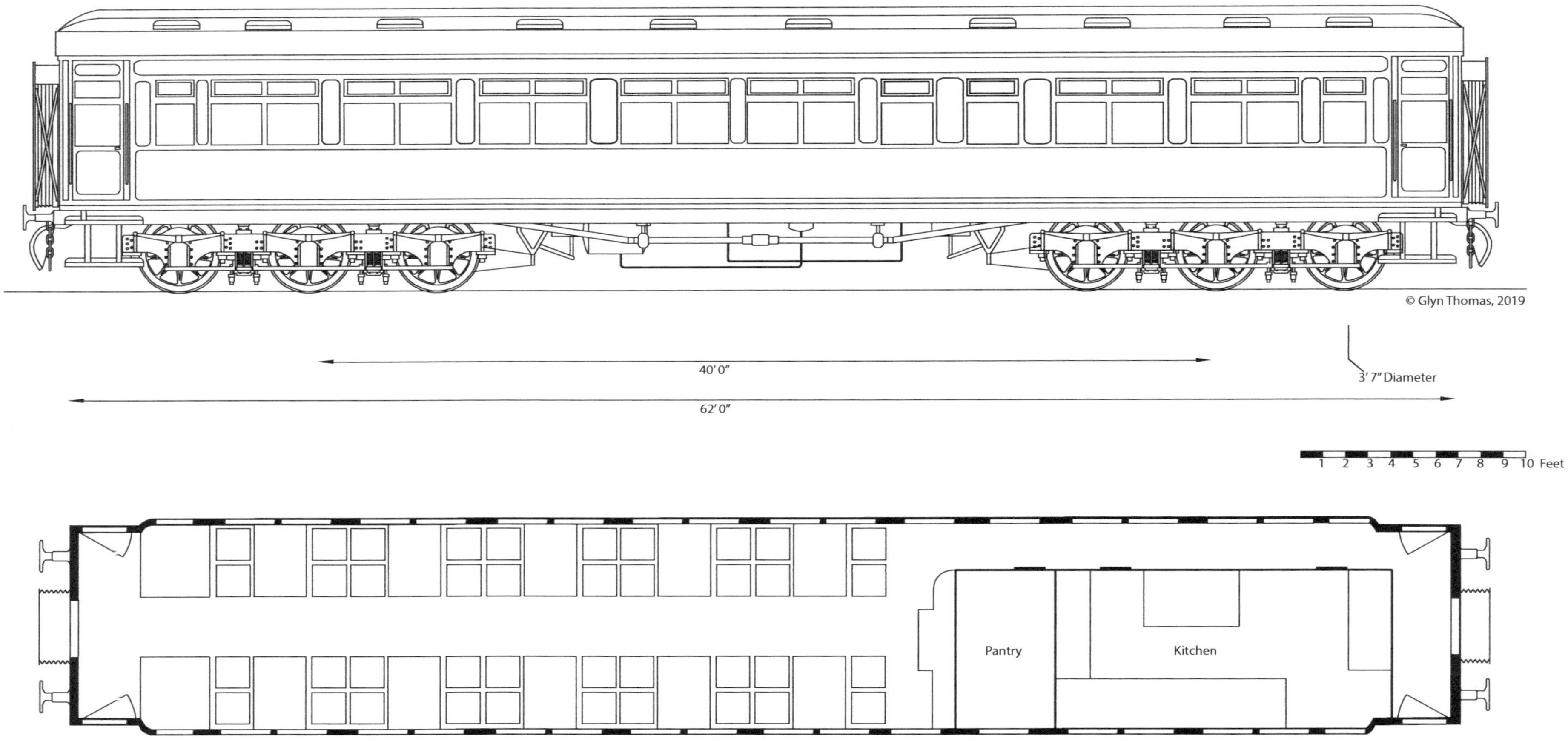

[Reference: Railway Engineer, October 1905]

Bogie Wheel-base	10’ 0”
Bogie Centres	40’
Wheel Diameter	3’ 7”

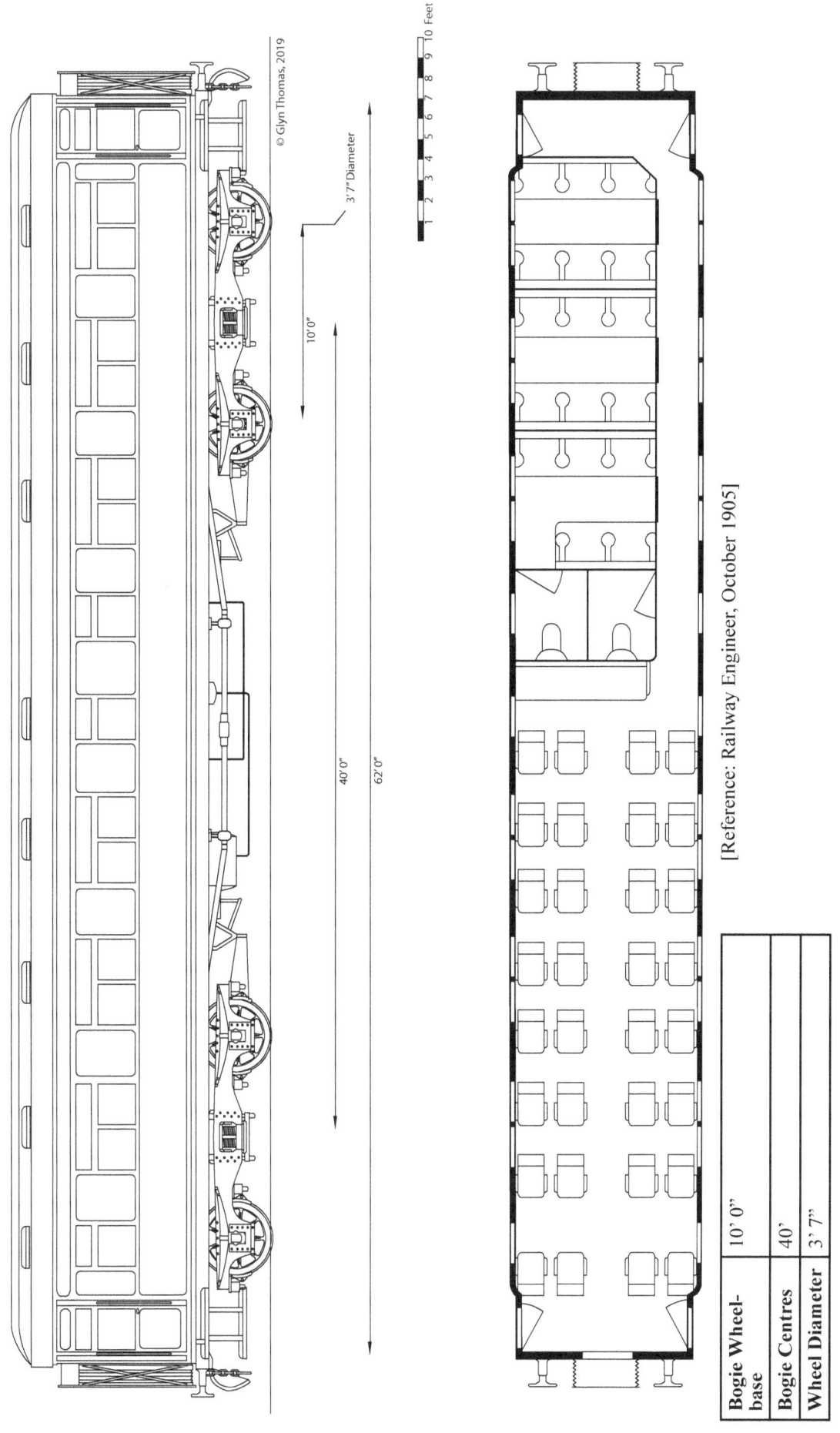

GIPR Race Special 1st Class Coach

© Glyn Thomas, 2019

3′7″ Diameter

10′0″

40′0″

62′0″

1 2 3 4 5 6 7 8 9 10 Feet

[Reference: Railway Engineer, October 1905]

Bogie Wheel-base	10′ 0″
Bogie Centres	40′
Wheel Diameter	3′ 7″

BNR Mail Coaches

Bengal Nagpur Railway Coach no. 922 [Chris Walker Collection, cjwbnr028]

The Bengal Nagpur Railway operated the Calcutta-Madras Mail train. In 1914 this was equipped with new coaches built on the Indian-standard underframe. A typical 8-coach train composition was: brake-3rd, 3rd, inter-3rd, inter-refreshment-3rd, 2nd-inter-3rd, 1st-2nd-servants, mail-baggage, restaurant. "Inter" class refers to an intermediate class between 3rd and 2nd class that was generally used by wealthy domestic passengers. The distance between Calcutta and Madras by rail is 1,032 miles, and the train was scheduled to complete this in 39 ½ hours. The final section between Waltair and Madras operated over the Madras and Southern Mahratta Railway (MSMR). These trains were initially hauled by the BNR's innovative De Glenn Atlantic steam locomotives.

Mail trains still run between Howrah and Chennai Central. The current (2020) SF Mail is train number 12839 and consists of 24 ICF coaches (luggage, 2nd, 2nd, 11 x sleeper cars, pantry, sleeper, 3 x 3-tier AC, 2 x 2-tier AC (1st), 1st-2nd AC composite, 2nd, luggage) hauled by a WAP-4 electric locomotive. The journey now takes 28 hours.

Bengal Nagpur Railway 1st-2nd Composite Coach no. 1122 [Chris Walker Collection, cjwbnr026]

Bengal Nagpur Railway Restaurant Car no. 907 [Chris Walker Collection, cjwbnr027]

BNR Mail 1st Class Coach

© Glyn Thomas, 2019

12'4"

67'0"

9'6"

1 2 3 4 5 6 7 8 9 10 Feet

[Reference: BNR Official Photographs and known dimensions]

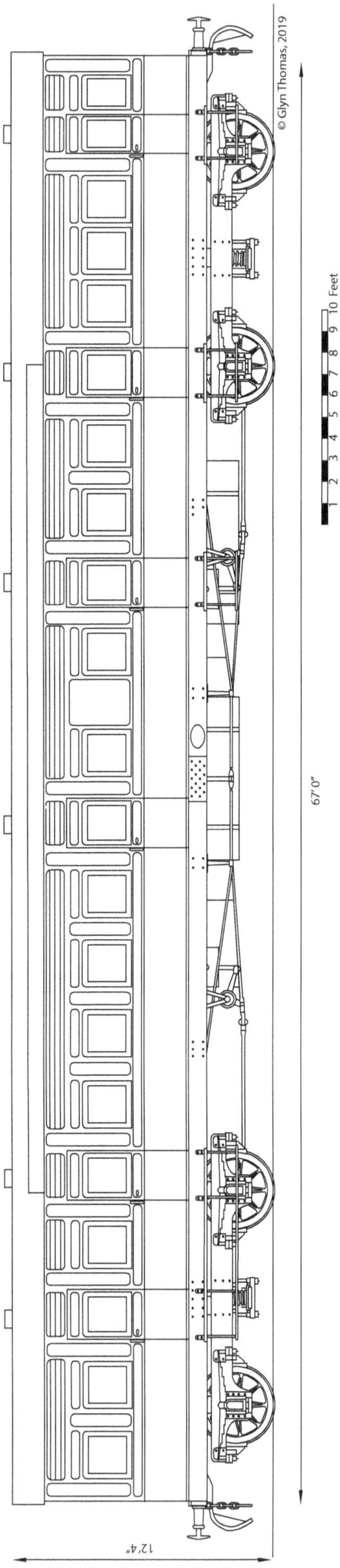

BNR Mail 1st-2nd Composite

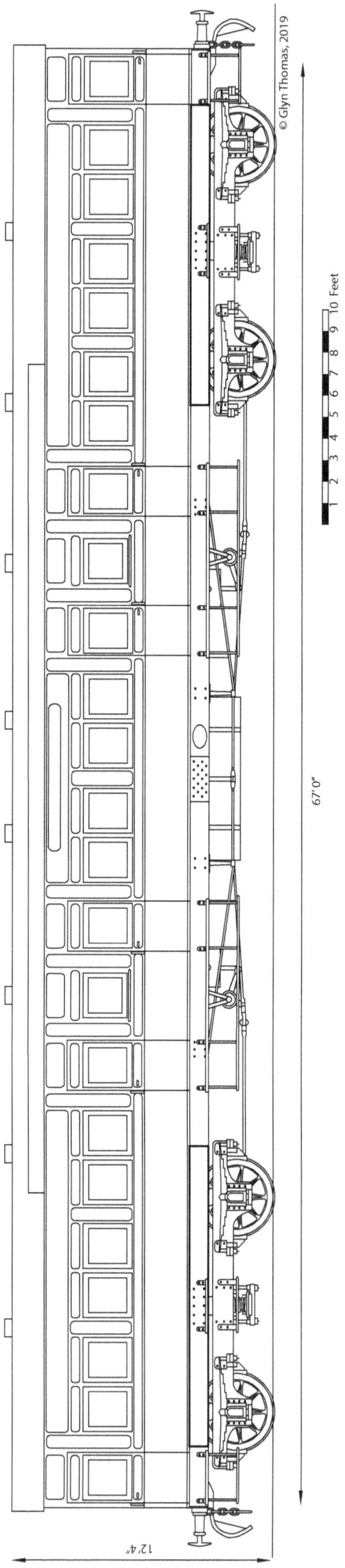

12'4"

67' 0"

© Glyn Thomas, 2019

1 2 3 4 5 6 7 8 9 10 Feet

[Reference: BNR Official Photographs and known dimensions]

BNR Mail 3rd Class Coach

12'4"

67' 0"

© Glyn Thomas, 2019

1 2 3 4 5 6 7 8 9 10 Feet

[Reference: BNR Official Photographs and known dimensions]

GIPR Military Train

GIPR Military Train Coach no. 4749 [Historical Railway Images, Flickr]

One of Britain's main reasons for developing Indian railways was to enable the transport of troops to hot-spots within the country and at its borders as quickly as possible. The need for this capability was underlined by the Indian Rebellion of 1857 which resulted in the loss of control of several major cities and considerable loss of life on both sides.

The military benefits of railways were proven during the Second Afghan War of 1878-1880, when troops were deployed to the frontier at a rate of 4,000 per day via eight trains of 500 troops each.

From the earliest days, India posed particular challenges for the safe transportation of troops. Rudyard Kipling's 1887 short story, "The Daughter of the Regiment", describes the devastating results of a cholera outbreak on a troop train caused by inadequate water supplies, and this was probably based on a real-life incident.

During the early part of the 20th Century, troops deploying from Britain would be shipped via the Suez Canal to Karachi, and then deployed throughout India by troop train organised by the North Western Railway (NWR). In 1915 disaster struck when a troop train became stranded in the Sind desert and 32 men died from heat-stroke. The Government of India was forced to act and soon afterwards, troop movements were changed. Incoming troops were shipped to Bombay and then forward to their final deployments using block trains supplied by the Great Indian Peninsula Railway (GIPR). Custom trains were designed by A. M. Bell (Carriage and Wagon Superintendent of the GIPR) and built at the railway's Matunga Carriage Works. These received considerable coverage in the railway press of the time including the Locomotive, Carriage and Wagon Review (1914, 1916, and 1917) and Engineer (1914). A major intention of these trains was to provide the ability to feed troops on the move, without the need to de-train at intermediate stations, and thus reduce deployment time.

Trains operated in fixed blocks of seven cars - initially they had a mess car at each end, troop cars, and an officer's car. Later, the mess cars became baggage cars with coffee shops and a pantry car was placed at the middle of the train. The troop cars where fitted with 22 rows of 3-tier bunks built of wooden slats on tubular steel frames that were originally designed for British troop ships. The officer's car had the standard corridor sleeping car layout. These trains sometimes operated with a standard GIPR restaurant car for officers' use. The troop cars could be used as regular third-class sleepers when not needed for military use.

Operationally, the trains originated on the Bombay Port Trust railway and joined the GIPR at Wadala junction.

Observed numbers include troop cars numbers. 4700 and 4749.

Indian Railways continues to operate military trains after Independence. Modern coaches are based on ICF designs and generally painted dark green - these run as entire trains or a single coach attached to a regular service train.

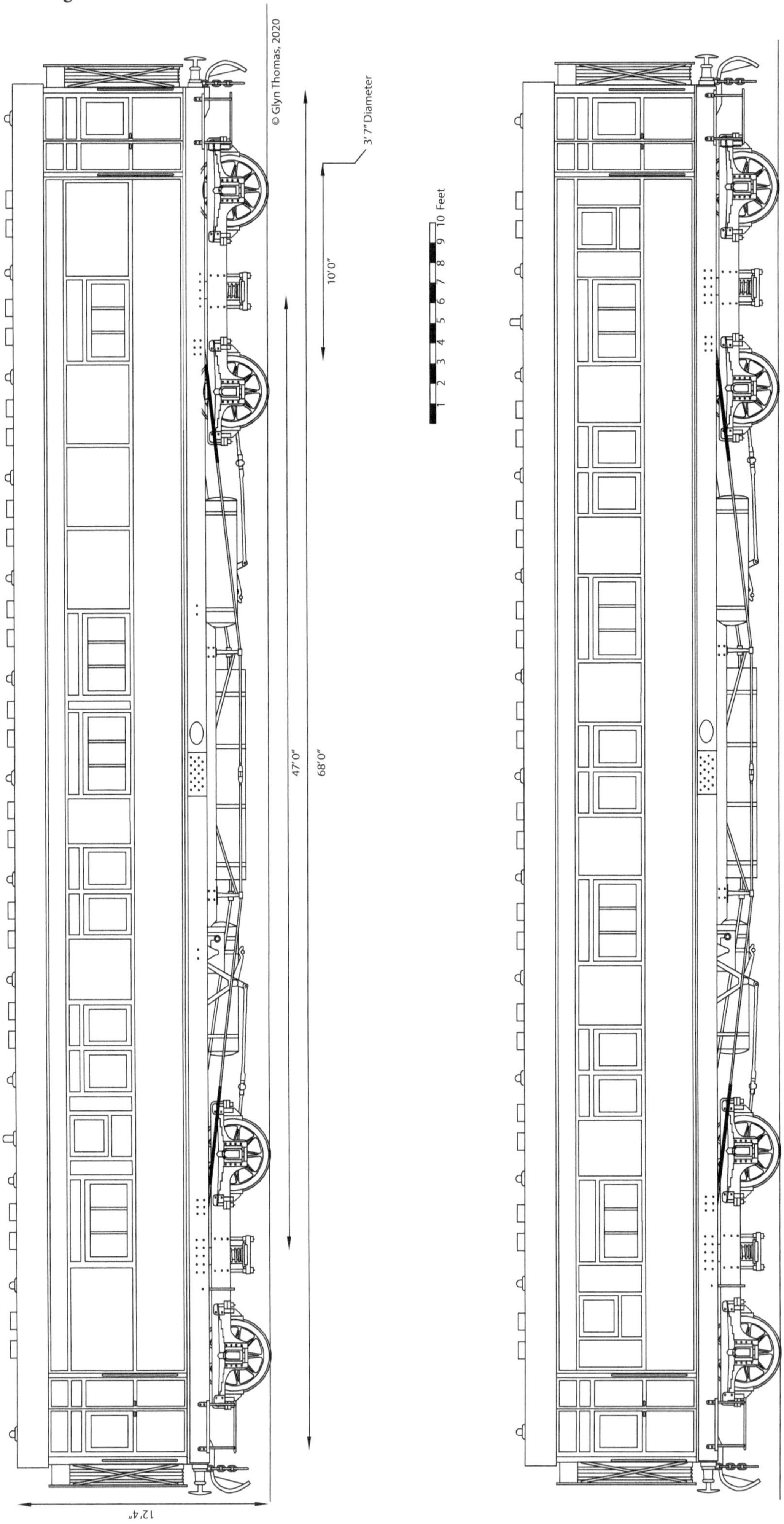
© Glyn Thomas, 2020
3'7" Diameter
1 2 3 4 5 6 7 8 9 10 Feet
10'0"
47'0"
68'0"
12'4"

GIPR Military Kitchen and Cold Store

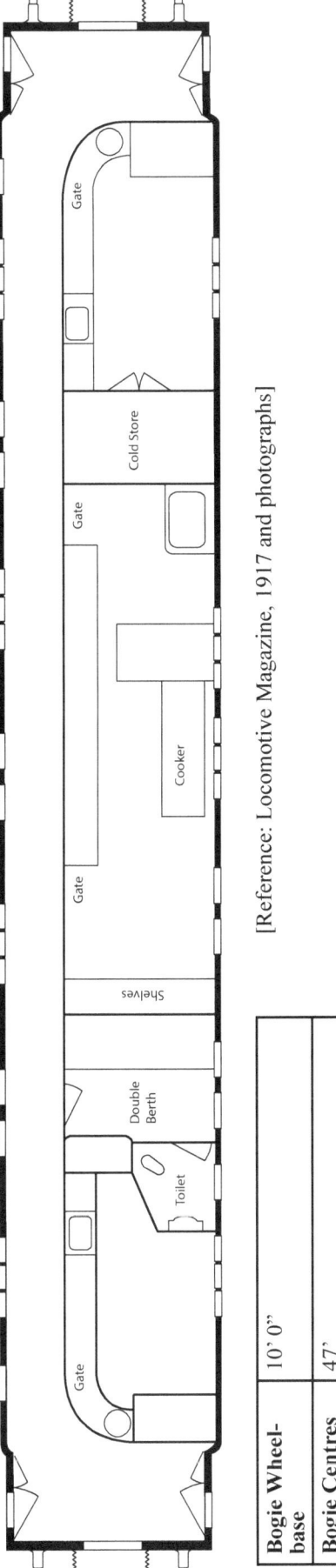

[Reference: Locomotive Magazine, 1917 and photographs]

Bogie Wheel-base	10' 0"
Bogie Centres	47'
Wheel Diameter	3' 7"

Kitchen and Cold Store (K&CS), 1917; note the "Government of India" designation in place of GIPR [Locomotive, Carriage and Wagon Review]

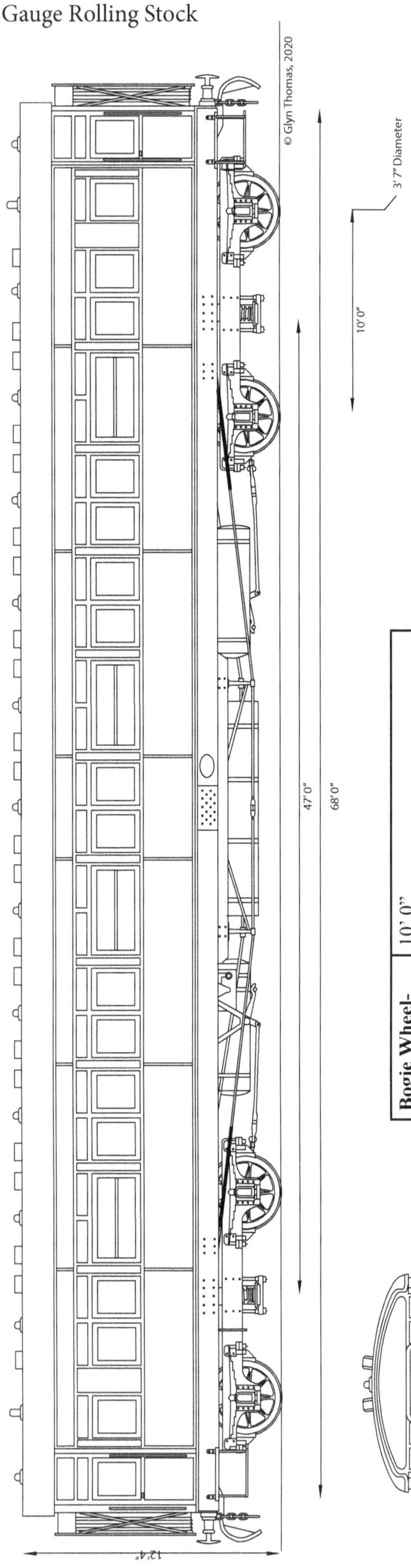

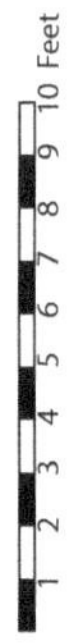

© Glyn Thomas, 2020
3'7" Diameter
10'0"
47'0"
68'0"
12'4"

1 2 3 4 5 6 7 8 9 10 Feet

[Reference: Railway Gazette, 1918]

Bogie Wheel-base	10' 0"
Bogie Centres	40'
Wheel Diameter	3' 7"
Capacity	66 soldiers, 110 third-class

10'0"

GIPR Military Enlisted Men's Coach

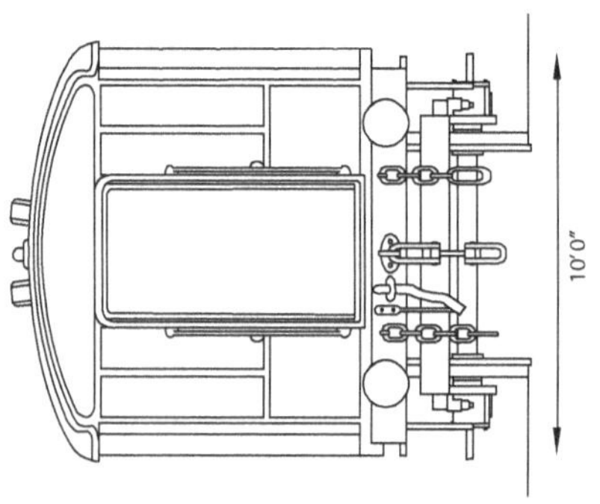

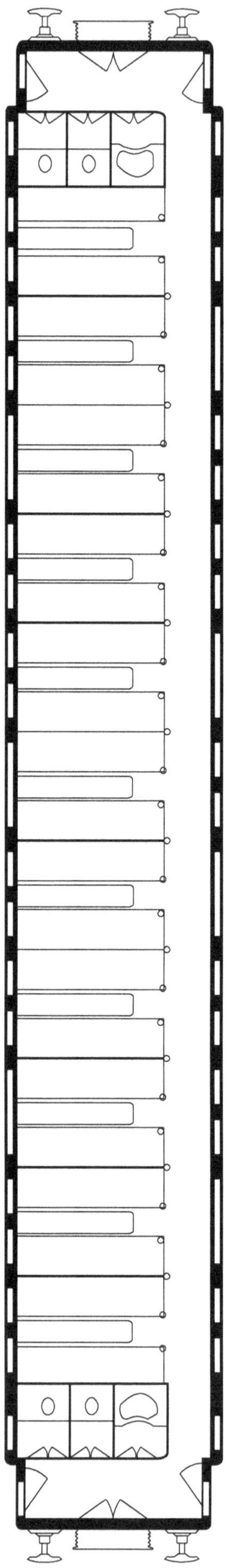

Broad-Gauge Rolling Stock

© Glyn Thomas, 2020

3'-7" Diameter

10' 0"

47' 0"

68' 0"

0 1 2 3 4 5 6 7 8 9 10 Feet

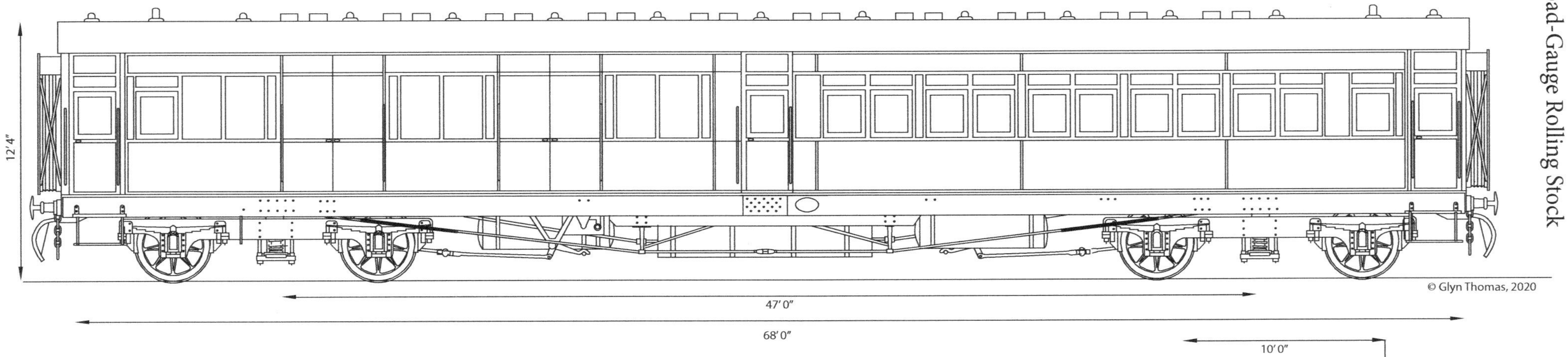

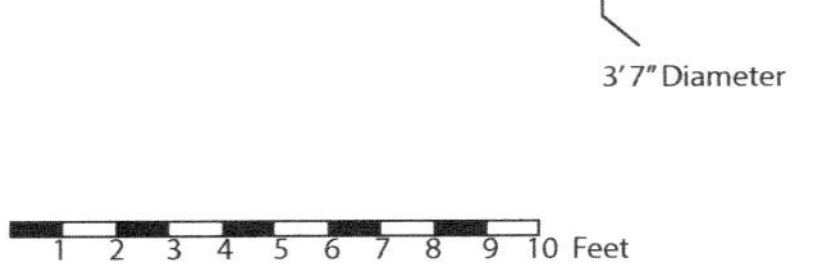

[Reference: Locomotive Magazine, 1917 and photographs]

GIPR Military Brake-Mess

12'4"

Bogie Wheel-base	10' 0"
Bogie Centres	40'
Wheel Diameter	3' 7"

MILITARY CAR

4700

Enlisted Men's Coach, 1914 [The Engineer]

SIR Coaches from the 1930s

SIR PT 2-6-4T no. 7 at Shoranur in 1947 [Kelland Collection, Bournemouth Railway Trust, 48156]

Diagrams of SIR coaches from the 1930s show how a more austere aesthetic had taken hold. The following coaches are shown. These were built locally by the SIR, probably using imported standard underframe components.

Luggage-brake vans built for passenger service in 1930. These took numbers 467-471. They were probably initially all louvered, but were modified in 1935 to have perforated zinc sheet on the lower panels.

Brake-third coaches built in 1933 and numbered 349-358.

Restaurant cars built in 1930 and numbered 4 and 5.

Third class coaches built in 1933 and numbered 242-246.

First class coaches built in 1935 and numbered 703-705.

First-second composite coach built in 1932 numbered 56.

Most of the passenger coaches had provision for sleeping, but the sleeping passenger numbers were not quoted in the diagram book.

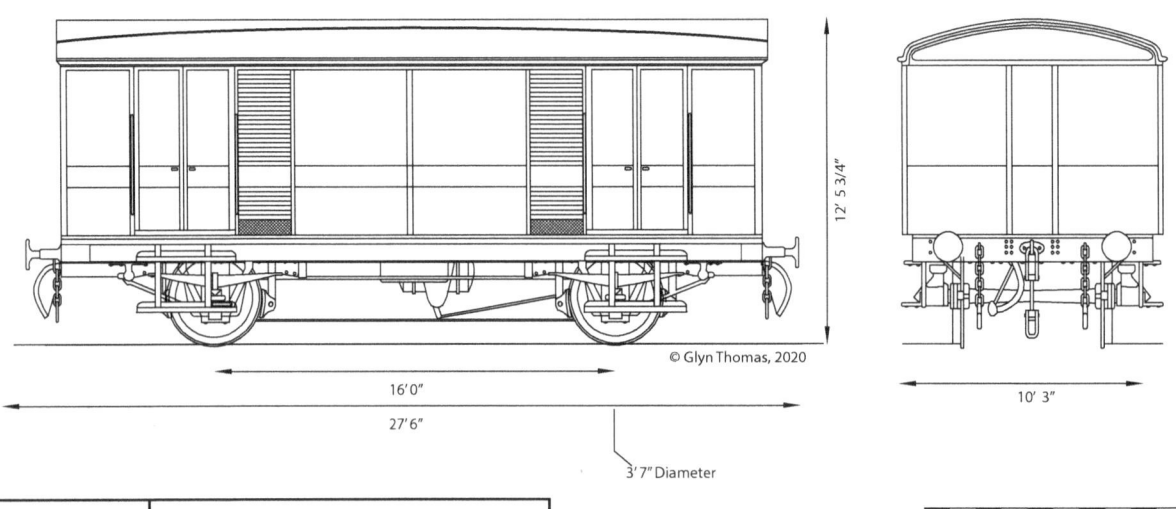

Wheelbase	16' 0"
Wheel Diameter	3' 7"
Tare Weight	13 tons 1 cwt 2 qtrs
Capacity	12 tons 10 cwt

[Reference: SIR diagram book via University of Otago, Ernie Webber Collection]

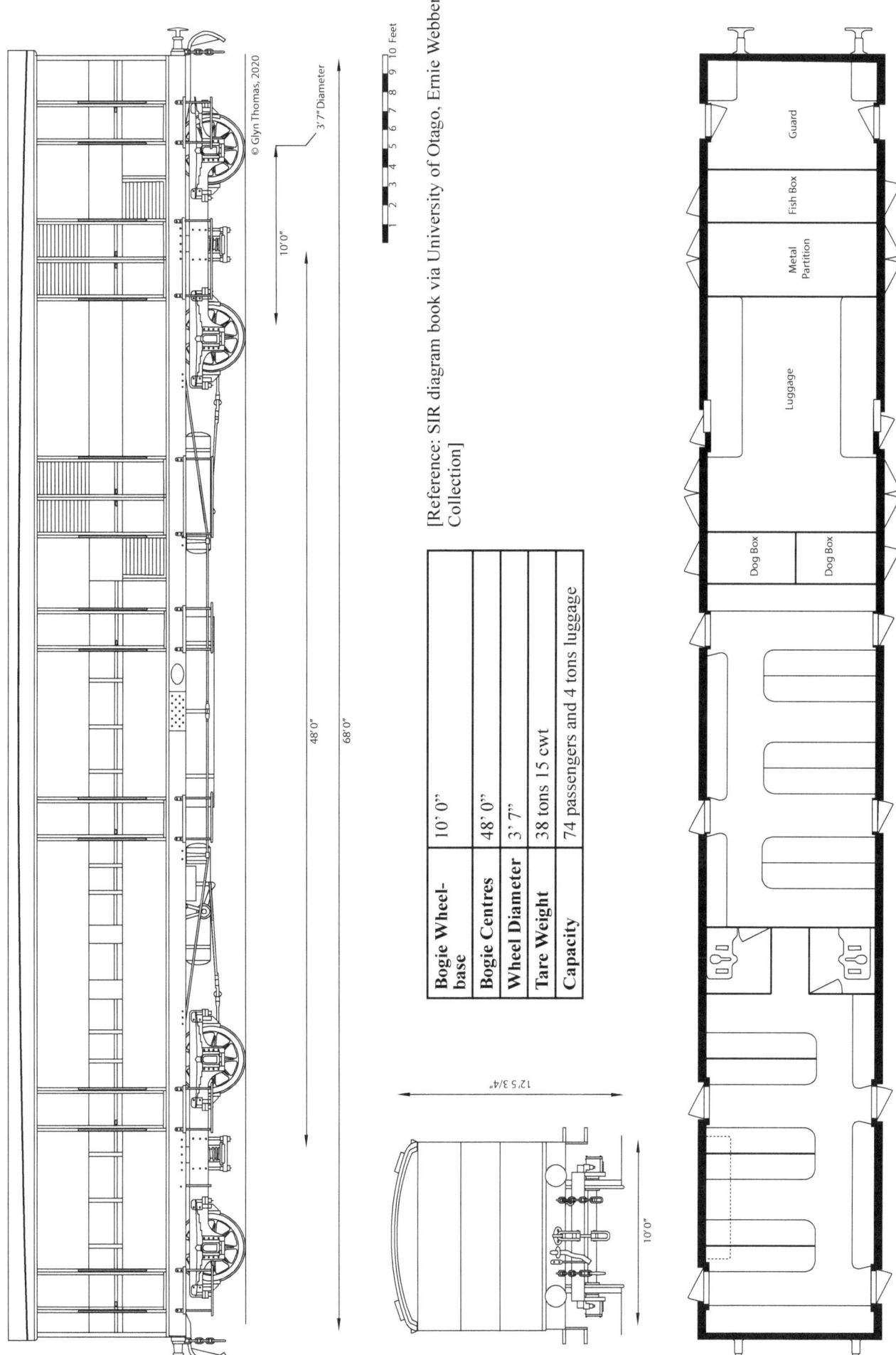

SIR Brake-3rd

© Glyn Thomas, 2020

3' 7" Diameter

10'0"

1 2 3 4 5 6 7 8 9 10 Feet

48' 0"

68' 0"

[Reference: SIR diagram book via University of Otago, Ernie Webber Collection]

Bogie Wheelbase	10' 0"
Bogie Centres	48' 0"
Wheel Diameter	3' 7"
Tare Weight	38 tons 15 cwt
Capacity	74 passengers and 4 tons luggage

12' 5 3/4"

10' 0"

Guard

Fish Box

Metal Partition

Luggage

Dog Box

Dog Box

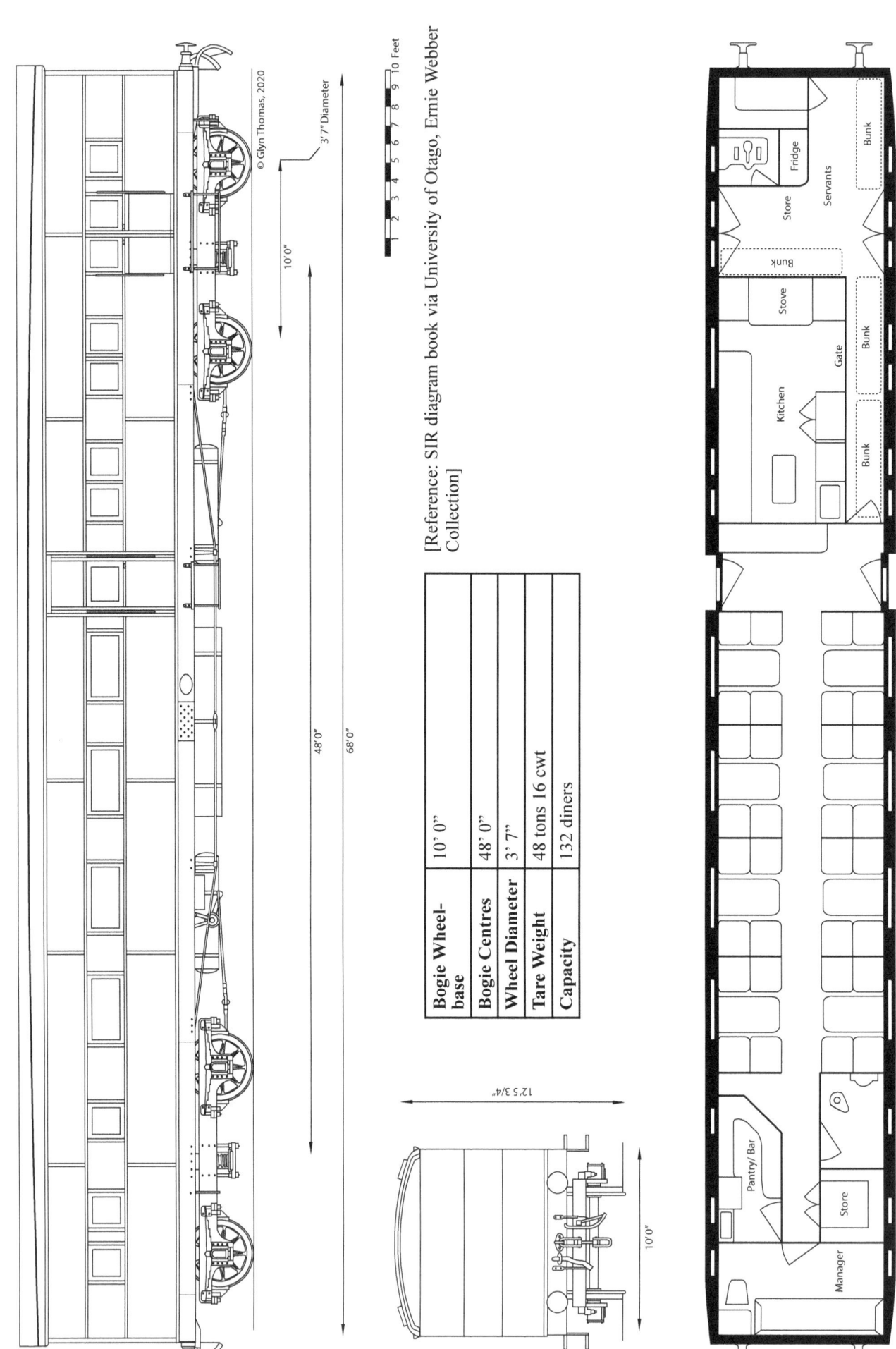

© Glyn Thomas, 2020

3' 7" Diameter

10' 0"

48' 0"

68' 0"

1 2 3 4 5 6 7 8 9 10 Feet

[Reference: SIR diagram book via University of Otago, Ernie Webber Collection]

12' 5 3/4"

10' 0"

Bogie Wheel-base	10' 0"
Bogie Centres	48' 0"
Wheel Diameter	3' 7"
Tare Weight	48 tons 16 cwt
Capacity	132 diners

Bunk

Fridge

Store

Servants

Bunk

Stove

Kitchen

Gate

Bunk

Bunk

Bunk

Pantry / Bar

Store

Manager

SIR Restaurant

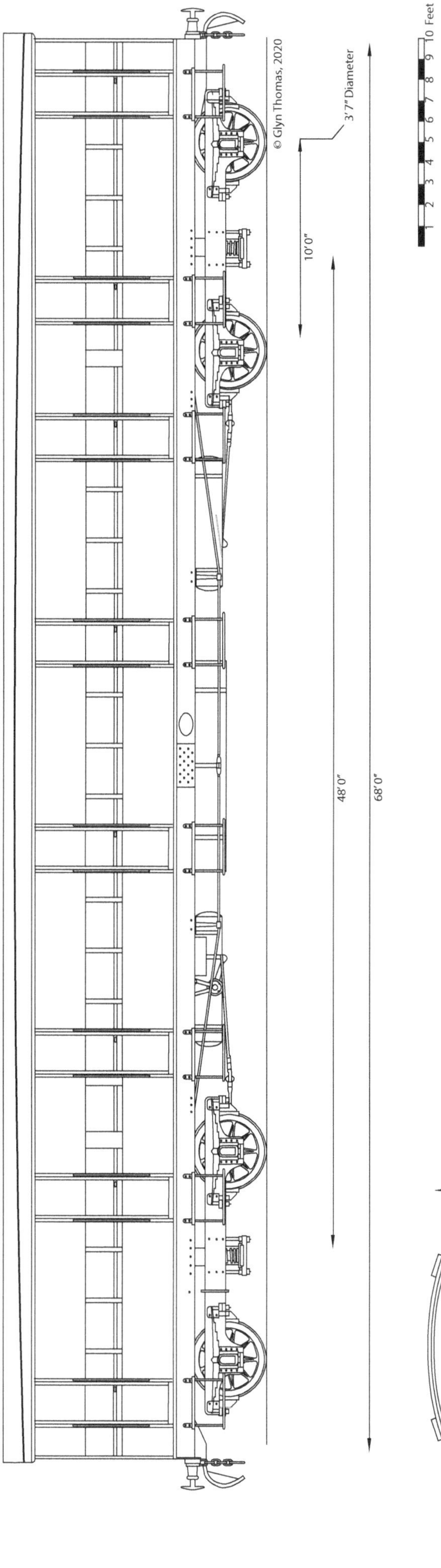

SIR 3rd Class Coach

© Glyn Thomas, 2020

3' 7" Diameter

10'0"

48'0"

68'0"

1 2 3 4 5 6 7 8 9 10 Feet

[Reference: SIR diagram book via University of Otago, Ernie Webber Collection]

Bogie Wheel-base	10' 0"
Bogie Centres	48' 0"
Wheel Diameter	3' 7"
Tare Weight	37 tons 2 cwt
Capacity	123 passengers

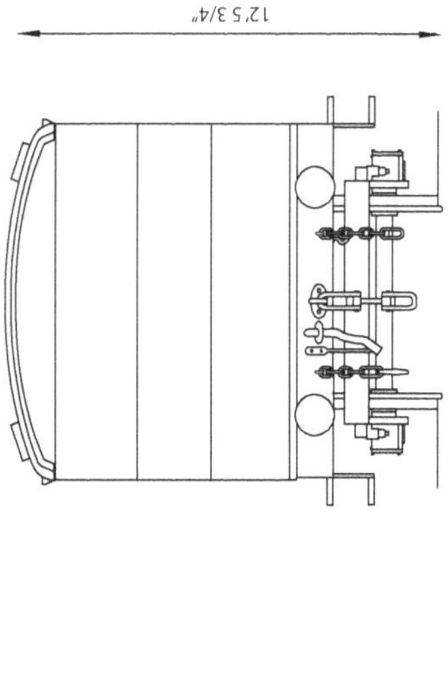

12' 5 3/4"

10'0"

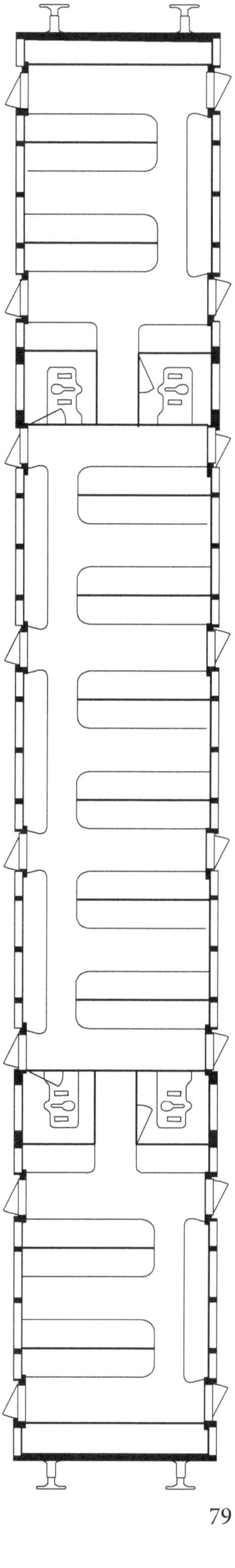

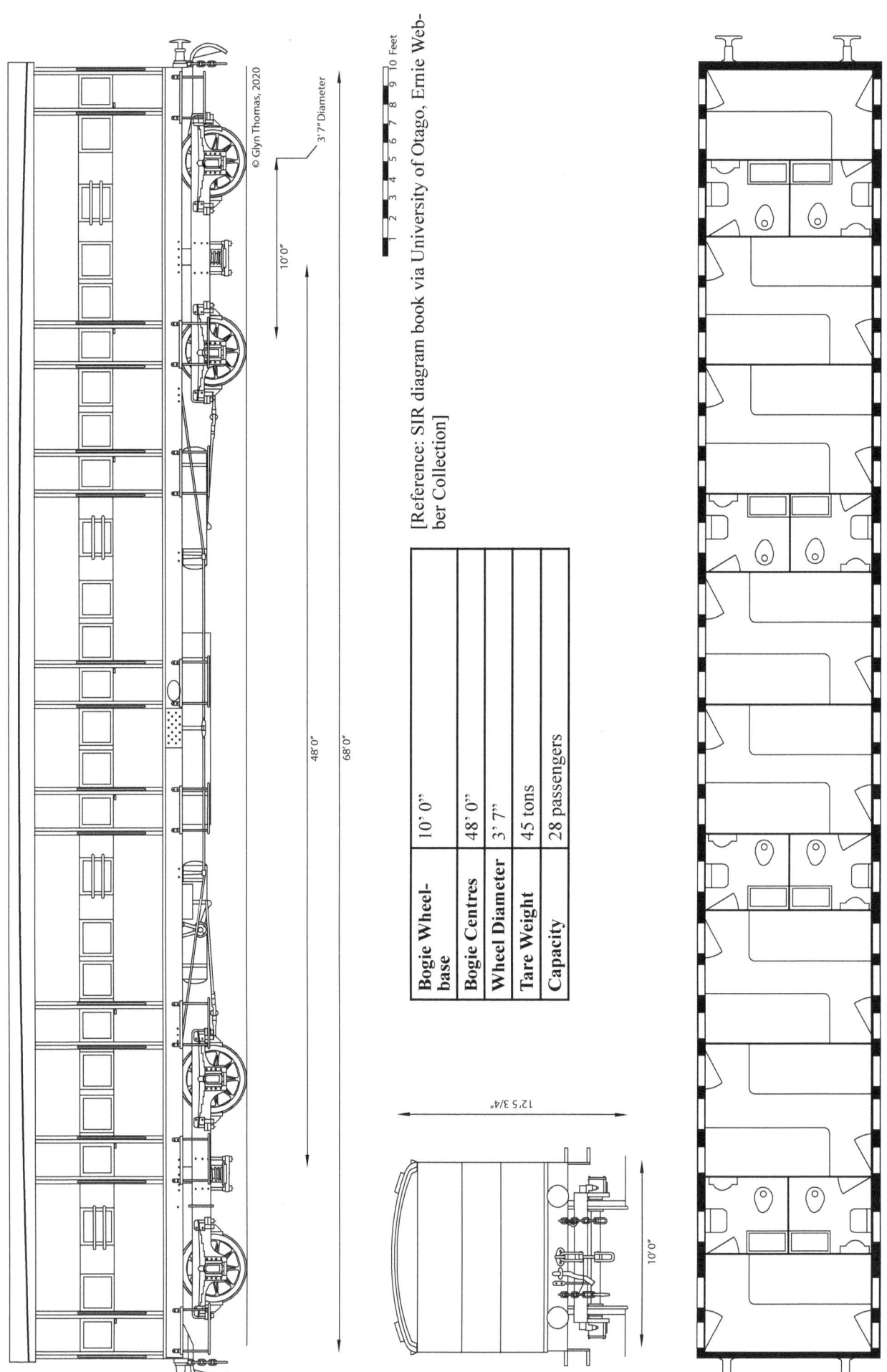

© Glyn Thomas, 2020

3'7" Diameter

10'0"

48'0"

68'0"

1 2 3 4 5 6 7 8 9 10 Feet

[Reference: SIR diagram book via University of Otago, Ernie Webber Collection]

Bogie Wheelbase	10' 0"
Bogie Centres	48' 0"
Wheel Diameter	3' 7"
Tare Weight	45 tons
Capacity	28 passengers

12' 5 3/4"

10' 0"

SIR 1st Class Coach

SIR 1st–2nd Composite

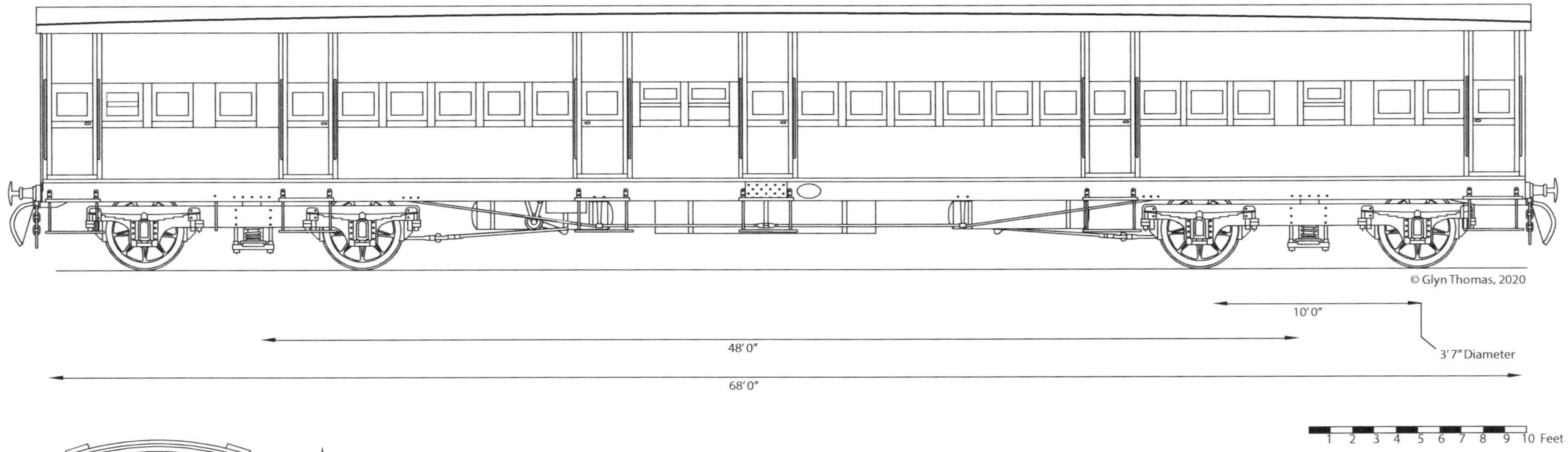

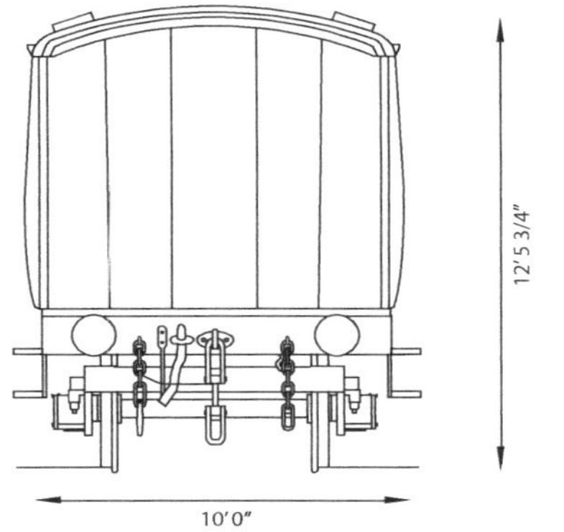

© Glyn Thomas, 2020

3'7" Diameter

10'0"

48'0"

68'0"

12' 5 3/4"

10'0"

2 3 4 5 6 7 8 9 10 Feet

[Reference: SIR diagram book via University of Otago, Ernie Webber Collection]

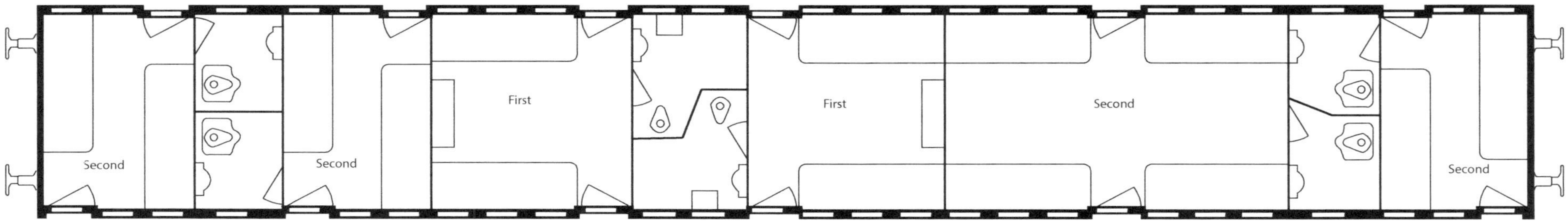

Bogie Wheelbase	10' 0"
Bogie Centres	48' 0"
Wheel Diameter	3' 7"
Tare Weight	41 tons 12 cwt
Capacity	12 first and 40 second class passengers

Second

Second

First

First

Second

Second

ICF Coaches

Western Railway Non-AC Second Class Sleeper no. 913381 at Mumbai in 2011 [Author]

As discussed in the introduction, following Independence there was deliberate policy by the Indian Government to become self-sufficient in the building of railway locomotives and rolling stock.

Over 26,000 ICF design coaches were built before they were superseded by a Linke Hofmann Busch (LHB) design introduced in the 1990s. The ICF itself switched to building LHB coaches in 2018.

There are numerous variations on the standard ICF design, including several with air conditioning.

Per the IRFCA, ICF coaches usually have a 4-, 5-, or 6-digit number, where the first two digits denote the year of construction.

The illustrations show a variety of ICF designs, including a 2004 design for a 3-tier second class sleeper that has a bulge in the roof to give the top sleeping passengers some headroom.

Central Railway AC 3-Tier Sleeper, no. 08112, and 2nd Class Sleeper no. 91300 at Mumbai in 2011 [Author]

Central Railway AC Chair Car 96153 at Mumbai in 2011 [Author]

Central Railway Second Class, Non-AC, 95612 at Mumbai in 2011 (note centre door) [Author]

Central Railway Second Class Brake with Disabled Access, Non-AC, 07710 at Mumbai in 2011 [Author]

Bogie Wheel-base	2896 mm
Bogie Centres	14,783 mm
Wheel Diameter	915 mm
Capacity	18 seated, 18 sleeping

[Reference: Indian Railway Plan]

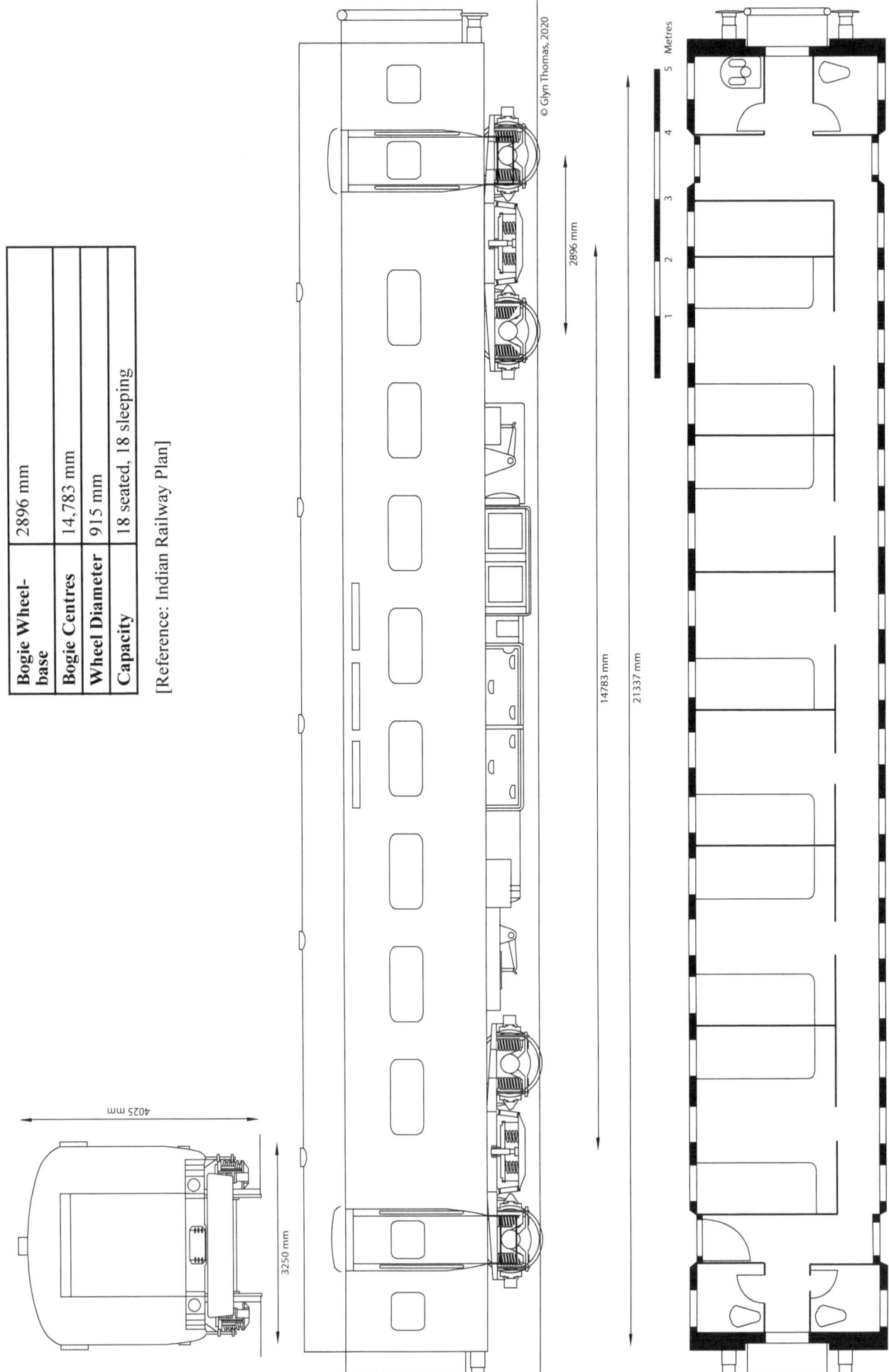

© Glyn Thomas, 2020

2896 mm

14783 mm

21337 mm

5 Metres

4

3

2

1

4025 mm

3250 mm

ICF 2-Tier 1st Class AC Sleeper

Bogie Wheel-base	2,896 mm
Bogie Centres	14,783 mm
Wheel Diameter	915 mm
Capacity	40 seated, 44 sleeping

[Reference: Photographs and known dimensions]

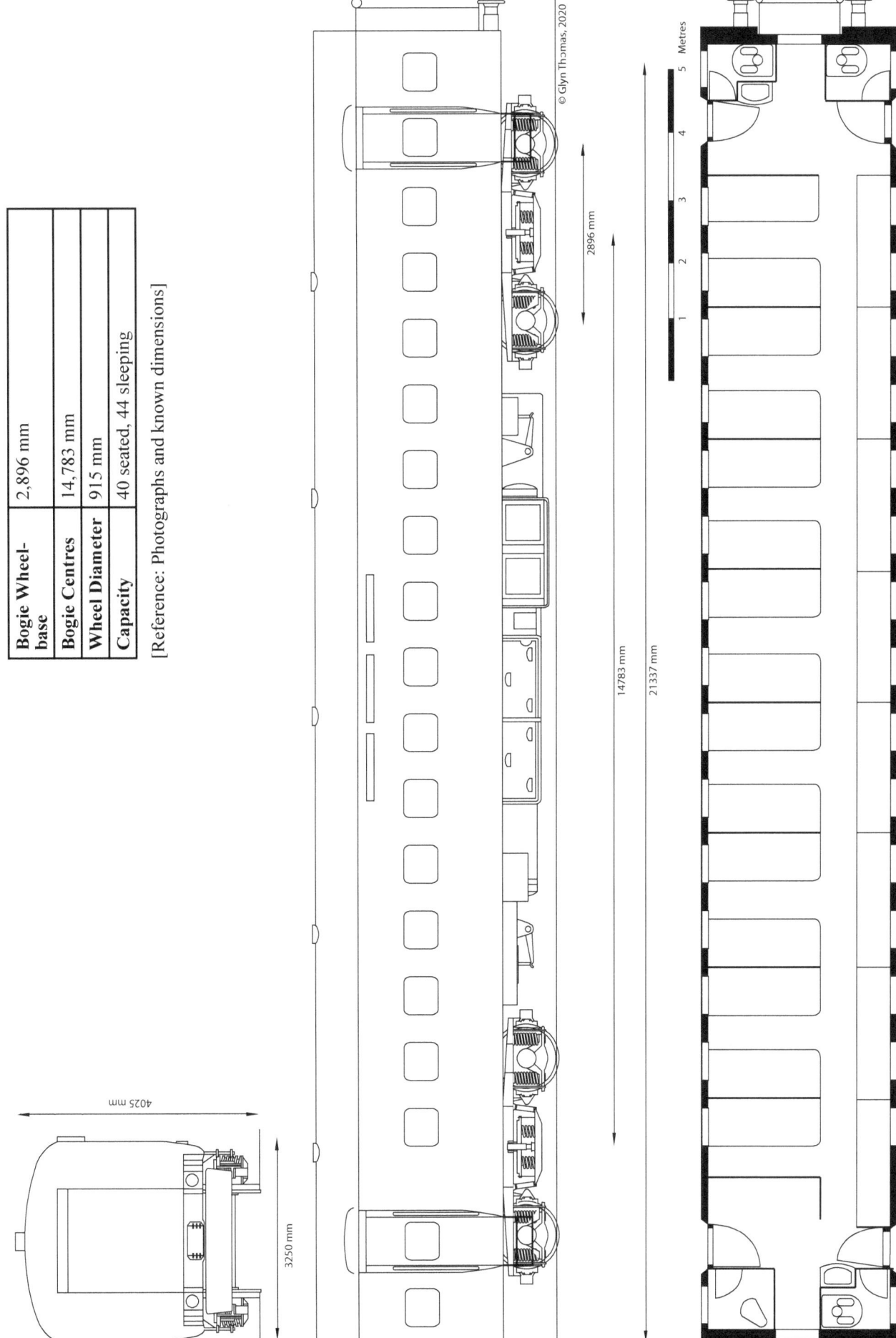

ICF 2-Tier 2nd Class AC Sleeper

© Glyn Thomas, 2020

Bogie Wheel-base	2,896 mm
Bogie Centres	14,783 mm
Wheel Diameter	915 mm
Capacity	26 seated, 20 sleeping

[Reference: Photographs and known dimensions]

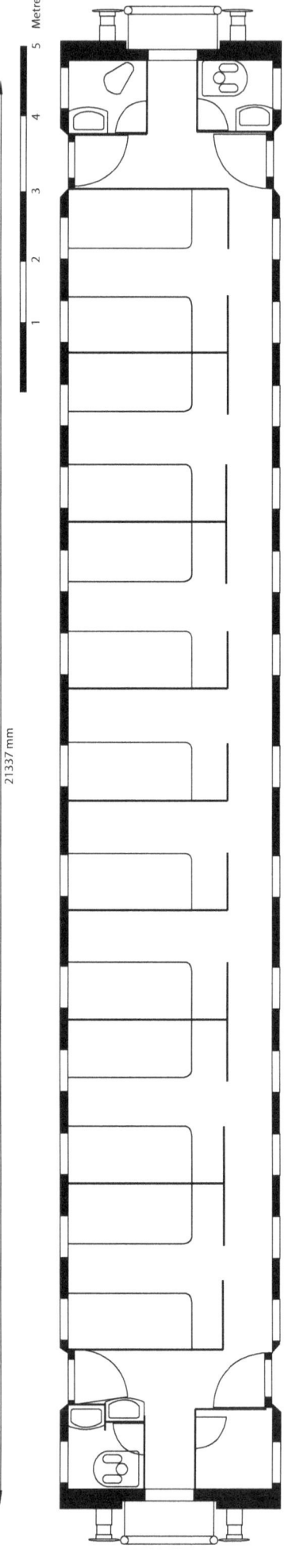

© Glyn Thomas, 2020

ICF 2-Tier 1st Class Non-AC Sleeper

Bogie Wheelbase	2,896 mm
Bogie Centres	14,783 mm
Wheel Diameter	915 mm

[Reference: Photographs and known dimensions]

ICF 3-Tier 2nd Class Non-AC Sleeper

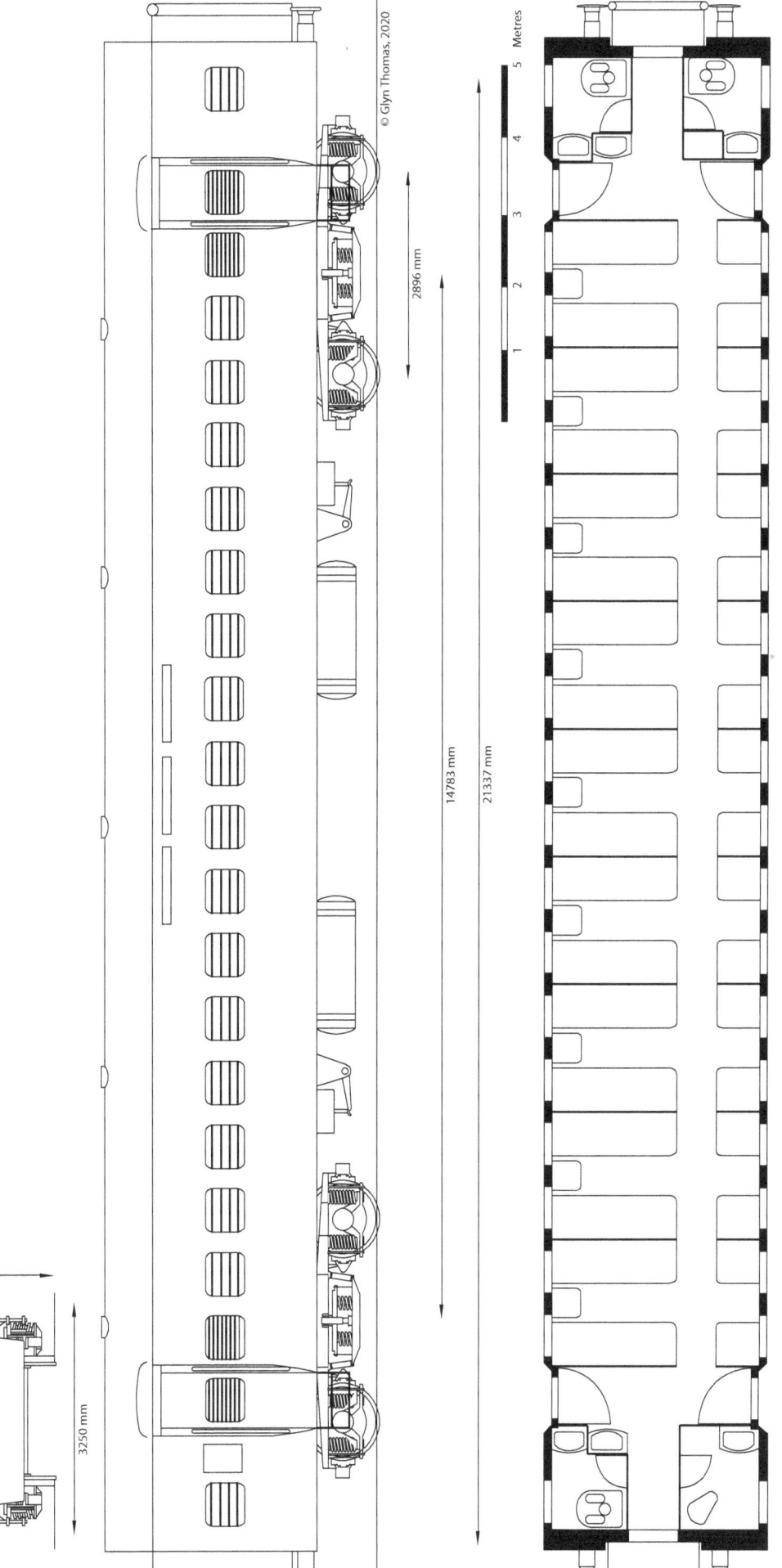

© Glyn Thomas, 2020

4025 mm

3250 mm

2896 mm

14783 mm

21337 mm

Metres

1 2 3 4 5

Bogie Wheelbase	2,896 mm
Bogie Centres	14,783 mm
Wheel Diameter	915 mm
Capacity	72 seated, 72 sleeping

[Reference: Indian Railway Plans]

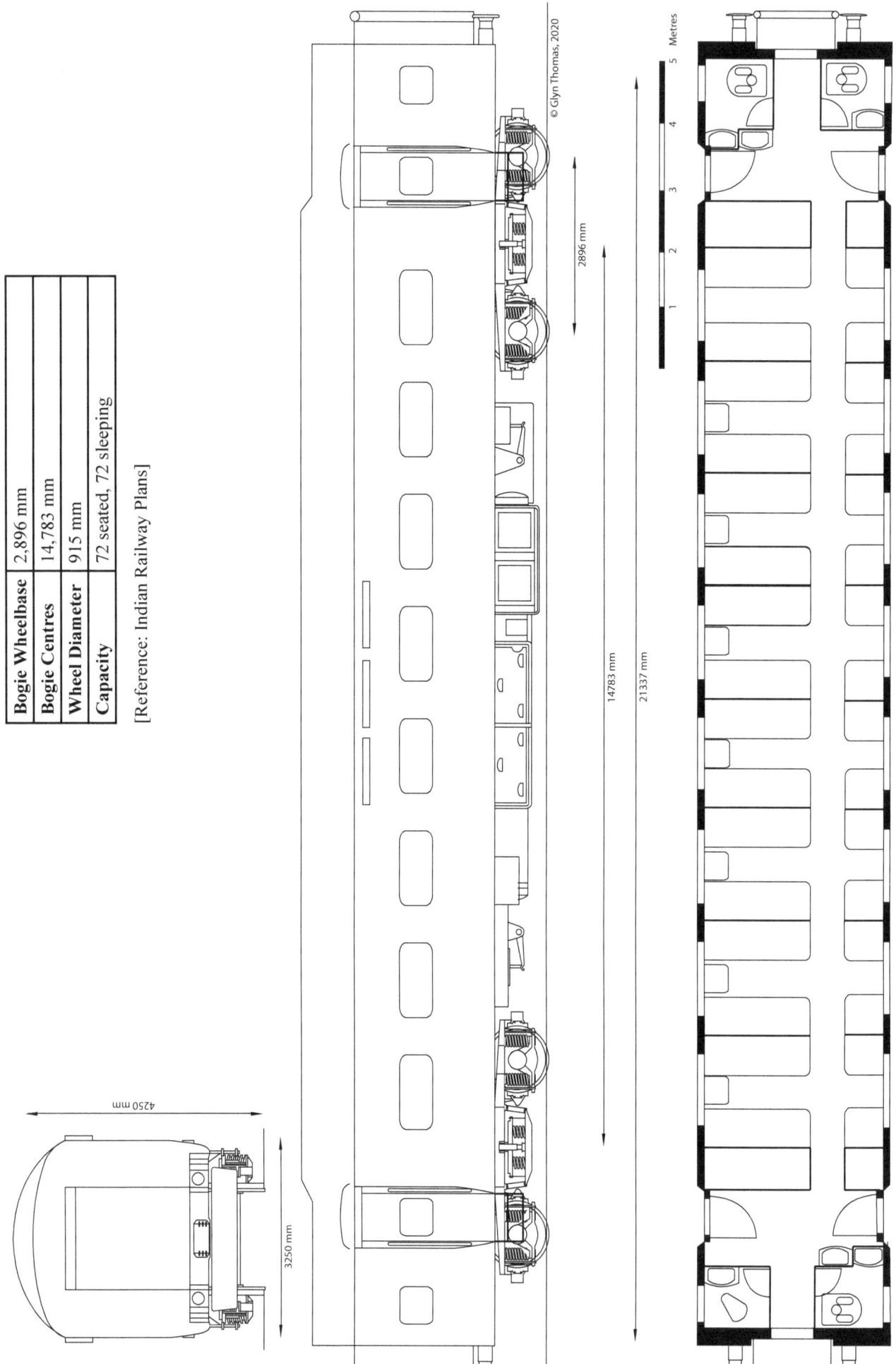

© Glyn Thomas, 2020

2896 mm

14783 mm

21337 mm

4250 mm

3250 mm

Metres

1 2 3 4 5

ICF 3-Tier 2nd Class AC Sleeper

Metre-Gauge Rolling Stock

4-Wheel Covered Vans

NF Covered Van no. 18615(?) at Jaipur in 1988 [Author]

Steel designs of 4-wheel vans for the metre-gauge were initially fairly evenly split between conventional flat sided designs with a corrugated iron roof, and the wagon-top design, where the sides are carried over seamlessly to the roof. Ultimately, the wagon-top design became the standard.

The wagon-top standard design for metre-gauge wagons was adopted earlier than its broad-gauge counterpart. A Metropolitan Cammell Railway Carriage and Wagon Co Ltd plan of 1899 shows an early example of the design (see Continental Modeller, January-February 1986 for a version by Jim Smith). The 1899 version had an 8' 9" wheelbase. In later versions, the wheelbase was extended to 10'.

Eastern Bengal State Railway Covered Van, 1904

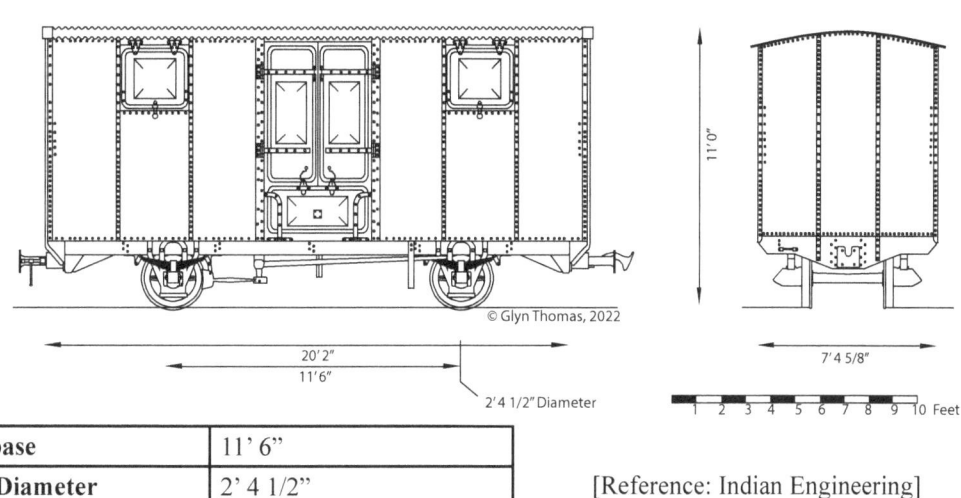

Wheelbase	11' 6"
Wheel Diameter	2' 4 1/2"

[Reference: Indian Engineering]

Metre-Gauge Rolling Stock

MA2 Covered Van 1927

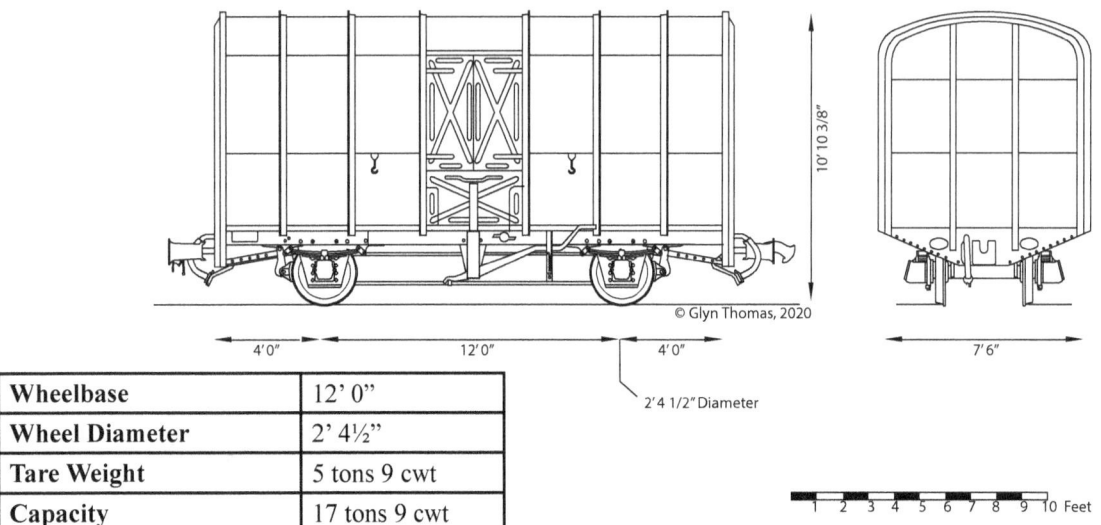

Wheelbase	12' 0"
Wheel Diameter	2' 4½"
Tare Weight	5 tons 9 cwt
Capacity	17 tons 9 cwt

The SIR received 1,210 of the MA2 type wagon in three batches between 1927 and 1929. These were numbered 1 to 1210. By the 1940s, numbers 141, 170, 299, and 892 had been removed from the roster, probably due to accidents.

Number 732 was classified MA2E and was adapted for transporting elephants.

[Reference: SIR diagram book via Ernie Webber Collection, Otago University]

MC Covered Van 1952

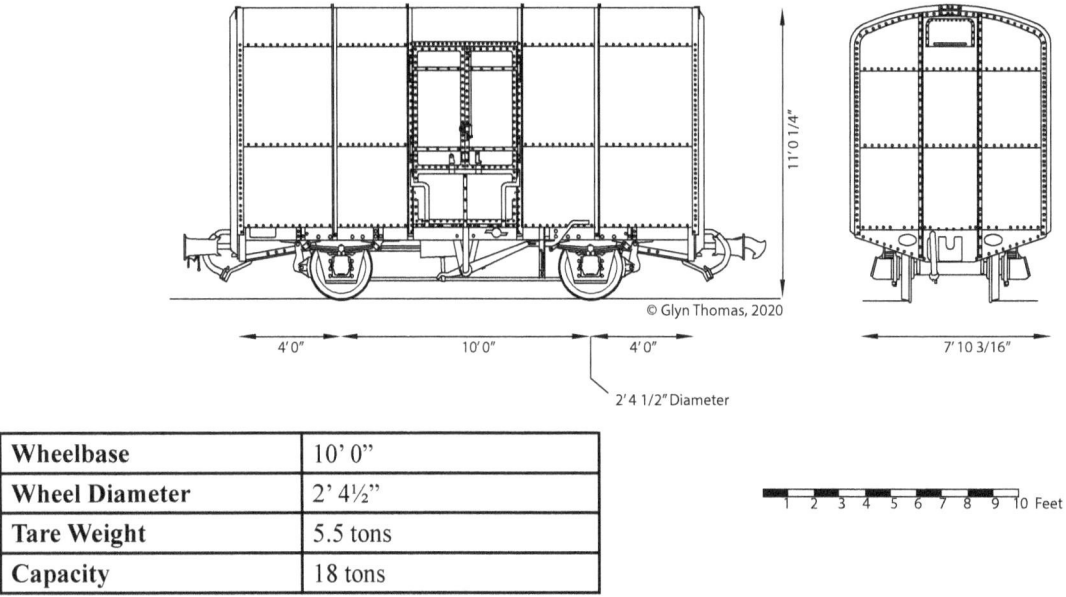

Wheelbase	10' 0"
Wheel Diameter	2' 4½"
Tare Weight	5.5 tons
Capacity	18 tons

MC Indian standard design built by Metropolitan Cammell Railway Carriage and Wagon Co Ltd in 1952.

The SIR operated 428 of these wagons built between 1931 and 1939 in five batches, numbered 1 to 428. By the 1940s numbers 335 and 342 had been removed from the roster. Other metre gauge lines probably operated similar numbers of vans.

[Reference: builder's diagram via Historical Model Railway Society]

Metre-Gauge Rolling Stock

Modern Covered Van

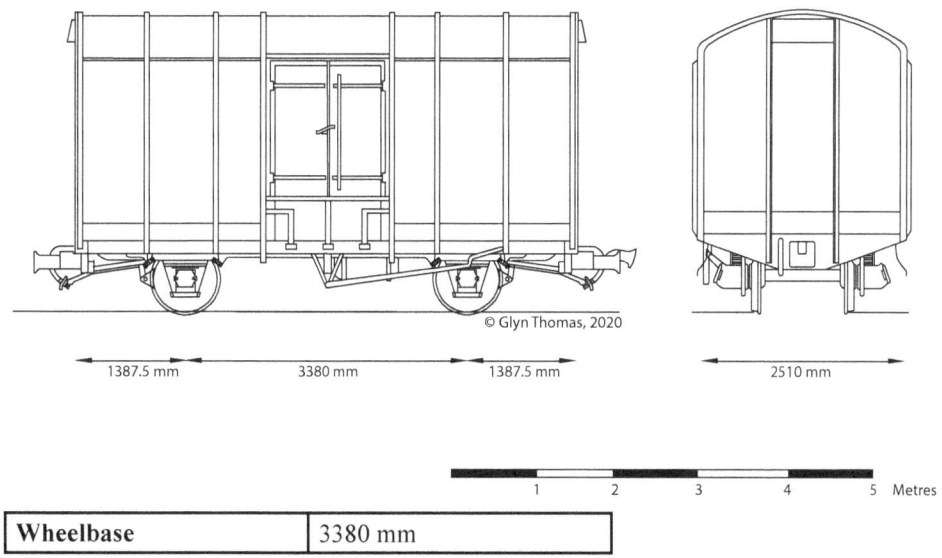

© Glyn Thomas, 2020

| 1387.5 mm | 3380 mm | 1387.5 mm | 2510 mm |

| 1 | 2 | 3 | 4 | 5 Metres |

Wheelbase	3380 mm

Indian Railways standard MG covered van. Large numbers of MC and equivalent 4-wheel vans were still in use in the 1970s and 1980s. However, as gauge conversion gathered pace, it appears that 4-wheeled vans were the first to be withdrawn.

[Reference: Pegasus Designs plans and Maintenance Manual for Wagons]

H. H. THE NIZAM'S STATE RAILWAYS.   Covered Goods Wagon.
Metre gauge. Length over headstocks, 18'. Width over headstocks, 7' 0¼". Length over buffers, 21' 10". Wheel base, 10'.
Weight, 5 tons 7 cwts. 3 qrs.

Gloucester Railway Carriage and Wagon Works Covered Van for the Nizam's State Railways [Historical Railway Images, Flickr]

4-Wheel Low-Sided Wagon

Low-sided Open Wagon being Switched by YG 2-8-2 3283 at Mahesana, 1981 [Author]

Low-sided open wagons can be used to carry unusual loads, in a similar manner to flat cars, or smaller amounts of granular products, such as ballast.

The illustrated wagon is of type MOM, built for Mysore State Railways. It was built by Metropolitan Cammell Carriage and Wagon Co Ltd. Seven wagons were ordered, at an unknown date, probably in the 1950s. [Reference: builder's diagram via the Historical Model Railway Society]

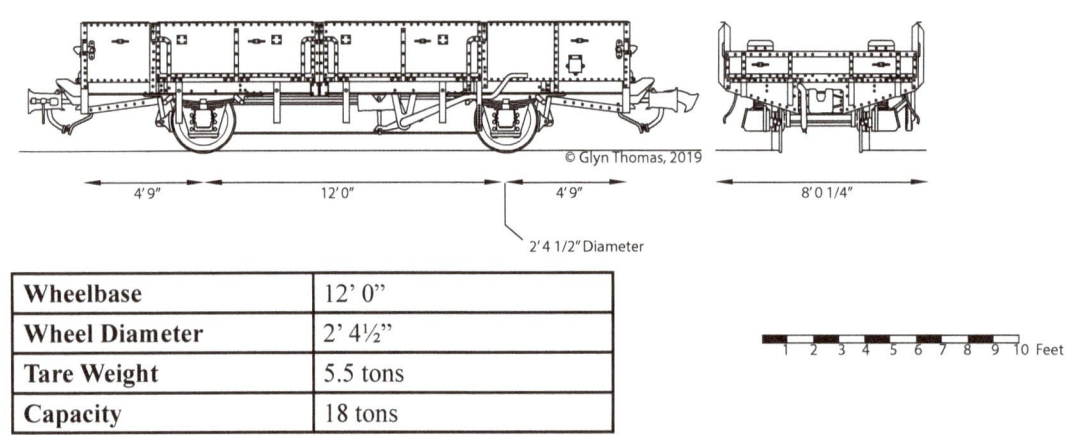

Wheelbase	12' 0"
Wheel Diameter	2' 4½"
Tare Weight	5.5 tons
Capacity	18 tons

4-Wheel Open Wagons

Long-wheelbase open wagon, NR5604(?) and covered Vans NE14533, WR28745, WR14126 (of a larger design) near Jaipur in 1989: [Author]

India has a long history of standardization of rolling stock. This was particularly prevalent on the metre-gauge railways, many of which were built by the state from the outset.

In 1913, the Railway Board issued a schedule that standardised the main dimensions of wagons on the broad- and metre-gauge. As discussed elsewhere, standardization eventually came under the purview of the Indian Railway Conference Association (IRCA). In 1921, they issued revised standards for both broad- and metre-gauge covering all the major wagon types and coach underframes. These standards totaled 274 diagrams.

Outlines of some of these designs appeared in Railway Engineer in 1923. Although the outlines are very basic, it is possible to extrapolate a credible impression of the standard MC/1 open wagon, as illustrated here.

It is not clear how many 4-wheel open wagons were produced, but it is likely that they would have been one of the most common types during the colonial era. Personal observation in the late steam era was that these were less common, and following the end of steam they were almost entirely supplanted by bogie open wagons.

MC-1

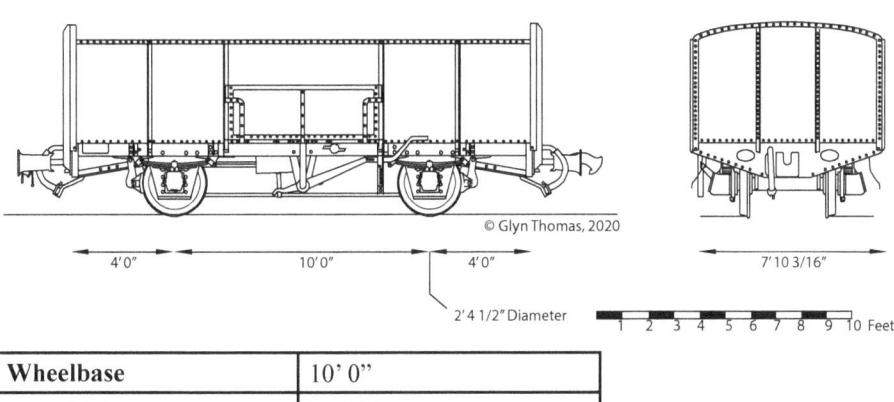

Wheelbase	10' 0"
Wheel Diameter	2' 4½"
Tare Weight	5 tons 2 cwt 1 qtr

[Reference: Railway Engineer, 1923]

MC-2

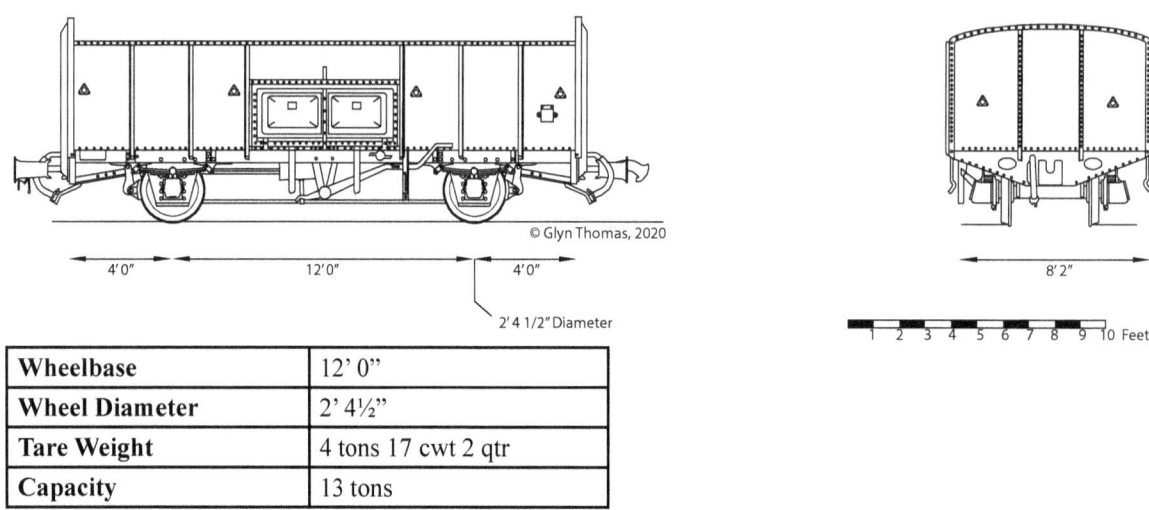

Wheelbase	12' 0"
Wheel Diameter	2' 4½"
Tare Weight	4 tons 17 cwt 2 qtr
Capacity	13 tons

[Reference: SIR diagram book via University of Otago, Ernie Webber Collection]

SIR MG 4-Wheel Fenced Open Wagon, 1933 [BRCW Photo, Julian Rainbow Collection]

4-Wheel Ballast Hopper

ABR Ballast Hopper, 1908 [Railway Engineer]

The illustration shows a 4-wheel hopper design built by Leeds Forge Co for the Assam Bengal Railway (ABR) and Burma Railways in 1908. These wagons are fitted with Jepson's Patent bottom discharge doors, operated by a worm gear. These were apparently built in large numbers for other Indian railways.

[Reference: Railway Engineer, December 1908]

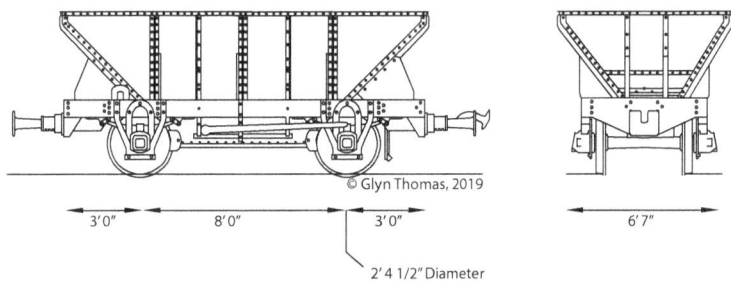

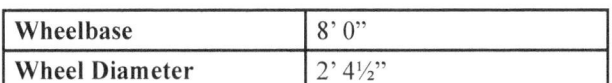

Wheelbase	8' 0"
Wheel Diameter	2' 4½"

Bogie Covered Vans

YDM4A no. 6206 with a train of bogie covered vans at Mahesana, on November 12th, 1975 [Brian Walker, BW1217, Transport Treasury]

As on the broad-gauge, bogie covered vans were a natural evolution of the van concept.

The first diagram shows a bogie van built by Metropolitan Carriage Wagon and Finance Co Ltd for the Eastern Bengal Railway (EBR) in 1912. This still features the older-style corrugated iron roof.

Indian Railways operated large numbers of 47' long MBC standard bogie vans. These were equivalent to two MC vans on the same underframe. It is possible to see several of these MBC vans around the remaining metre-gauge networks today, although there is little freight traffic any more.

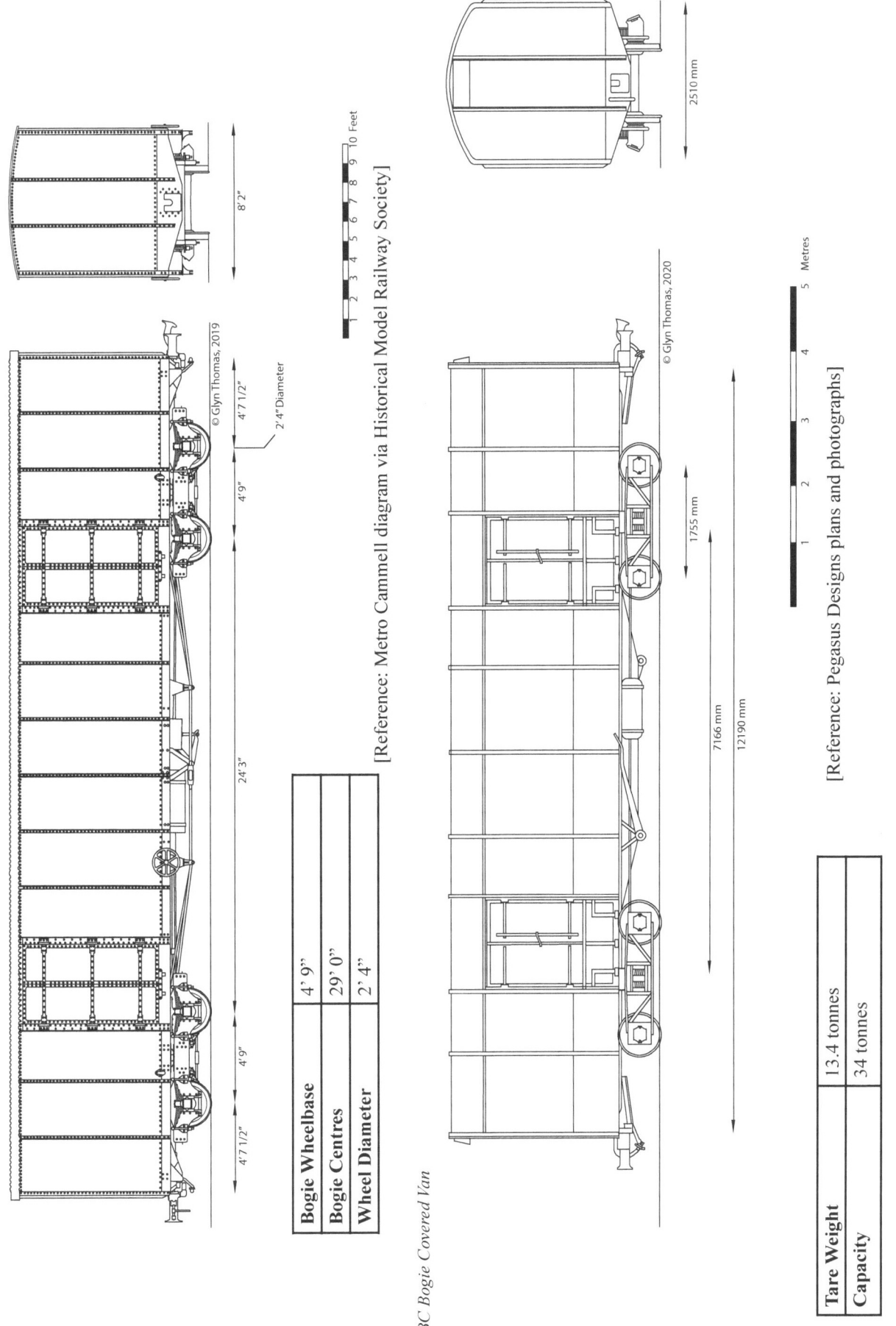

EBR Bogie Covered Van

IR MBC Bogie Covered Van

[Reference: Metro Cammell diagram via Historical Model Railway Society]

© Glyn Thomas, 2019

© Glyn Thomas, 2020

[Reference: Pegasus Designs plans and photographs]

Bogie Wheelbase	4' 9"
Bogie Centres	29' 0"
Wheel Diameter	2' 4"

| Tare Weight | 13.4 tonnes |
| Capacity | 34 tonnes |

Bogie Open Wagons

Sheffield-Twinberrow MG Bogie Open, 1908 [Locomotive, Carriage and Wagon Review]

Most Indian steel metre-gauge bogie wagons were fairly similar designs, either low-sided or high-sided, with various door configurations. The first example illustrated here is for the Nilgiri rack railway and has a unique feature of a rack brake on one bogie. It appears that the mechanism for this was manual only, and separate conventional vacuum brakes were also fitted.

In 1908, the Locomotive Carriage and Wagon Review ran a series of articles extolling the virtues of the Sheffield-Twinberrow system of rolling stock. Pressed steel structural components were used to increase the capacity of wagons while minimizing tare weight, and bogie designs were generally preferred. These designs clearly influenced by earlier work by Calthrop on the Barsi Light Railway (see the narrow gauge section), and were broadly adopted in India. The illustration shows a bogie open wagon fitted with Sheffield-Twinberrow bogies, and is based on dimensions from the article.

Nilgiri Bogie Open Wagon 1905

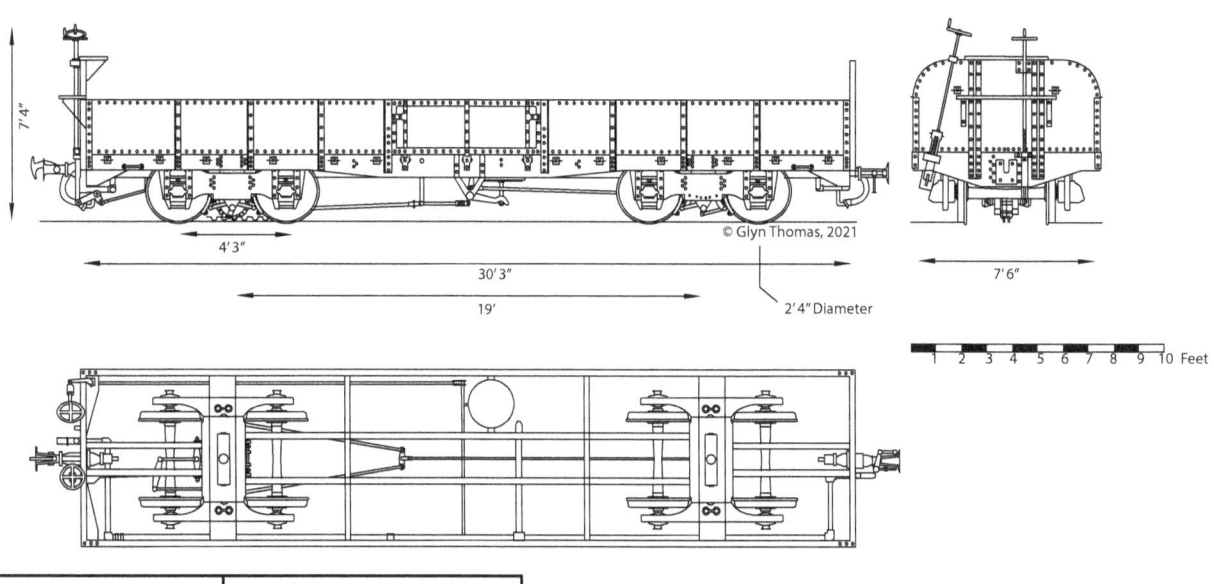

Bogie Wheelbase	4' 3"
Bogie Centres	19' 0"
Wheel Diameter	2' 4"
Tare Weight	7 tons 14 cwt
Capacity	20 tons

[Reference: Indian Engineering, 1907]

Bogie Open Wagon 1908

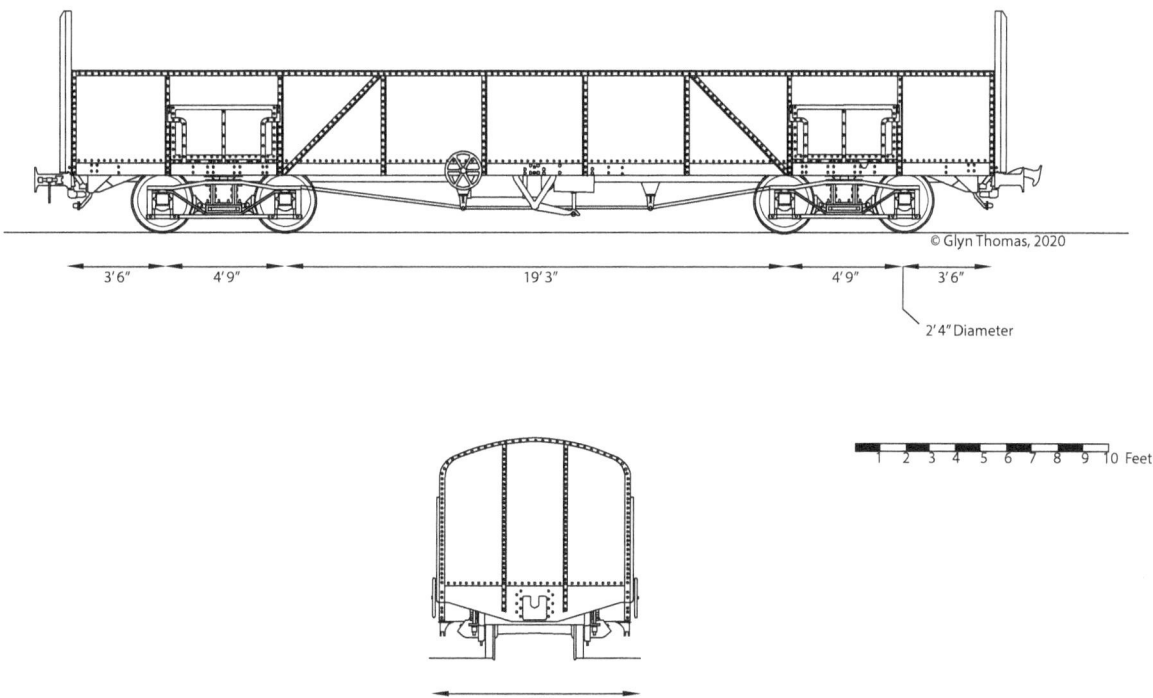

Bogie Wheelbase	4' 9"
Bogie Centres	24' 0"
Wheel Diameter	2' 4"
Tare Weight	7 tons 16 cwt
Capacity	24 tons

[Reference: Photographs and dimensions from The Locomotive, 1908]

Cochin State Forest Tramway Stock

CSFT train at Chalakudy c. 1910 [Scientific American]

During the colonial era, the region of Cochin (now Kerala) in southwest India was a princely state ruled by the Maharajah of Cochin. The principle resource of the region was high quality teak and rosewood timber from huge tracts of rain forest. The British were quick to recognise the value of the timber, and there was uncontrolled logging and land clearance for agriculture of the more accessible lands through most of the 19th Century.

In 1895, Sir James Thompson approached the Maharajah with a proposal to improve management of the forest. This resulted in the 1897 establishment of the role of Forest Officer reporting to the Maharajah. Plans were initiated to halt logging in overworked areas, and extend forestry activities inland. Surveys of the inland rivers concluded that it wouldn't be practical to float logs out of the forest, so a tramway was proposed instead. The initial plan in 1901 was for a 12 miles line to be worked by gravity inclines and manual labour, but the plan rapidly expanded to 49.5 miles with locomotive power. The line opened throughout in 1907 and was considered an 'engineering marvel' with two clusters of gravity worked inclines, and numerous zig-zags on the locomotive-worked sections in between.

Unfortunately, the proposed forestry management plan was never implemented and the Cochin State Forest Tramway accelerated and expanded degradation of the forest. By the 1920's there were growing calls for closure of the tramway due to climate change caused by destruction of the environment. The State's Finance Committee recommended closure in 1926, but the line survived and continued to drive exploitation of the forest.

By Independence, the value of the tramway was severely diminished because land close to the line was worked out, and roads had been built to access other parts of the forest. The line ceased operation in 1951, but was retained with the prospect of being used for tourism. The tourist line plans didn't materialise and the line was abandoned in 1963. Soon afterwards, part of the trackbed was submerged under Parambikulam reservoir.

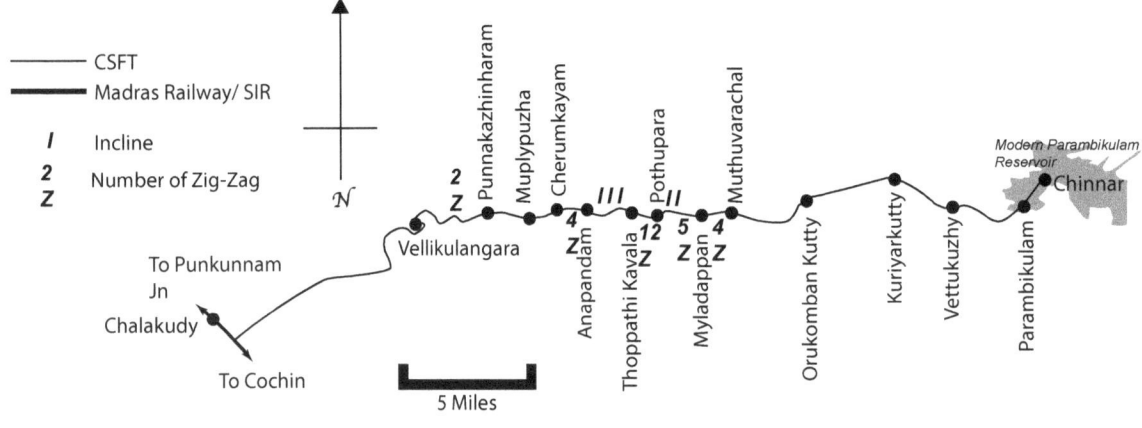

CSFT Route

Metre-Gauge Rolling Stock

Until 2013, organised tours were offered to hike parts of the remaining trackbed, but these are no longer permitted because the forest has been designated as a tiger reserve. There are tentative plans to establish a tramway museum at the old workshops in Chalakudy, which may include some remaining wagons. It is reported that an early engineering model of the line could be seen in the Kerala museum, but it's not been possible to confirm it is still on display.

Modern writers are quick to fault colonial exploitation of the forest for imperial gains. However, revenue from forestry was a major source of income for Cochin state, and funded the construction of a modern port at Kerala and other infrastructure improvements.

The tramway was built to metre gauge, presumably to permit interchange with the state railway (which was metre gauge at that time), although the couplings used different, so it is unlikely that interchange did occur. Locomotives and rolling stock for the line were supplied by Orenstein and Koppel. Seven 0-6-0Ts and one 0-8-0T of typical O&K design operated the line. O&K also provided cranes and other logging equipment, while P&W MacLellan of Glasgow provided bridges. P&W MacLellan was also a major importer of teak into Britain.

70 pairs of disconnect logging trucks by O&K were the primary rolling stock on the line. Disconnect log trucks are simple 4-wheel trucks supporting a rotating cradle. The trucks can be coupled together when unloaded. When loaded, the trucks are uncoupled and logs are suspended between the cradles and chained to each car. This method is very flexible, permitting a wide variety of lengths and diameters of logs to be accommodated.

An unusual Indian adaptation of general logging practice was the use of elephants to haul logs from the cutting areas to loading points on the tramway.

Rolling stock was augmented with tenders for the locomotives and at least one 'salon' coach, which were probably built at Chalakudy using log truck underframes. It was possible for tourists to charter a coach on the line and stay overnight at forest lodges.

There is a detailed history of the line, the "Cochin State Forest Tramway Journal" by Devan Varma available free of charge on the IRFCA website.

The provided diagrams are based on O&K catalogue entries and photographs, and therefore may not be 100% accurate. If the museum at Chalakudy opens, it may be possible to measure the prototype in future.

Other Forestry Railways on the Subcontinent

"Industrial Locomotives of India and South Asia" by Simon Darvill lists at least 13 other forestry railways and tramways across India, Pakistan and dependent islands. These ranged from small lines operated manually or with elephants, to major systems. In general, it was much more common for forestry lines to be laid to 2' gauge. Equipment often came from O&K in the early days, and John Fowler of Leeds later.

The Raipur Forest Tramway was a 68 mile 2' gauge line from Kurud to Ekawari, built in 1924-27 and operating until 1943. Seven locomotives worked on the line including five of the B-class 0-4-0ST design used on the Darjeeling Himalayan Railway (DHR).

The Goalpara Forest Tramway (Kachugaon Light Railway) was started in 1900 and eventually extended a 2' gauge line 45.5 miles from Kachugaon to Fakirgaram and beyond in northern Assam. It was initially worked by O&K 0-4-0T and 0-6-0T locos. Andrew Barclay 0-4-2T locomotives from the Jorhat Provincial Railway (see 2' gauge rolling stock) were trialled here when that line closed in 1944, but were in too poor condition and they were replaced with newer Bagnall 0-4-2Ts from Martin and Co. A 4-wheel diesel hydraulic locomotive built by SAN of India was purchased in 1979. The line operated until 1988 when political unrest made logging impractical. The Kachugaon terminus is now the site of a major refugee camp.

The preserved Changa Manga Forest Tramway in Pakistan is probably the best remaining example of these lines.

Dedicated logging lines understate the amount of railway-related logging that took place in India. Construction of main lines through forested areas often included logging concessions for sleeper production and commercial forestry.

Metre-Gauge Rolling Stock

Disconnect Logging Trucks

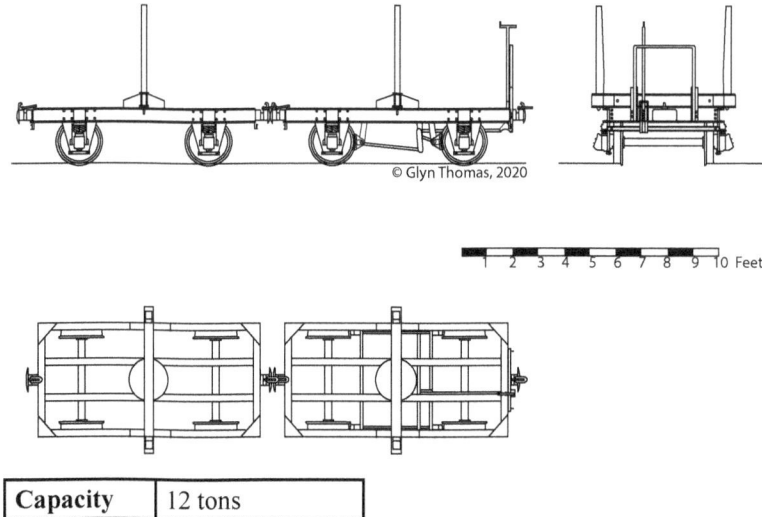

© Glyn Thomas, 2020

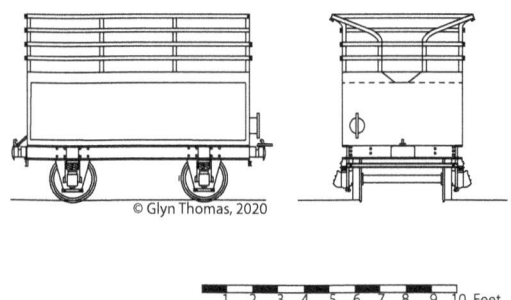

Capacity	12 tons

Tender for Locomotives

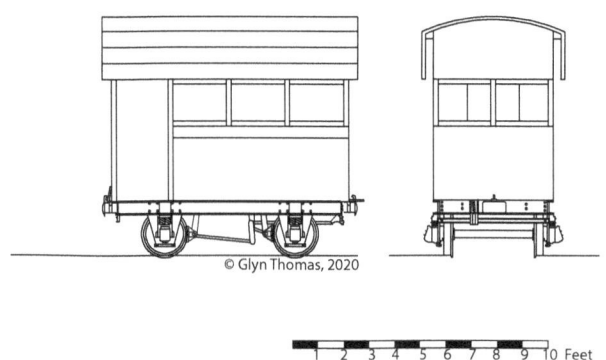

© Glyn Thomas, 2020

Salon Coach

© Glyn Thomas, 2020

Bogie Tank Wagons

MG BTP Tank Wagons at Patalpani on the Akola-Mhow line on August 24th, 2015 [Jay Balakrishna, YouTube]

Bogie tanks wagons were quite common on the metre gauge lines. Initially, they were used mainly for water and petrol (using designs with different valve arrangements).

The first diagram illustrates a 1930 standard design for the conveyance of petrol by an unknown builder. 20 were supplied direct to SIR and numbered 1-20. A further wagon of the same design and year was transferred from the South Central Railway after Independence and numbered 21. 6 of these wagons, numbered 7, 8, 9, 11, 16, and 20 were transferred overseas, probably after Independence. The class was classified MBTP. This class was through-piped, but not vacuum braked directly.

In later years, the bogie tank wagon appears to have been one of the most common types of wagon remaining on the metre-gauge. The second plan is scaled from photos of the modern design and was probably intended to carry water (many of these wagons were shipped to dry areas during times of drought).

SIR MBTP Tank Wagon

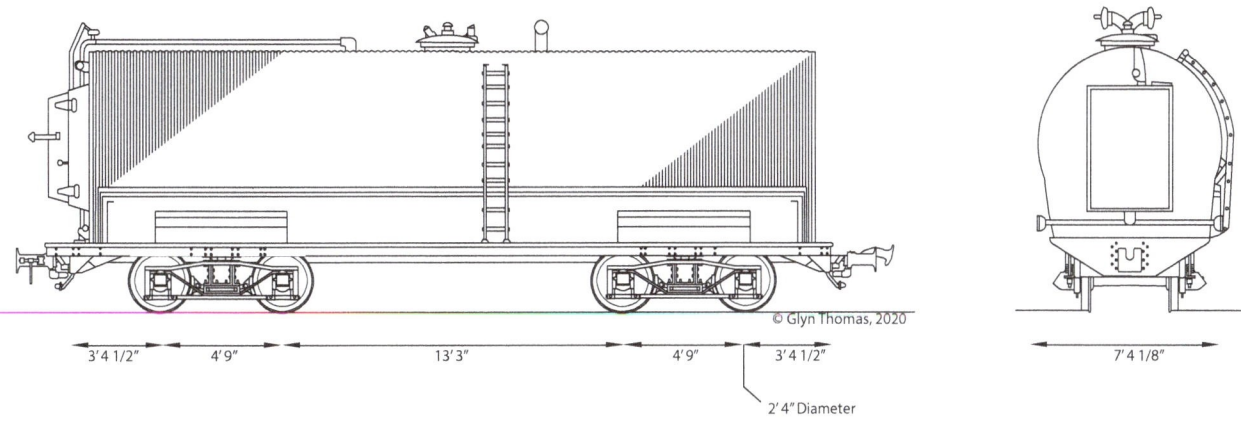

Bogie Wheelbase	4' 9"
Bogie Centres	18' 0"
Wheel Diameter	2' 4"
Tare Weight	17 tons 2 cwt 24 qtrs
Capacity	5300 Gallons

[Reference: SIR diagram book via University of Otago, Ernie Webber Collection]

IR MBTW Tank Wagon

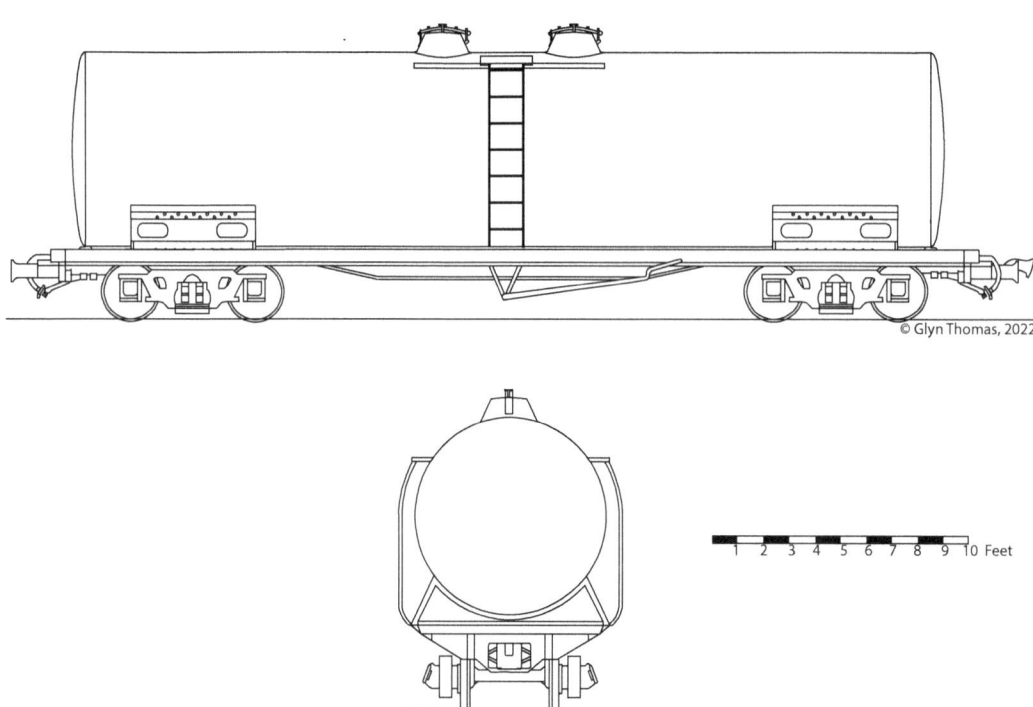

[Reference: Maintenance Manual for Wagons and Photographs]

Flatcar

MG Flatcars being shunted by a pair of YG 2-8-2s ant Ajmer in 1979 [David Churchill, DHRS]

As with the broad-gauge, metre-gauge railways need a number of flat cars to handle unusual loads that are difficult to carry in covered wagons or sided open wagons.

The illustration below shows the SIR design for a flatcar classified MBR. These were designed to carry rails, but were probably also used for other purposes. 10 were built in 1930 and assigned numbers 1 to 10. All were transferred overseas, probably to the Middle East during World War 2.

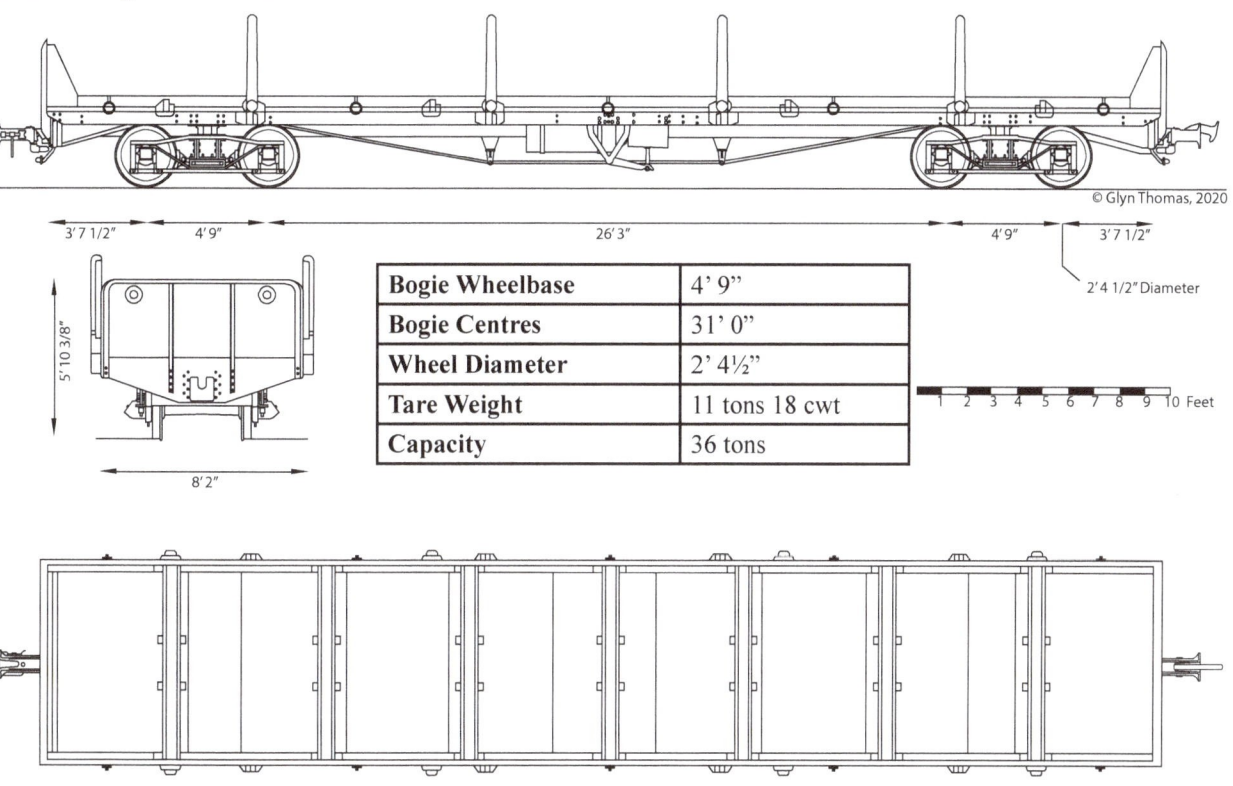

Bogie Wheelbase	4' 9"
Bogie Centres	31' 0"
Wheel Diameter	2' 4½"
Tare Weight	11 tons 18 cwt
Capacity	36 tons

[Reference: SIR diagram book via University of Otago, Ernie Webber Collection]

Brake Vans

NR brake van MBVG no. 2239 at Londa Junction. in 1989 [Author]

Brake vans remained common on metre gauge freights until the end of steam. These were usually of 4-wheel designs.

Standard metre-gauge brake vans were classified MBVG. There was some variation within the class so modellers should consult photos for details.

SIR SBV Brake Van

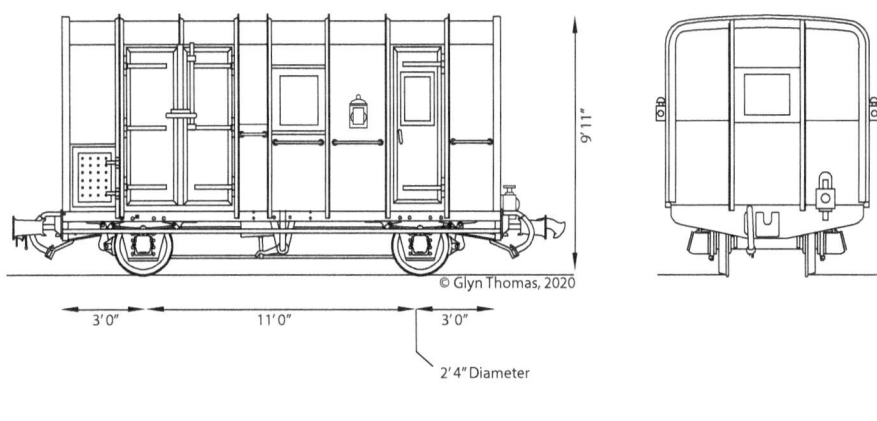

Wheelbase	10' 0"
Wheel Diameter	2' 4"
Tare Weight	12 tons 7 cwt
Capacity	3 ton

SIR brake van design, built on the standard MBVG underframe. 16 were built in 1932, numbered 108 to 123. A further batch was built in 1935, with 11 remaining on the line the 1940s, numbered 124, 125, 128-132, and 143-146.

[Reference: SIR diagram book via University of Otago, Ernie Webber Collection]

Metre-Gauge Rolling Stock

SIR SBV Brake Van

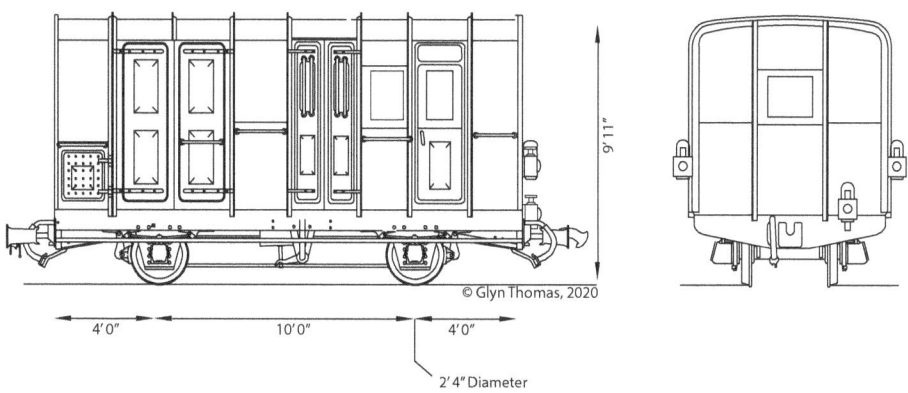

Wheelbase	11' 0"
Wheel Diameter	2' 4"
Tare Weight	13 tons 3 cwt
Capacity	1 ton

A later version of the SBV type for SIR. There were 11 of these on the line, built in 1945. and numbered 163 to 173.

[Reference: SIR diagram book via University of Otago, Ernie Webber Collection]

IR MBVG Brake Van

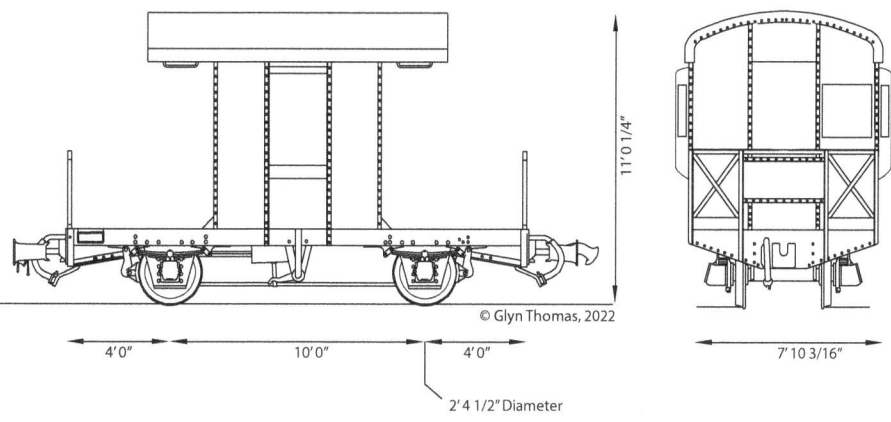

Wheelbase	10' 0"
Wheel Diameter	2' 4 ½"
Tare Weight	9.5 tons
Capacity	

This illustration shows a Northern Railway design, based on an example seen at Golden Rock in 1985.

[Reference: Photographs and known dimensions]

EBR 4-Wheel Coaches

Early postcard view of Mhow (originally built by the Holkar State Railway in 1874, later Rajputana Malwa Railway and BB-CIR), showing typical MG 4-wheel coaches similar to the EBR examples [Julian Rainbow Collection]

In 1899, the Railway Engineer ran a series of articles illustrating 4- and 6-wheel coaches for the Eastern Bengal Railway (EBR) metre-gauge. The illustrations show a third-class coach and a 1st-2nd class composite.

EBR 1st-2nd Composite Coach

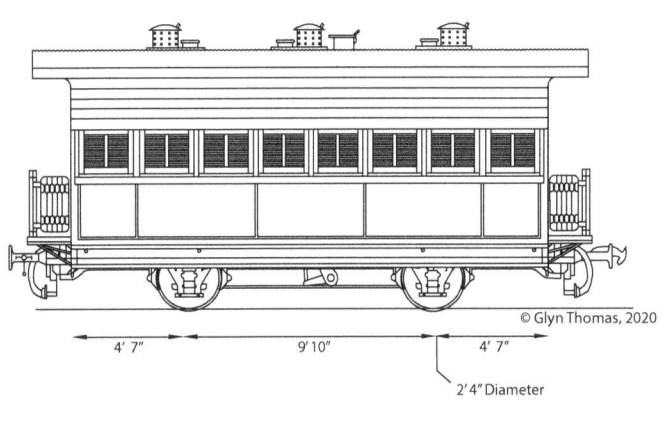

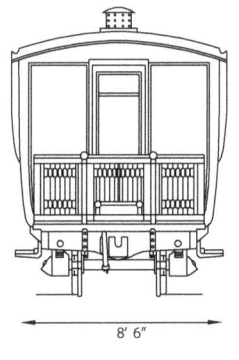

4' 7" 9' 10" 4' 7"

2' 4" Diameter

8' 6"

© Glyn Thomas, 2020

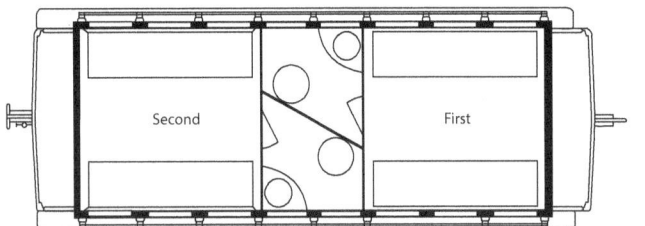

Second   First

1 2 3 4 5 6 7 8 9 10 Feet

Wheelbase	9' 10"
Wheel Diameter	2' 4"

[Reference: Railway Engineer, 1899]

Metre-Gauge Rolling Stock

EBR 3rd Class Coach

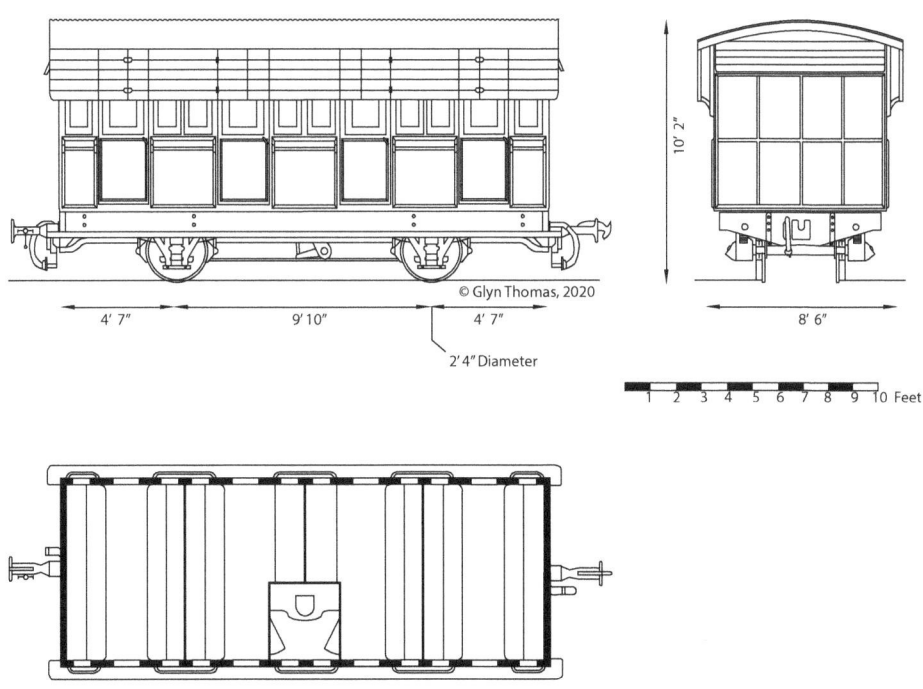

Wheelbase	9' 10"
Wheel Diameter	2' 4"

[Reference: Railway Engineer, 1899]

EBR 1st-2nd Class Composite Coach

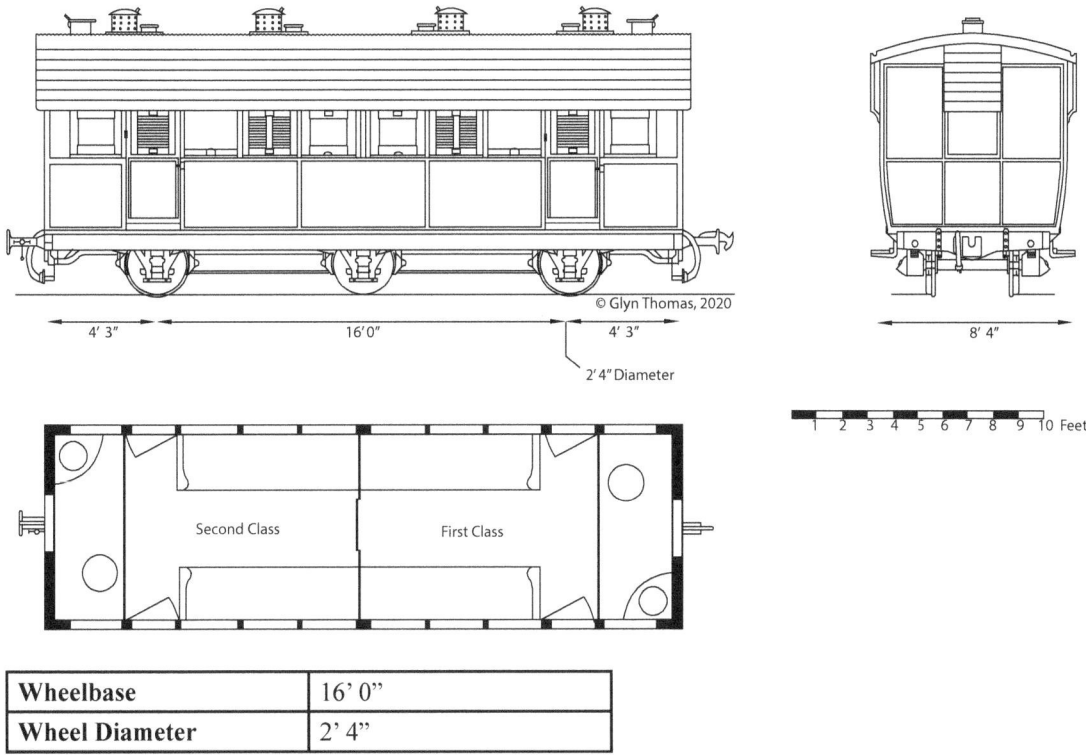

Wheelbase	16' 0"
Wheel Diameter	2' 4"

[Reference: Railway Engineer, 1899]

Saurashtra Railway Coach

Metre-Gauge Inspection Saloon on the Western Railway at Ahmedabad in 2005; this coach is similar in appearance to the coach in the diagram [Abhijit Lokre, IRFCA]

The Saurashtra Railway was formed as a state railway in 1948 to take over the princely states' metre-gauge lines, including the Bhavnagar State Railway, Gondal Railway, Porbandar Railway, Jamnagar & Dwarka Railway, Morvi Railway, Dhrangadhra Railway, Okhamandal State Railway, Junagadh State Railway, Baria State Railway, and Rajpipla Railway. The railway was short-lived in this form and was subsequently merged into the Western Railway in 1951.

This plan is based on an example in the Western Railway diagram book c.1995. These second-class coaches were built in 1951 to 1952 and classed ES, numbered 652-661, and ESY numbed 662. The ESY version presumably had a section reserved for ladies, per the post-Independence classification scheme.

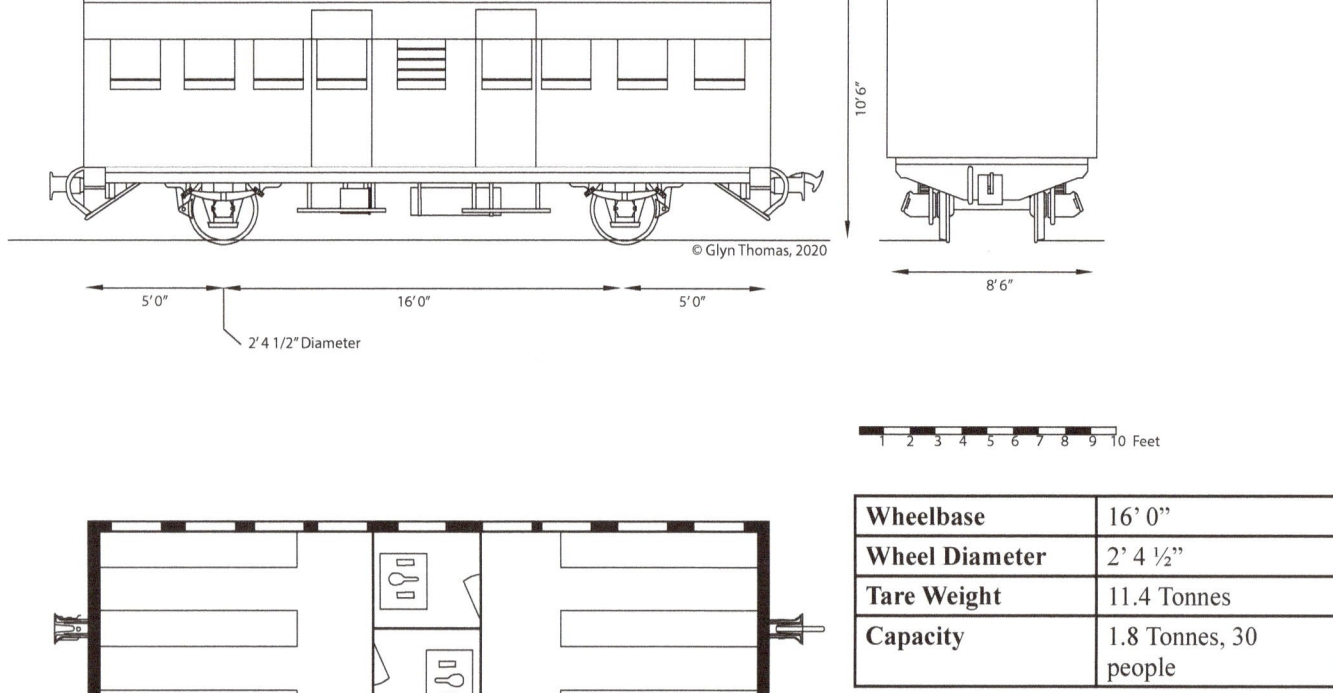

Wheelbase	16' 0"
Wheel Diameter	2' 4 ½"
Tare Weight	11.4 Tonnes
Capacity	1.8 Tonnes, 30 people

[Reference: Western Railway diagram book via Ken Walker]

1930s Coaches

A train connecting with a ferry to Ceylon stands on Dhanushkodi Pier in 1929. The nearest coach is similar to the brake-3rd illustrated below [Chris Walker Collection, cjwsir008]

This section covers plans for metre-gauge coaches built during the inter-war years.

SIR Tourist Coach [Chris Walker Collection, cjwsir018]

SIR Third-Class Tourist Coach [Chris Walker Collection, cjwsir019]

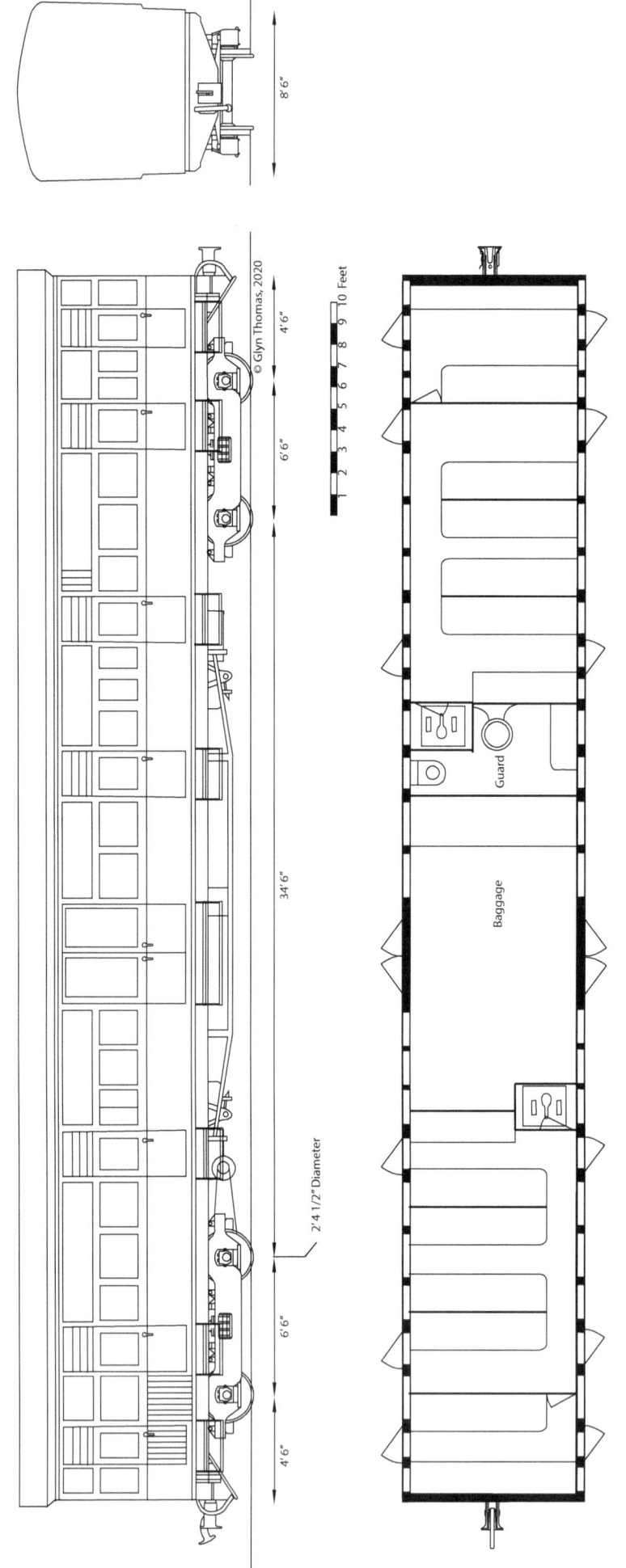

BBCIR Brake-3rd

© Glyn Thomas, 2020

1 2 3 4 5 6 7 8 9 10 Feet

8' 6"

4' 6"   6' 6"   34' 6"   6' 6"   4' 6"

2' 4 1/2" Diameter

Bogie Wheelbase	6' 6"
Bogie Centres	41' 0"
Wheel Diameter	2' 4 ½"
Tare Weight	21.5 Tons
Capacity	7.9 Tons Luggage and 56 passengers

A second-baggage coach built by the Bombay, Baroda, and Central India Railway (BBCIR). The BBCIR operated an extensive metre-gauge network in western India. In 1951, the BBCIR was merged into the Western Railway. This coach was illustrated in the Western Railway diagram book c.1995 as a late survivor of a design that probably saw other variations when built. These coaches were built between 1927 and 1939 and were originally classified as third-class, code TLR. In 1974 they were reclassified as SLR to indicate the elimination of third-class. Known numbers and details are shown in the following table.

Old Number	New Number	Year Built	Bogies
1107	1807	1927	IRCA
1119	1619	1928	IRCA
1128	1728	1929	IRCA
840	1840	1939	Sheffield Diamond
858	1858	1939	Sheffield Diamond
869	1869	1939	Sheffield Diamond

[Reference: Western Railway diagram book via Ken Walker]

Metre-Gauge Rolling Stock

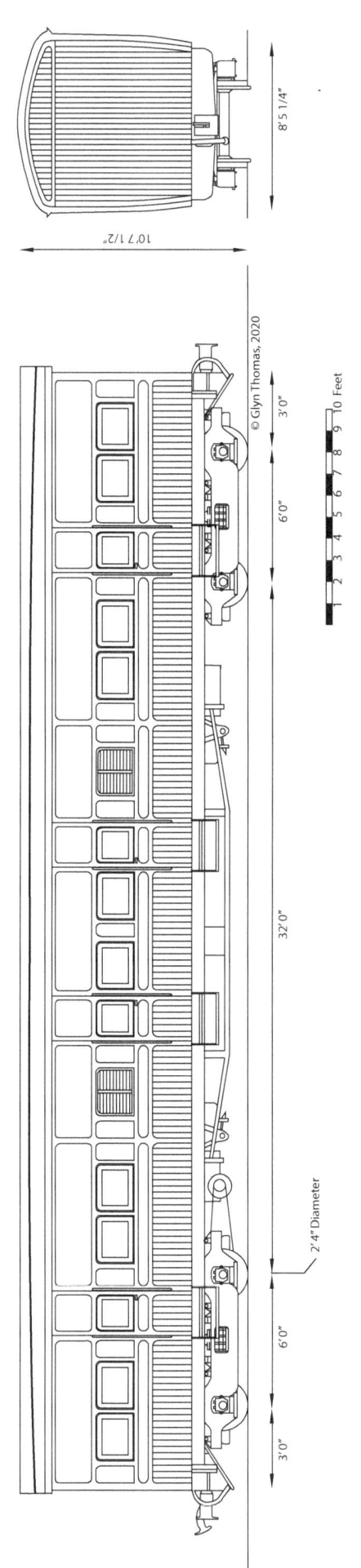

SIR 2nd Class Coach

8' 5 1/4"

10' 7 1/2"

© Glyn Thomas, 2020

3'0" 6'0"

1 2 3 4 5 6 7 8 9 10 Feet

32' 0"

2' 4" Diameter

6'0" 3'0"

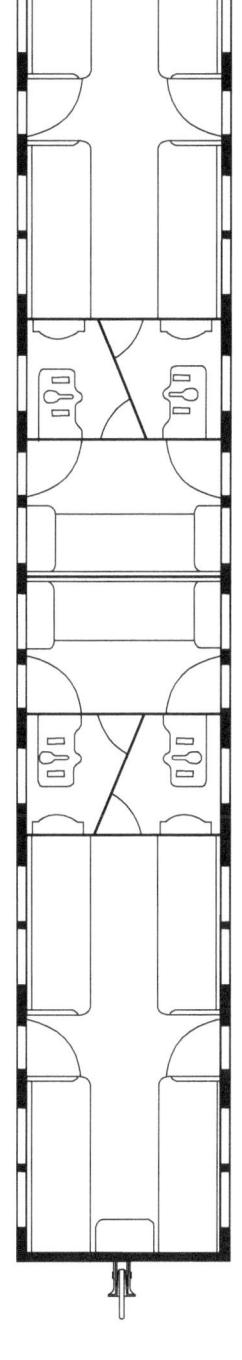

Second class 2-tier sleeper built by the SIR. Two were built in 1925 (nos. 1 and 2), and one in 1928 (no. 3). Unusually, the cost to the railway is known: 32,550 Rupees.

Bogie Wheelbase	6' 0"
Bogie Centres	38' 0"
Wheel Diameter	2' 4"
Tare Weight	21 tons 5 cwt
Capacity	40 seated or 20 sleeping

[Reference: SIR diagram book via University of Otago, Ernie Webber Collection]

© Glyn Thomas, 2020

8' 5 1/4"

10' 7 1/2"

4'3" 6'6" 34'6" 6'6" 4'3"

2' 4 1/2" Diameter

1 2 3 4 5 6 7 8 9 10 Feet

SIR 1st Class Coach

First class sleeper for the SIR. Four were built in 1929 (nos. 7,8,9,10).

Bogie Wheelbase	6' 6"
Bogie Centres	41' 0"
Wheel Diameter	2' 4 ½"
Tare Weight	23 tons 9 cwt
Capacity	20 seated or 10 sleeping

[Reference: SIR diagram book via University of Otago, Ernie Webber Collection]

Metre-Gauge Rolling Stock

SIR Brake-3rd

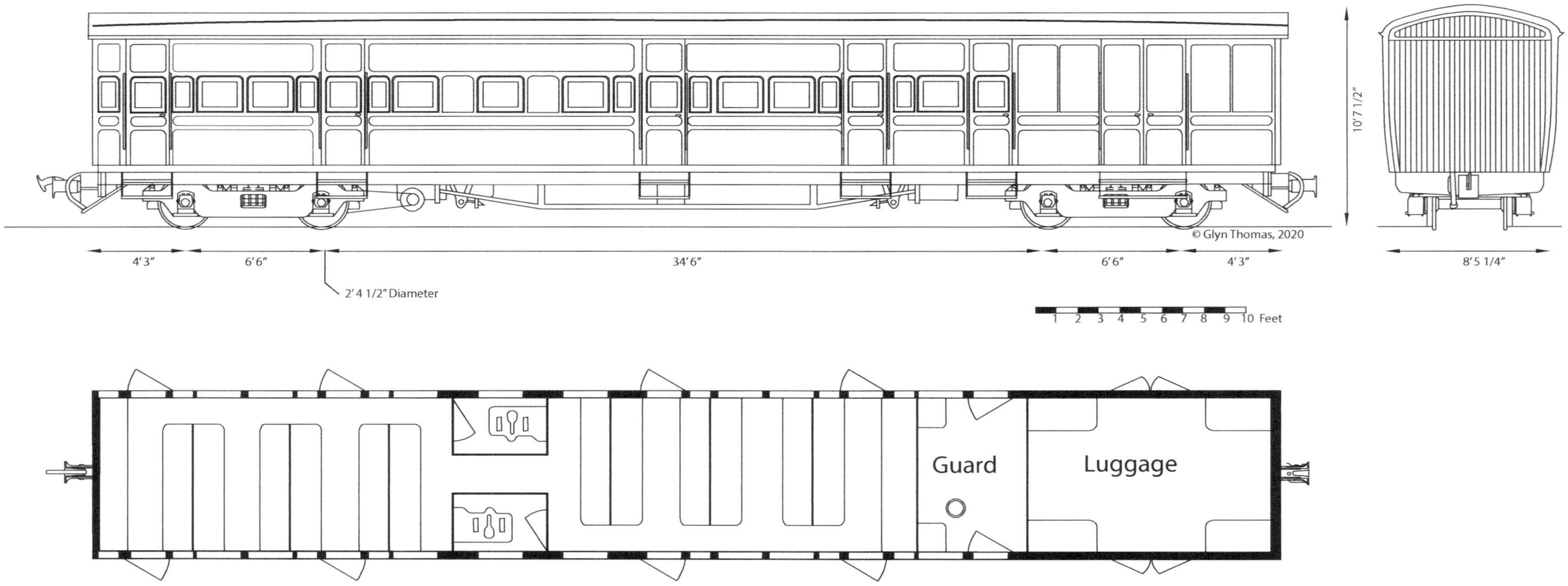

8' 5 1/4"

10' 7 1/2"

© Glyn Thomas, 2020

4' 3"   6' 6"   34' 6"   6' 6"   4' 3"

2' 4 1/2" Diameter

1 2 3 4 5 6 7 8 9 10 Feet

Luggage

Guard

Third-luggage composite. 12 were built in 1929, numbered 41-52. 3 were built in 1934, numbered 54-56 - these were removed from the SIR roster before the 1940s, possibly transferred elsewhere.

Bogie Wheelbase	6' 6"
Bogie Centres	41' 0"
Wheel Diameter	2' 4 ½"
Tare Weight	20 tons 17 cwt
Capacity	56 passengers and 4 tons luggage

[Reference: SIR diagram book via University of Otago, Ernie Webber Collection]

115

8' 5 1/4"

10' 9"

© Glyn Thomas, 2020

4'3" 6'6"

1 2 3 4 5 6 7 8 9 10 Feet

34'6"

2' 4 1/2" Diameter

6'6" 4'3"

SIR 2nd-3rd Composite

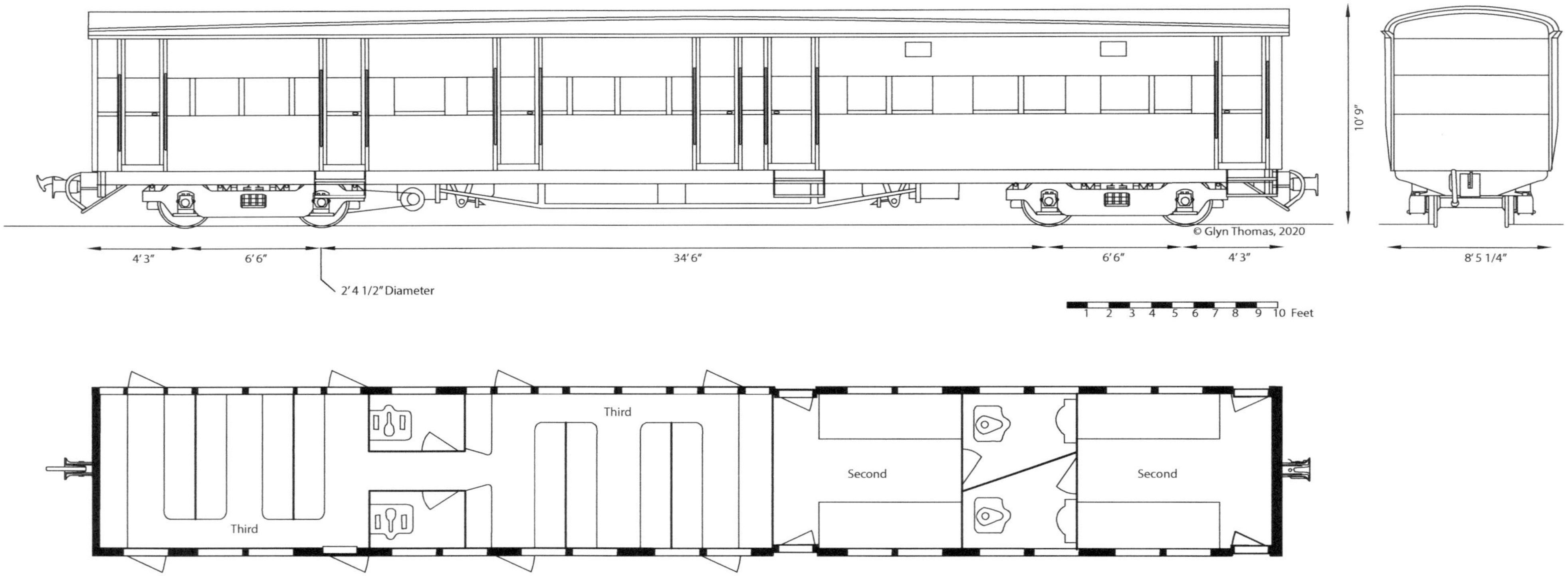

Second

Second

Third

Third

The SIR built four of these 2nd-3rd composite coaches in 1935 and numbered them 1 to 4.

Bogie Wheelbase	6' 6"
Bogie Centres	41' 0"
Wheel Diameter	2' 4 ½"
Tare Weight	23 tons 18 cwt
Capacity	16 second and 44 third class passengers

[Reference: SIR diagram book via University of Otago, Ernie Webber Collection]

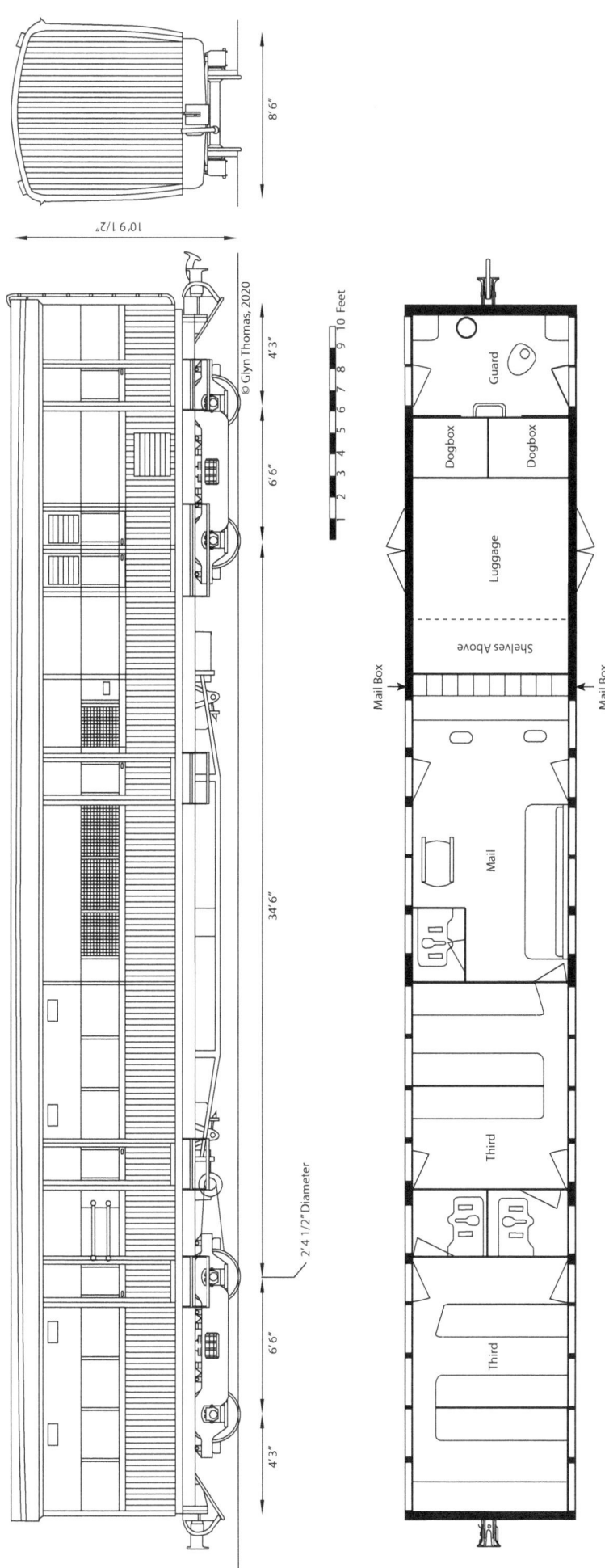

SIR 3rd-Post-Luggage Coach

The SIR built three of these 3rd-post-luggage coaches in 1938 and numbered them 15, 16, and 17.

Bogie Wheelbase	6' 6"
Bogie Centres	41' 0"
Wheel Diameter	2' 4 ½"
Tare Weight	22 tons 12 cwt
Capacity	28 third class passengers and 4 tons of luggage

[Reference: SIR diagram book via University of Otago, Ernie Webber Collection]

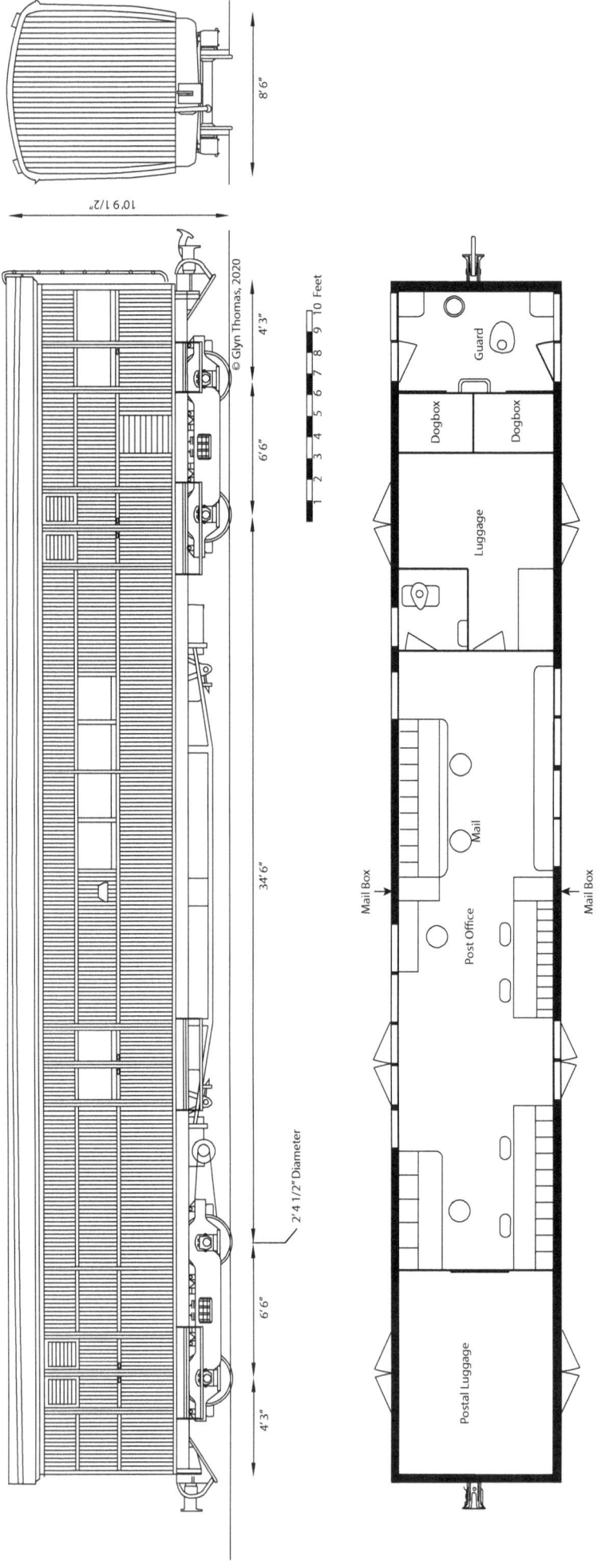

SIR Post-Luggage Coach

The SIR built two of these post-luggage coaches in 1941 and numbered them 1 and 2.

Bogie Wheelbase	6' 6"
Bogie Centres	41' 0"
Wheel Diameter	2' 4 ½"
Tare Weight	21 tons 2 cwt
Capacity	7 tons of luggage

[Reference: SIR diagram book via University of Otago, Ernie Webber Collection]

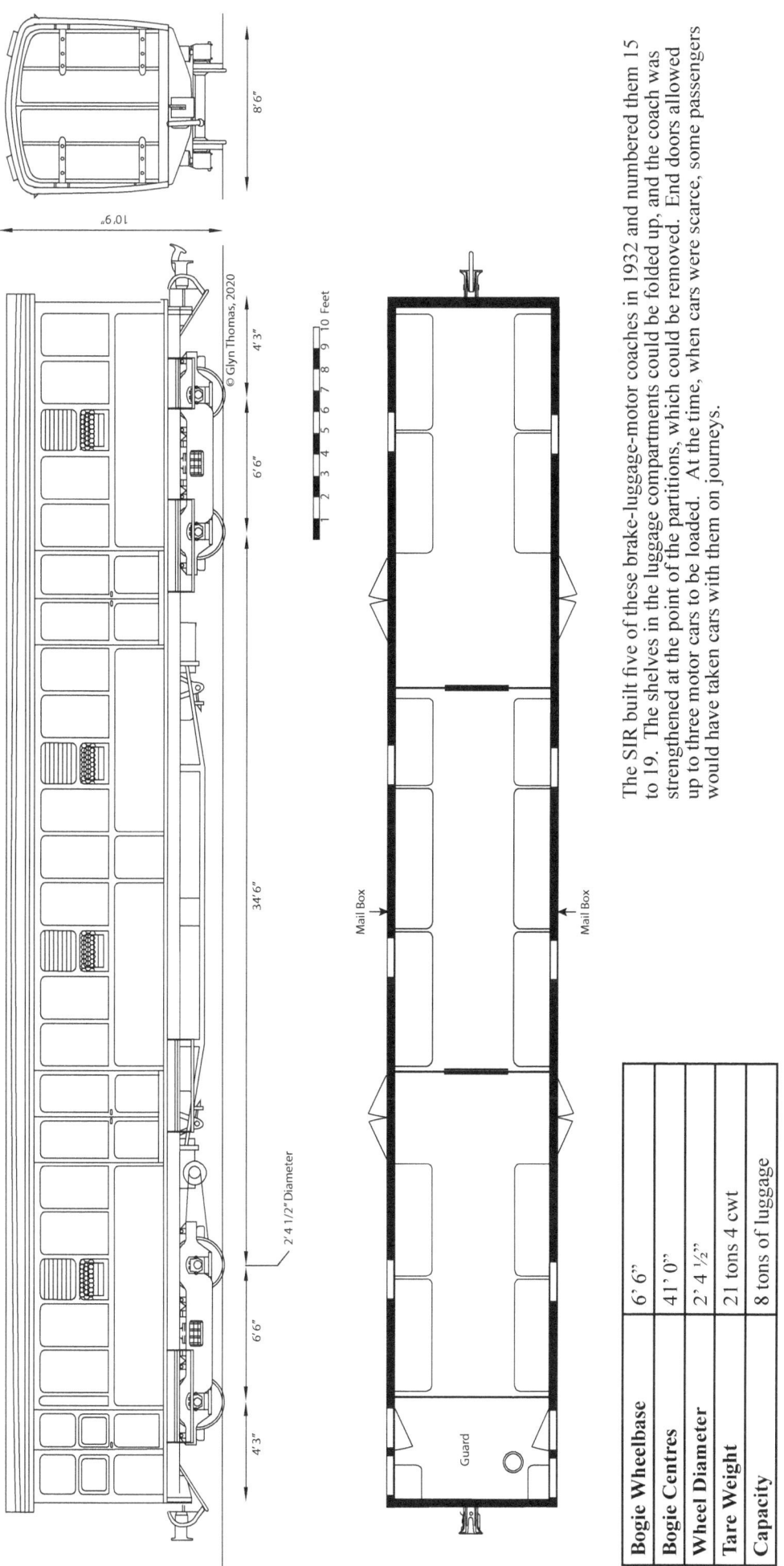

SIR Brake-Parcel-Motor Coach

© Glyn Thomas, 2020

10 Feet

1 2 3 4 5 6 7 8 9

8'6"

10'6"

4'3"   6'6"   34'6"   6'6"   4'3"

2' 4 1/2" Diameter

Mail Box

Mail Box

Guard

The SIR built five of these brake-luggage-motor coaches in 1932 and numbered them 15 to 19. The shelves in the luggage compartments could be folded up, and the coach was strengthened at the point of the partitions, which could be removed. End doors allowed up to three motor cars to be loaded. At the time, when cars were scarce, some passengers would have taken cars with them on journeys.

Bogie Wheelbase	6' 6"
Bogie Centres	41' 0"
Wheel Diameter	2' 4 ½"
Tare Weight	21 tons 4 cwt
Capacity	8 tons of luggage

[Reference: SIR diagram book via University of Otago, Ernie Webber Collection]

SIR Tourist Coach

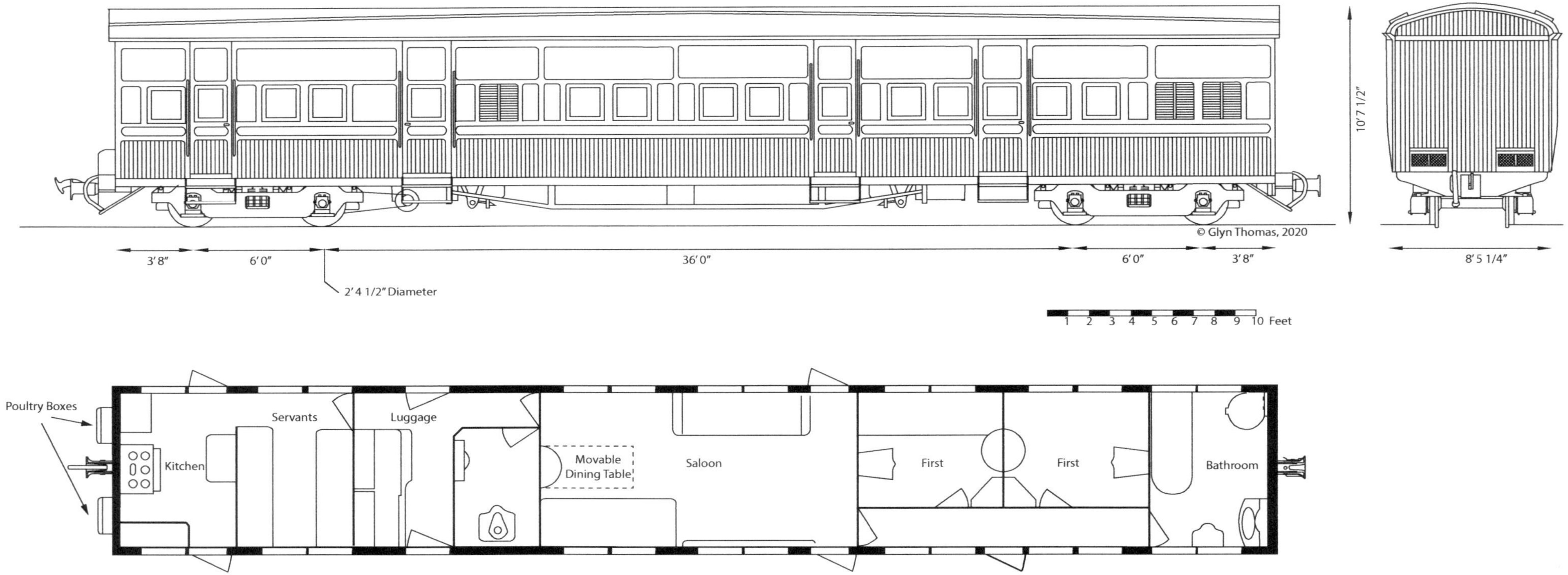

© Glyn Thomas, 2020

8' 5 1/4"

10' 7 1/2"

3' 8" 6' 0" 36' 0" 6' 0" 3' 8"

2' 4 1/2" Diameter

1 2 3 4 5 6 7 8 9 10 Feet

Bathroom

First

First

Saloon

Movable Dining Table

Luggage

Servants

Kitchen

Poultry Boxes

The SIR built two of these tourist coaches in 1924-1925 and numbered them 1 and 2. At the time the railway promoted luxury tourism by train. Families or small groups could charter one of these coaches and have it attached to service trains to tour points of interest. These coaches cost 29,302 rupees.

Bogie Wheelbase	6' 6"
Bogie Centres	41' 0"
Wheel Diameter	2' 4 ½"
Tare Weight	23 tons
Capacity	Approx 4 tourists and up to 4 servants

[Reference: SIR diagram book via University of Otago, Ernie Webber Collection]

IRS Coaches

YG 2-8-2 no. 4028 with a train of IRS coaches at Mahesana in 1981 [Author]

The diagrams in this section illustrate metre-gauge coaches built on standard Indian Railway Standard (IRS) underframes and bogies. Coaches to these designs still formed the mainstay of the metre-gauge fleet into the late steam era. The designs include examples built in railway workshops as well as independent builders such as Jessop and MAN.

IRS SYLR Coach at Sholapur in 2001 [Prakash Tendulkar, IRFCA]

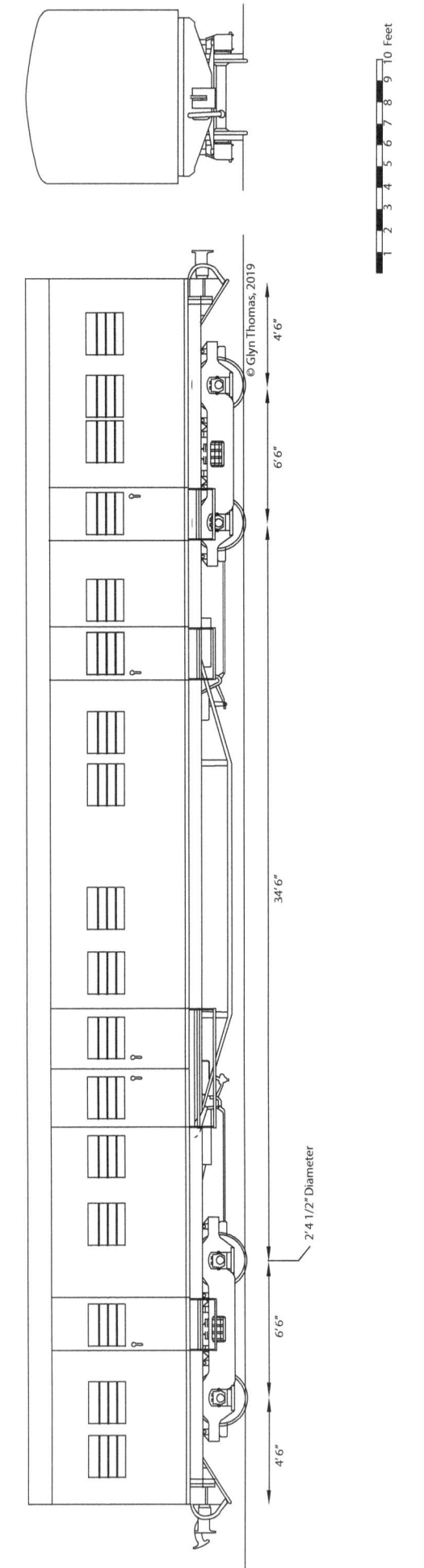

IRS 1st Class Cabin Coach

© Glyn Thomas, 2019

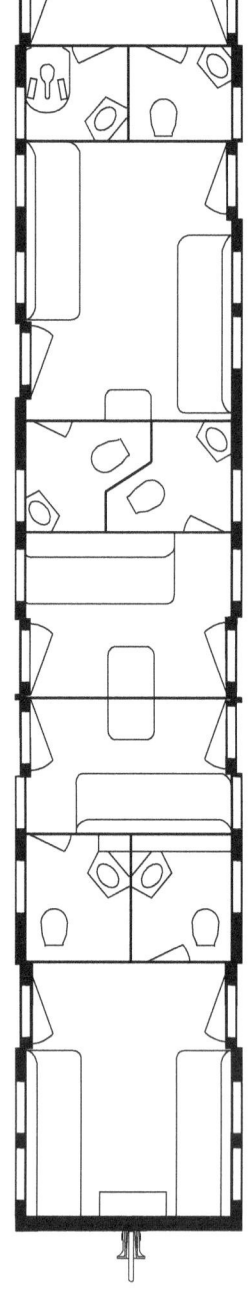

Design for first-class cabin cars, which permitted travellers to journey in relative privacy. Five coaches of this type were built in 1954, numbered 501-505. These survived into the 1990s. The two smaller compartments were air-conditioned.

Bogie Wheelbase	6' 6"
Bogie Centres	41' 0"
Wheel Diameter	2' 4 ½"
Tare Weight	34 Tons
Capacity	31 seated or 18 sleeping

[Reference: Western Railway diagram book via Ken Walker]

Metre-Gauge Rolling Stock

IRS 2-Tier 1st–2nd Composite Sleeper

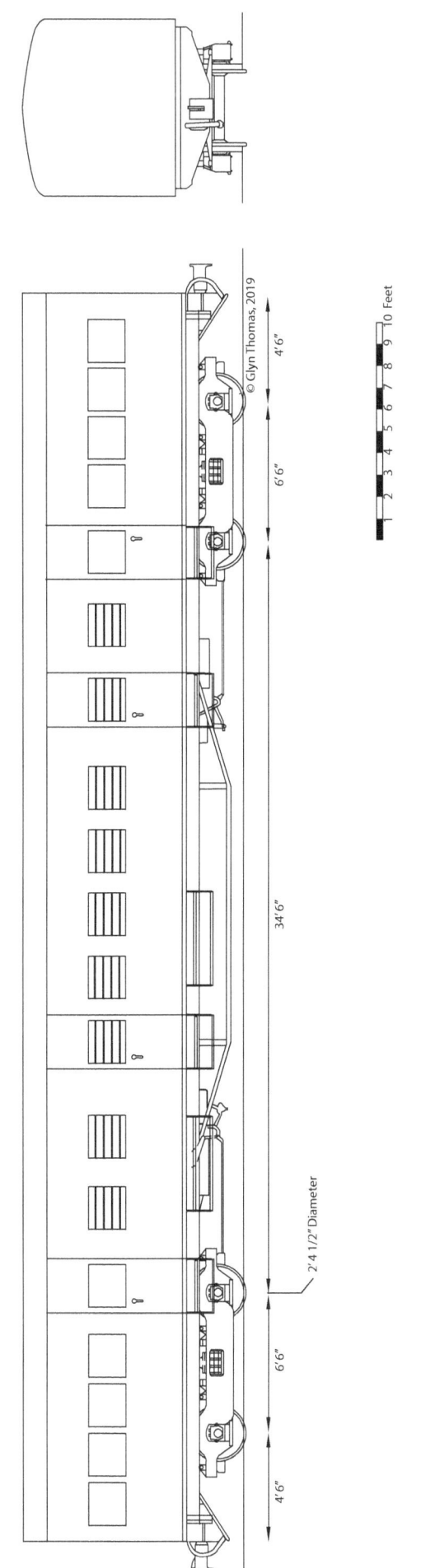

© Glyn Thomas, 2019

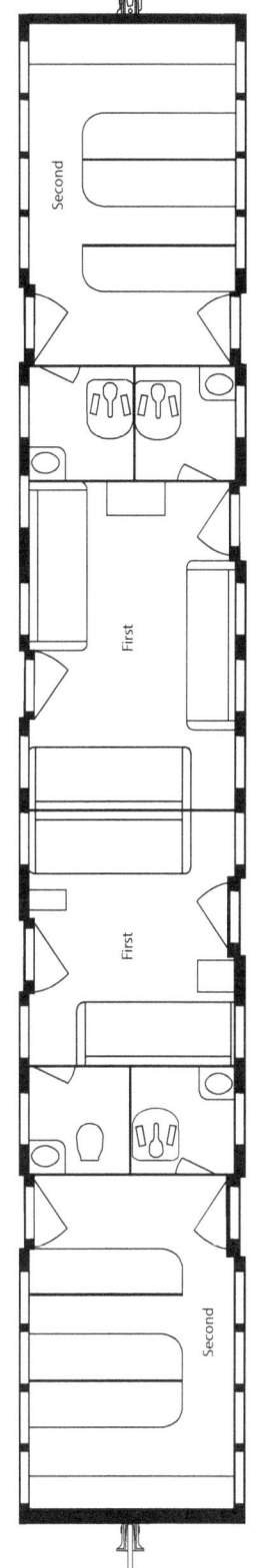

Wooden-body composite first-second coaches. Illustrative numbers are shown in the following table. All these with the exception of 34508 were still running in 1995.

Bogie Wheelbase	6' 6"
Bogie Centres	41' 0"
Wheel Diameter	2' 4 ½"
Tare Weight	27.43 Tons
Capacity	1st Class: 15 seated (10 sleeping)
	2nd Class: 34 seated

Number	Date
34508	1958
34510	1958
34515	1959
34522	1959
34523	1960

[Reference: Western Railway diagram book via Ken Walker]

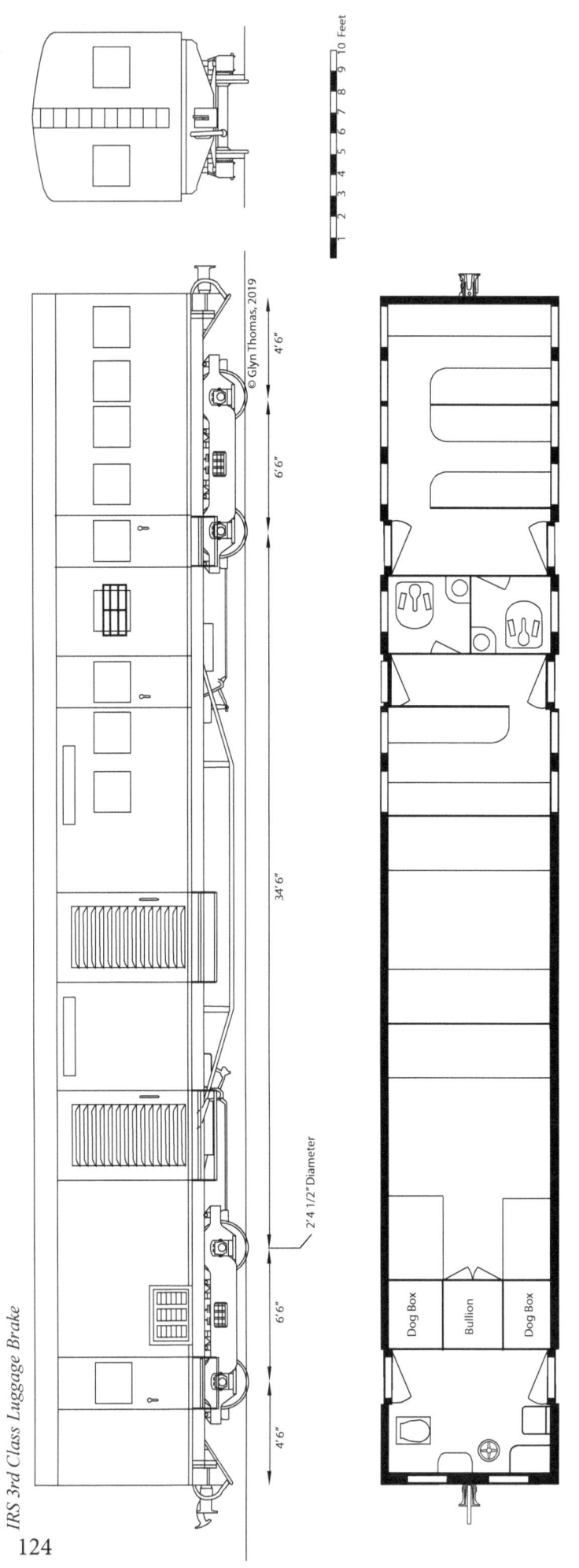

IRS 3rd Class Luggage Brake

© Glyn Thomas, 2019

4'6"   6'6"   6'6"   4'6"

34'6"

2' 4 1/2" Diameter

1 2 3 4 5 6 7 8 9 10 Feet

| Dog Box | Bullion | Dog Box |

Bogie Wheelbase	6' 6"
Bogie Centres	41' 0"
Wheel Diameter	2' 4 ½"
Tare Weight	34 Tons
Capacity	26 passengers, guard, and 5.5 Tons luggage (total 8 Tons)

This class of combination third-luggage-brake was built by Jodhpur workshop. They were original-ly classified as TLR, changed to SLR in 1974. Known details are provided in the table below. The design includes a dog box on each side of the luggage compartment with external ventilation. There is also a bullion safe. The guard is provided with a European-style toilet, while passengers get two Indian-style toilets.

Number	Year Built	Withdrawal Date (if known)
1670	1958	1988
1671	1958	1977
1672	1958	
1673	1959	1990
1674	1959	1939
1675	1959	1939
1676	1959	1991
1677	1959	1980

[Reference: Western Railway diagram book via Ken Walker]

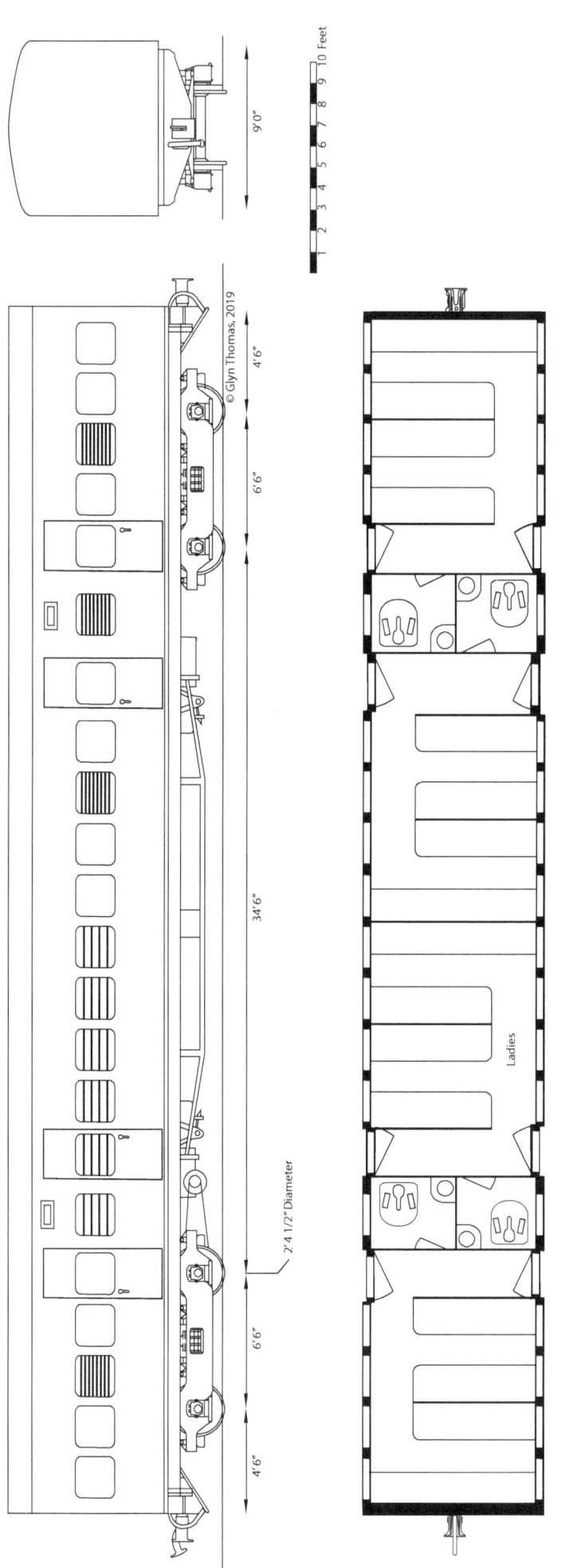

IRS 2nd Class Coach

© Glyn Thomas, 2019

9'0"

4'6"

6'6"

34'6"

2' 4 1/2" Diameter

6'6"

4'6"

1 2 3 4 5 6 7 8 9 10 Feet

Ladies

A class of 12 third-class coaches, built by Jessop and Co. in 1951 and featuring shell bodies. These coaches were finished in BKR Shop. They were initially classified GT or GTY (with ladies compartment), changed to GS and GSY after 1974. Some of these survived into the 1990s.

Bogie Wheelbase	6' 6"
Bogie Centres	41' 0"
Wheel Diameter	2' 4 ½"
Tare Weight	36 Tons
Capacity	68 passengers

[Reference: Western Railway diagram book via Ken Walker]

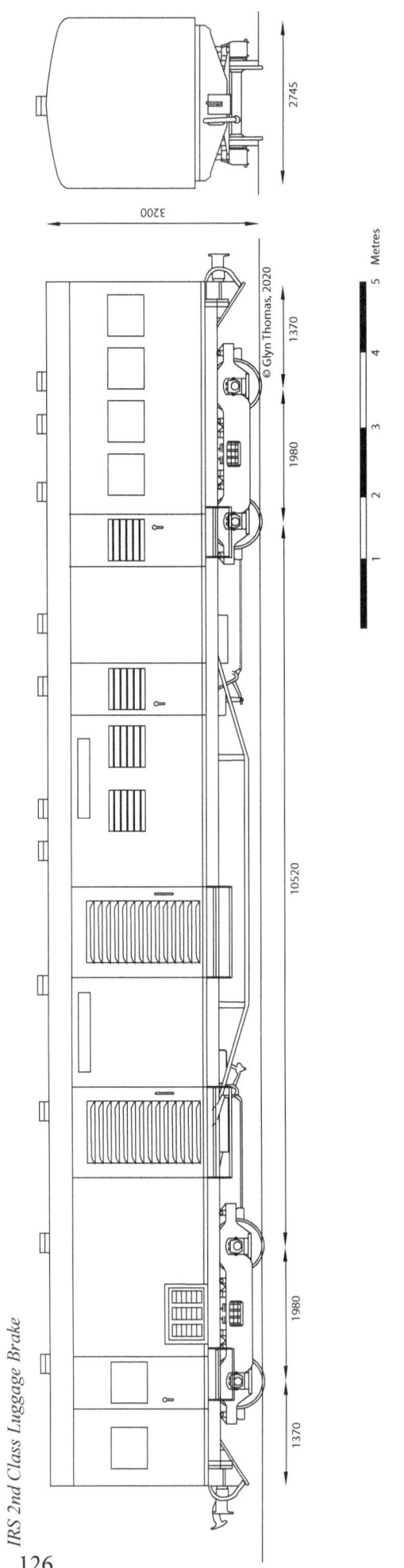

IRS 2nd Class Luggage Brake

126

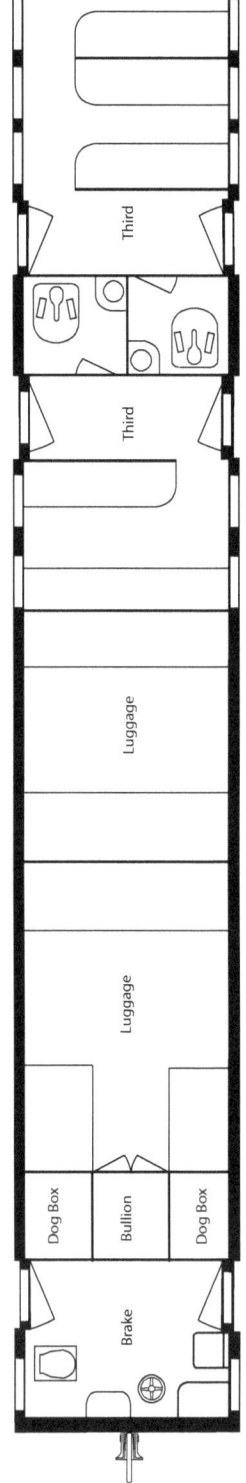

Bogie Wheelbase	1,980 mm
Bogie Centres	12,500 mm
Tare Weight	26.52 tonnes
Capacity	32 passengers, guard, and 5.59 tonnes of luggage

This shell-body class is very similar to the TLR third-luggage-brake coaches illustrated above, but were built as second-luggage-brake (SLR) at the outset. Known numbers and build dates are shown in the table below (this was probably originally a larger class as evidenced by the number gaps).

Number	Build Date
33201	1958
33203	1958
33261	1961
33262	1961
33265	1961
33269	1961
33270	1961
33273	1961

33269 was the last member of the class in operation by 1995.

[Reference: Western Railway diagram book via Ken Walker]

Metre-Gauge Rolling Stock

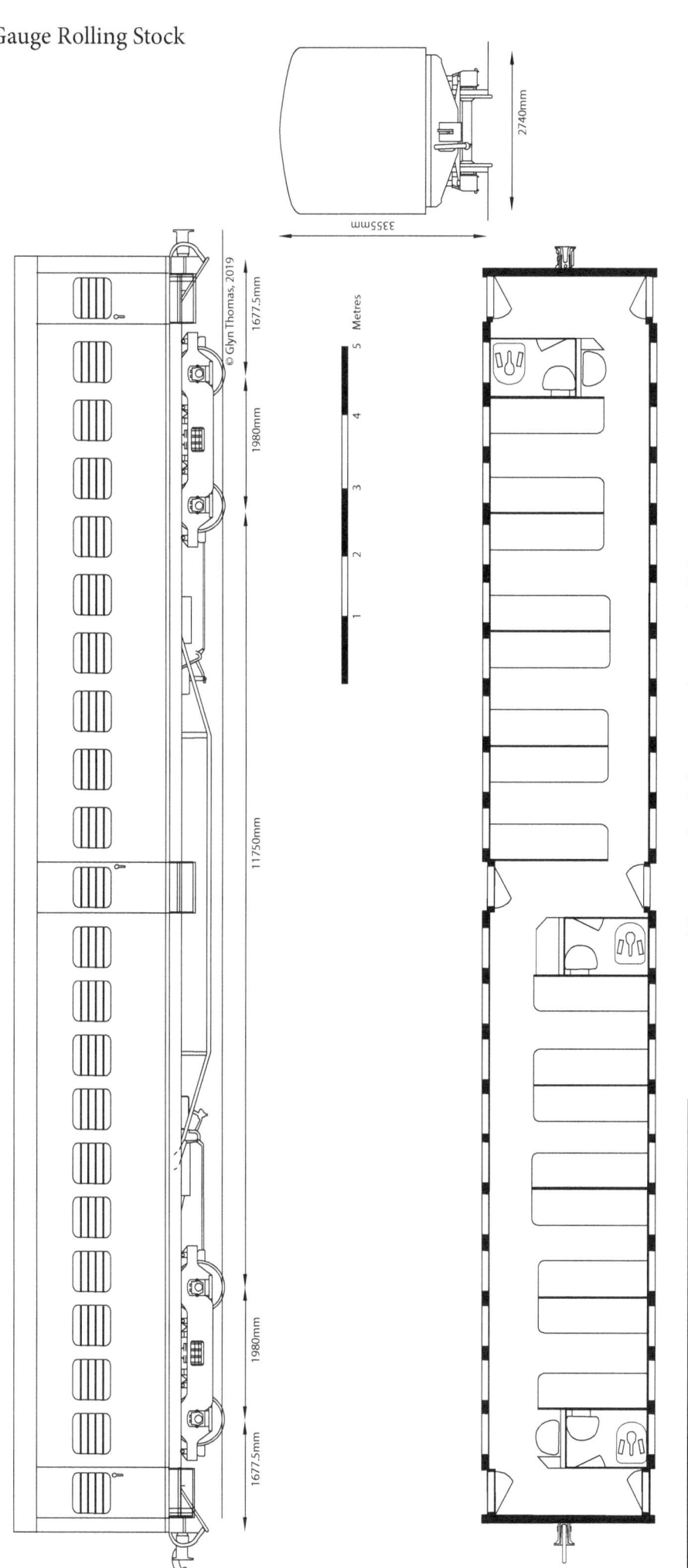

IRS 2nd Class Coach

© Glyn Thomas, 2019

1677.5mm 1980mm 11750mm 1980mm 1677.5mm

2740mm

3355mm

1 2 3 4 5 Metres

These two-tiered sleeper coaches were built by Jessop and Co. They were originally classified as third-class, code GTCW. In 1974 they were reclassified as second class, code GSCW. Numbers 2901 - 2917 were built in 1971, and 2918-2943 were built in 1972. The following coaches were transferred to NER in 1994: 2902, 2906, 2909, 2910, 2911, 2913, 2927, 2928, 2931, 2935, 2938, and 2939. The following coaches were withdrawn before 1995: 2904, 2905, 2915, 2916, 2921, 2925, 2926, 2941.

Bogie Wheelbase	1,980 mm
Bogie Centres	13,715 mm
Wheel Diameter	724 mm
Tare Weight	27.7 t
Capacity	64 seated and 16 sleeping

[Reference: Western Railway diagram book via Ken Walker]

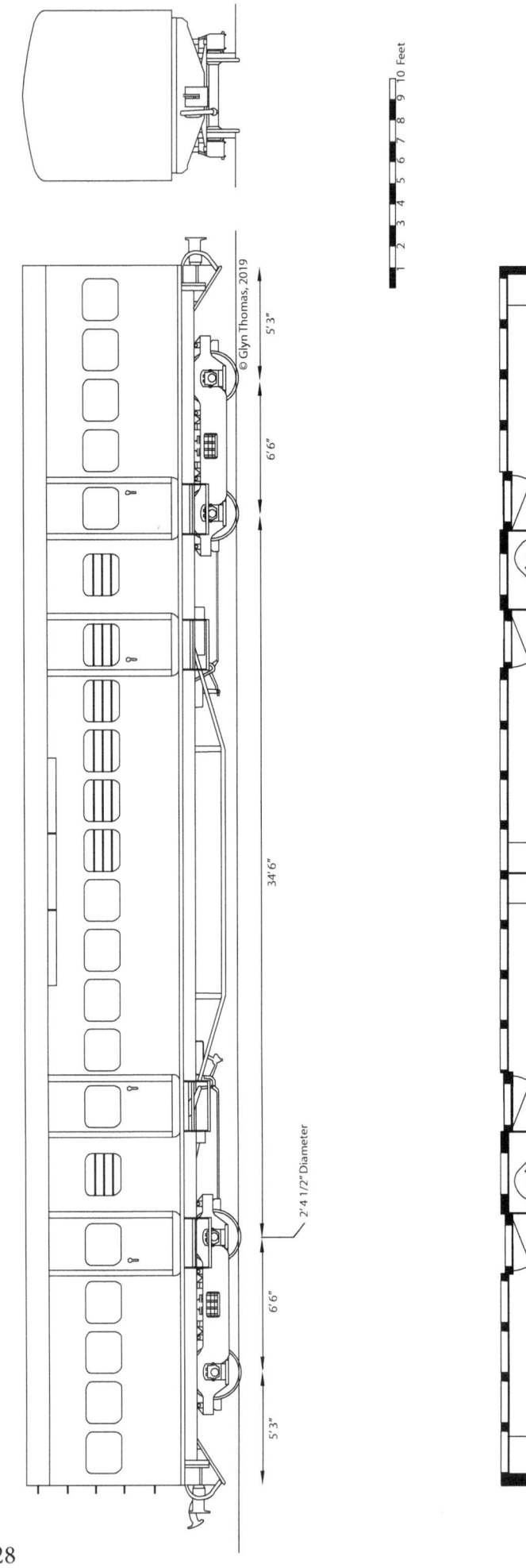

IRS MAN 2nd Class Coach

© Glyn Thomas, 2019

5' 3" 6' 6" 34' 6" 6' 6" 5' 3"

2' 4 1/2" Diameter

This diagram shows a second class coach built by MAN in 1951. No details are available on the number built or disposition, although some apparently survived into the 1990s. Note the barred windows on the ladies section and toilets. Indian Railways provided barred windows throughout on later coaches.

Bogie Wheelbase	6' 6"
Bogie Centres	40' 6"
Wheel Diameter	2' 4 ½"
Tare Weight	
Capacity	

[Reference: Western Railway diagram book via Ken Walker]

ICF Coaches

MG Coach 32225 on the Akola-Mhow line, August 24th, 2015 [Jay Balakrishna - YouTube]

Integrated Coach Factory started producing 1st-class metre-gauge coaches in 1960, and 3rd-class coaches in 1963. In later years, an air-conditioned variant was introduced.

By the 1990s, the ICF designs had largely superseded the older IRS designs on metre-gauge trains, aided by widespread gauge-conversion initiatives. At the time of writing (2020), ICF coaches themselves are being scrapped because there are only a few metre-gauge routes remaining.

MG SYLR ICF Coach on the Mysore-Chamarajanagar train, 2003 [Jay Balakrishna - YouTube]

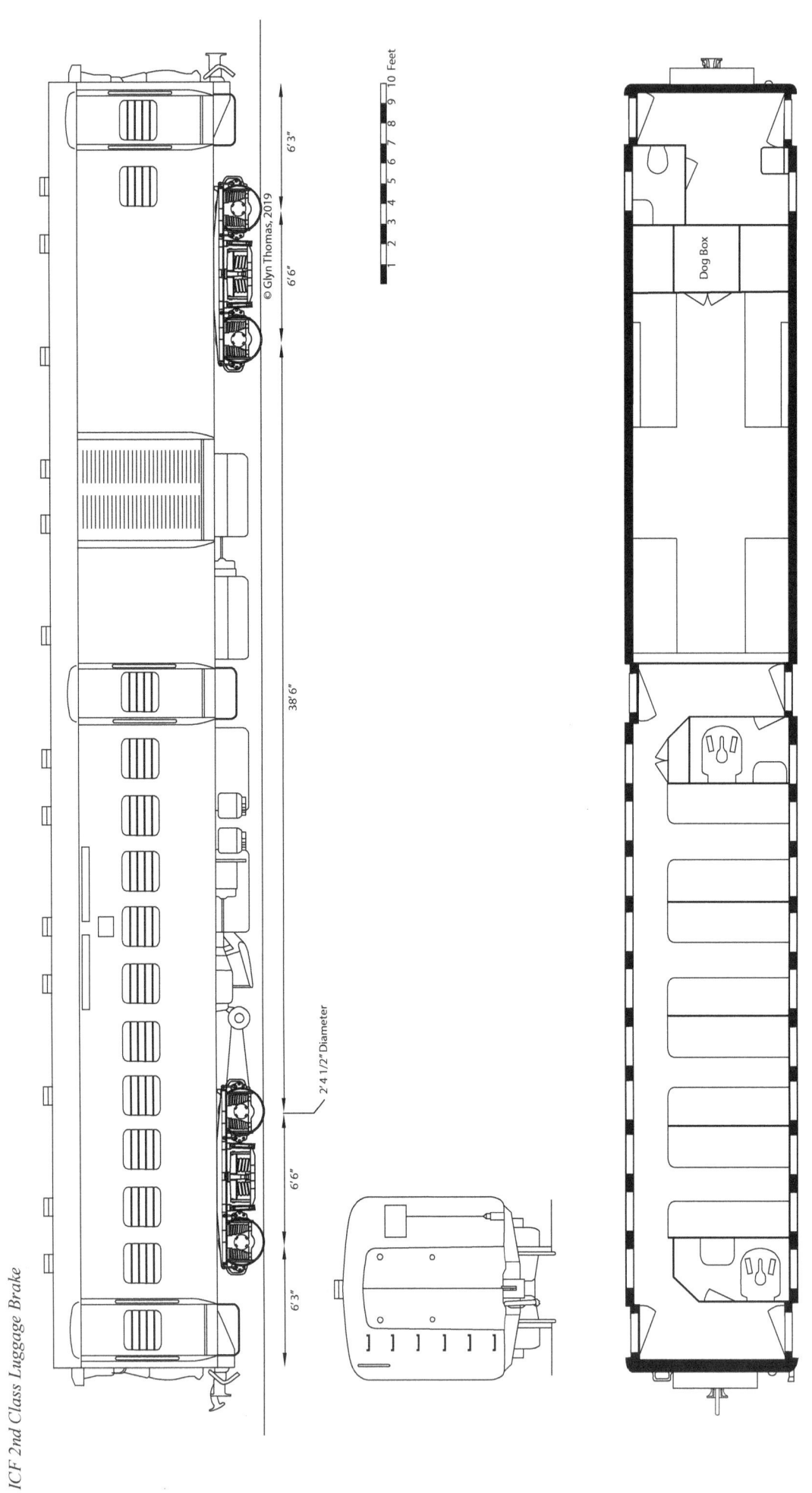

ICF 2nd Class Luggage Brake

© Glyn Thomas, 2019

1 2 3 4 5 6 7 8 9 10 Feet

6' 3"

6' 6"

38' 6"

2' 4 1/2" Diameter

6' 6"

6' 3"

Dog Box

Lightweight third-class-luggage-brake coach, classed TLR. Some included a section reserved for ladies, classed TYLR. These wee reclassified to SLR or SYLR when third-class was eliminated in 1974.

[Reference: Western Railway Diagram Book, c. 1995, Ken Walker Collection]

Bogie Wheelbase	6' 6"
Bogie Centres	45' 0"
Wheel Diameter	2' 4 ½"
Tare Weight	30.2 Tonnes
Capacity	32 passengers and 4.25 Tonnes luggage

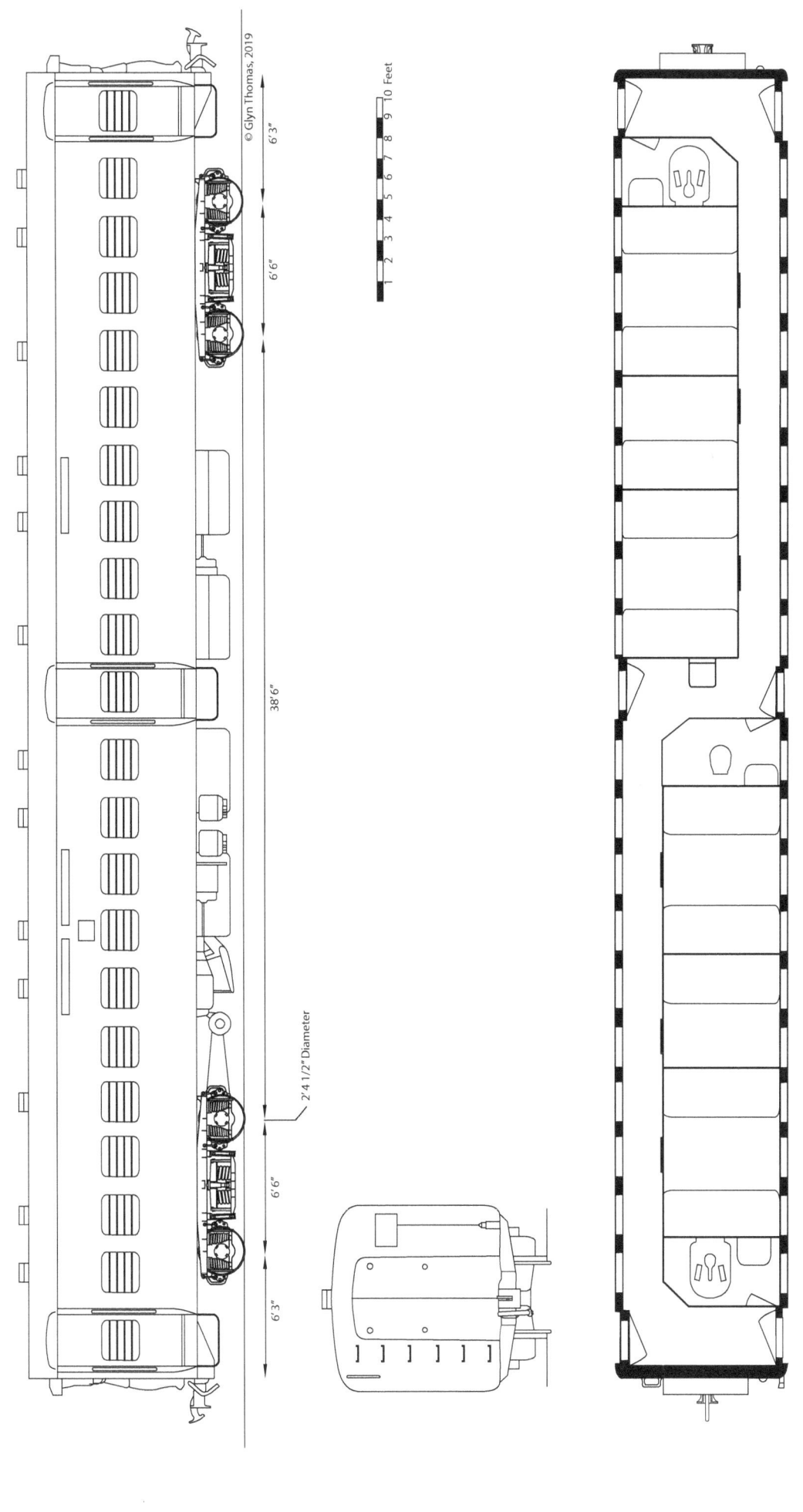

ICF 1st Class Coach

© Glyn Thomas, 2019

6' 3"

6' 6"

38' 6"

2' 4 1/2" Diameter

6' 6"

6' 3"

1 2 3 4 5 6 7 8 9 10 Feet

The ICF lightweight first-class steel coach with two-tier bunks.

[Reference: Western Railway Diagram Book, c. 1995, Ken Walker Collection]

Bogie Wheelbase	6' 6"
Bogie Centres	45' 0"
Wheel Diameter	2' 4 ½"
Tare Weight	29.1 Tonnes
Capacity	30 seated or 20 sleepers

131

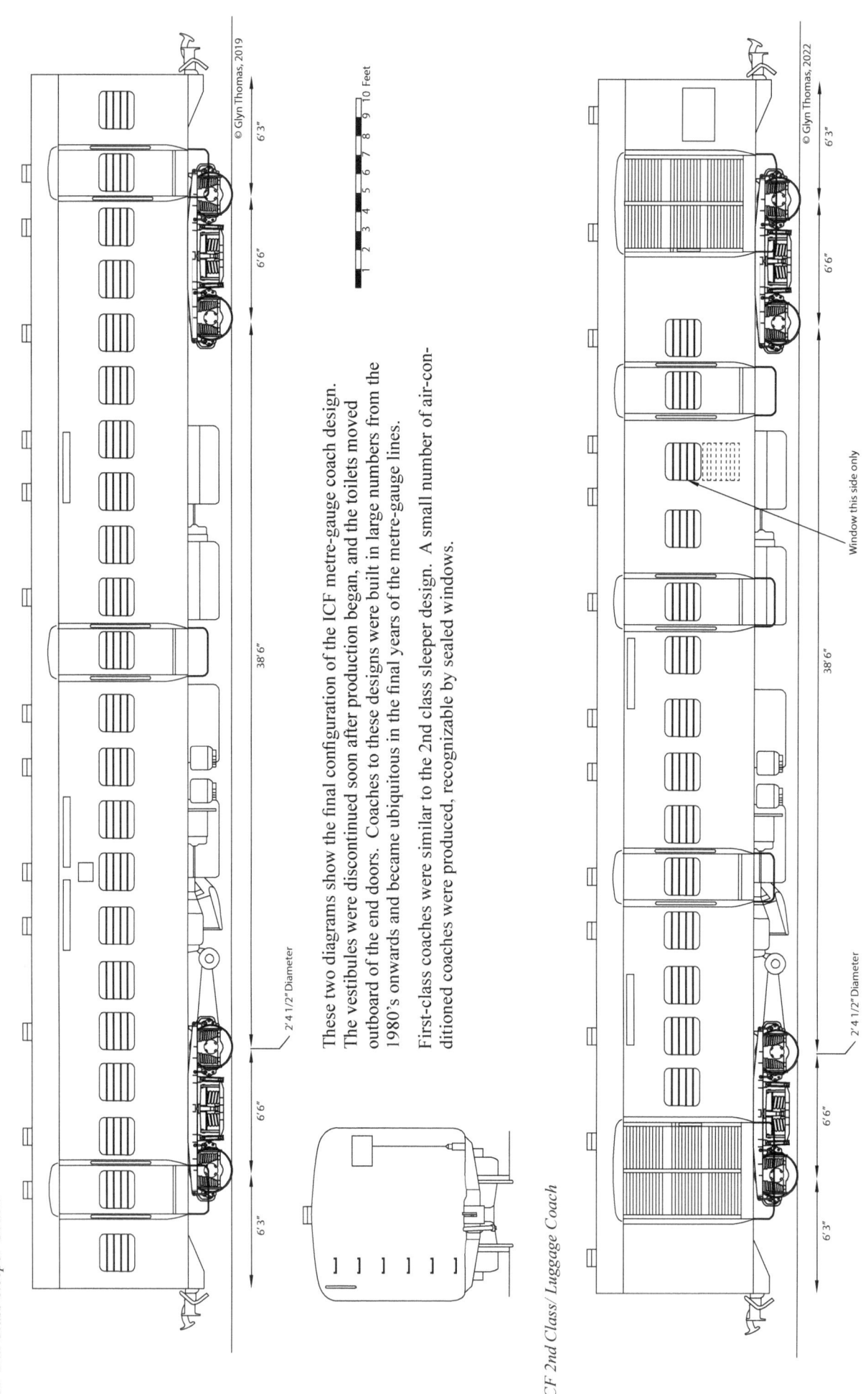

ICF 2nd Class Sleeper Coach

ICF 2nd Class/ Luggage Coach

These two diagrams show the final configuration of the ICF metre-gauge coach design. The vestibules were discontinued soon after production began, and the toilets moved outboard of the end doors. Coaches to these designs were built in large numbers from the 1980's onwards and became ubiquitous in the final years of the metre-gauge lines.

First-class coaches were similar to the 2nd class sleeper design. A small number of air-conditioned coaches were produced, recognizable by sealed windows.

© Glyn Thomas, 2019

© Glyn Thomas, 2022

1 2 3 4 5 6 7 8 9 10 Feet

6'3"

6'6"

38'6"

6'6"

6'3"

2' 4 1/2" Diameter

Window this side only

2' 6" Gauge Rolling Stock

4-Wheel Open Wagons

Leeds Foundry Sheffield-Twinberrow 4-Wheel Open Wagon for the Barsi Light Railway, 1908 [Locomotive, Carriage and Wagon Review]

The diagrams for this section are largely prepared based on a BBCIR (Gaekwar's Baroda State Railway) diagram book that was obtained by the (now defunct) Indian Railway Study Group run by Kelvin White. In addition, a 4-wheel design for the Barsi Light Railway is also provided, based on known dimensions.

Gaekwar's Baroda State Railway (GBSR) was the first narrow-gauge railway in India, commissioned by the Princely State of Baroda in 1862. GBSR operated a network of lines centred on Dabhoi and linking Goyagate (Pratapnagar), Chandod, Bodeli and Samalaya Jn. At independence, it was merged into BBCIR, and ultimately became part of the Western Railway. In the 21st Century, former GBSR lines have largely been converted to broad-gauge. Small museums have been established at Pratapnagar and Dabhoi.

Barsi Light Railway 4-Wheel Open Wagon, 1908

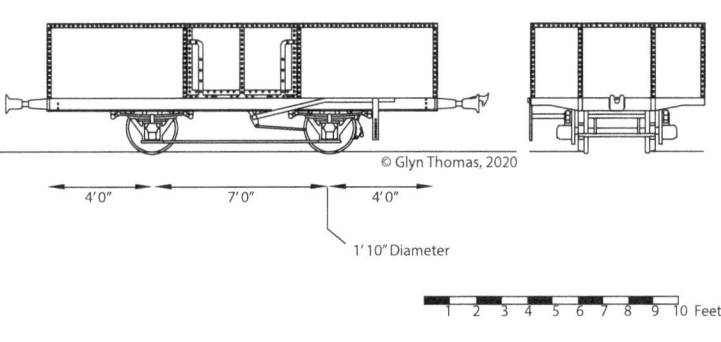

Wheelbase	7' 0"
Wheel Diameter	1' 10"
Tare Weight	2 tons 6 cwt
Capacity	8 tons

[Reference: Dimensions from Locomotive Carriage and Wagon Review, 1908]

2' 6" Gauge Rolling Stock

Timber Wagon

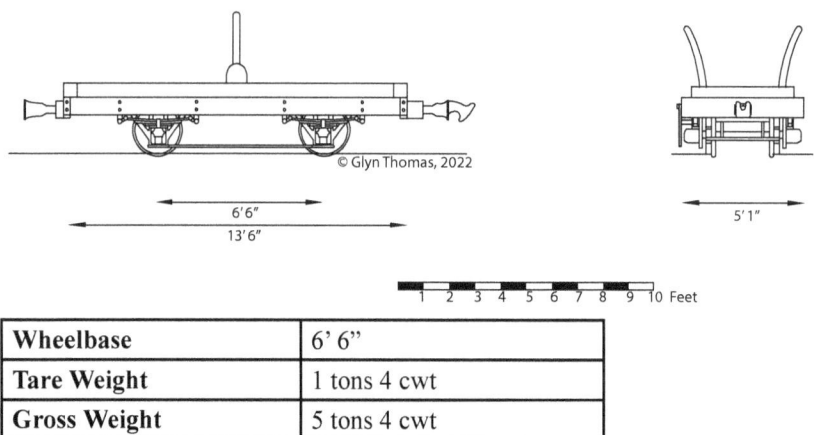

© Glyn Thomas, 2022

6' 6"
13' 6"

5' 1"

1 2 3 4 5 6 7 8 9 10 Feet

Wheelbase	6' 6"
Tare Weight	1 tons 4 cwt
Gross Weight	5 tons 4 cwt

[Reference: BBCIR Diagram Book via Kelvin White]

Low-Sided Open Wagon

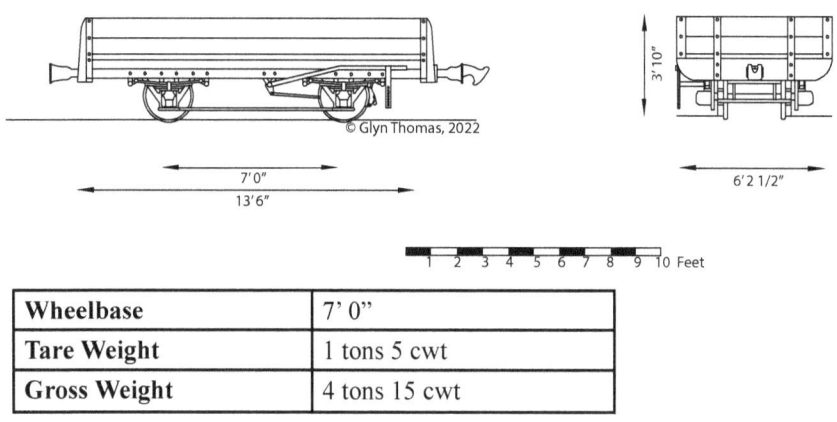

© Glyn Thomas, 2022

7' 0"
13' 6"

3' 10"

6' 2 1/2"

1 2 3 4 5 6 7 8 9 10 Feet

Wheelbase	7' 0"
Tare Weight	1 tons 5 cwt
Gross Weight	4 tons 15 cwt

[Reference: BBCIR Diagram Book via Kelvin White]

Low-Sided Open Wagon, 1911

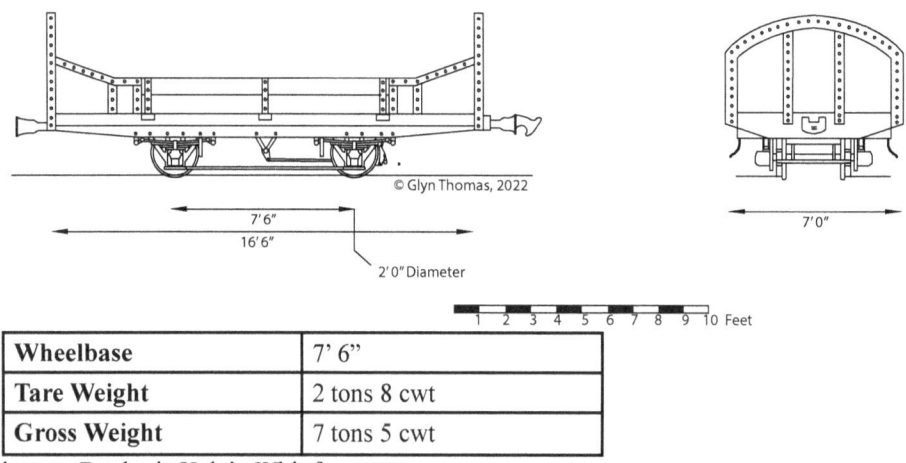

© Glyn Thomas, 2022

7' 6"
16' 6"

2' 0" Diameter

7' 0"

1 2 3 4 5 6 7 8 9 10 Feet

Wheelbase	7' 6"
Tare Weight	2 tons 8 cwt
Gross Weight	7 tons 5 cwt

[Reference: BBCIR Diagram Book via Kelvin White]

Type ML on GBSR, 16 built in 1910 and a further 8 in 1911. Manual brake, possibly with an end lever, not shown. Some survived to be re-rated in metric tonnes. Loading guidance provided for bauxite and sand. This appears to have been a very common design on the narrow-gauge.

Bogie Open Wagons

A major influence on the development of narrow-gauge locomotives and rolling stock in India was the engineer of the Barsi Light Railway (BLR), Everard Calthrop. Calthrop started his career as a locomotive inspector on the GIPR, tasked with identifying potential branchlines. He proposed the creation of the BLR and subsequently became the line's consulting engineer.

Calthrop was influential in advocating a standard 5-ton axle load throughout the train, to suit lightweight track construction. He matched this with large multi-axle locomotives and bogie rolling stock to retain high capacity within this constraint. The model was so successful that it influenced many colonial narrow gauge lines that followed, and even translated to metre and broad gauge lines via the Sheffield-Twinberrow system of wagon construction.

The illustrations in this section are drawn from a number of sources, including the BBCIR (GBSR) diagram book referenced elsewhere.

Madras Railway Bogie Open Wagon 1905

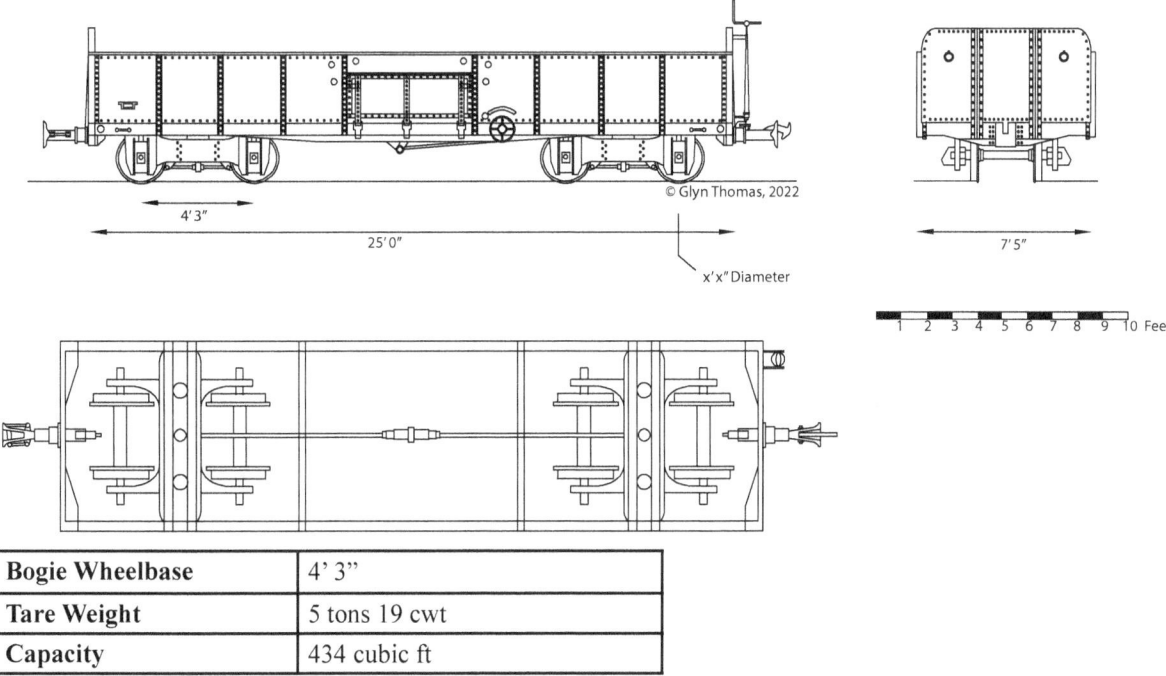

© Glyn Thomas, 2022

Bogie Wheelbase	4' 3"
Tare Weight	5 tons 19 cwt
Capacity	434 cubic ft

[Reference: Indian Engineer, 1905]

This type was reportedly built for famine relief lines in Southern India.

Low-Sided Bogie Open Wagon without Doors

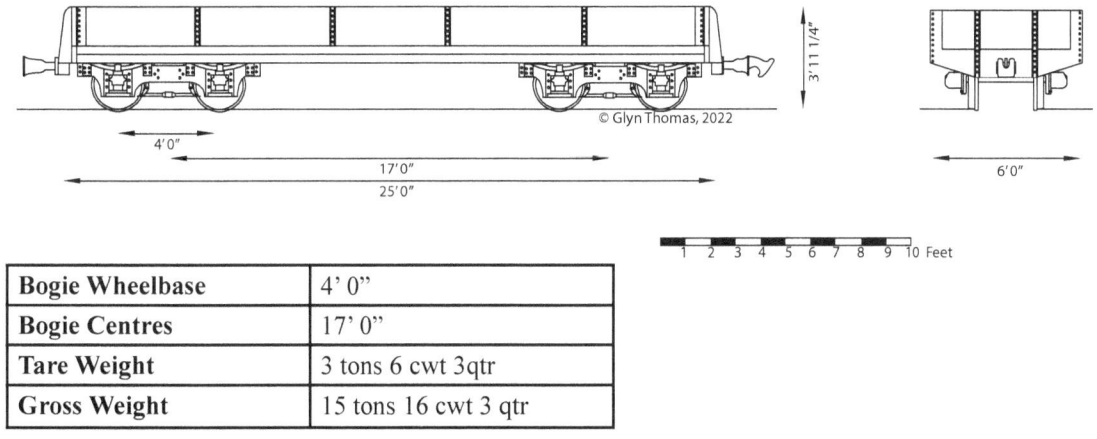

© Glyn Thomas, 2022

Bogie Wheelbase	4' 0"
Bogie Centres	17' 0"
Tare Weight	3 tons 6 cwt 3qtr
Gross Weight	15 tons 16 cwt 3 qtr

[Reference: BBCIR Diagram Book via Kelvin White]

It is possible that the entire side could be dropped for loading.

2' 6" Gauge Rolling Stock

BNR Bogie Open Wagon 1907

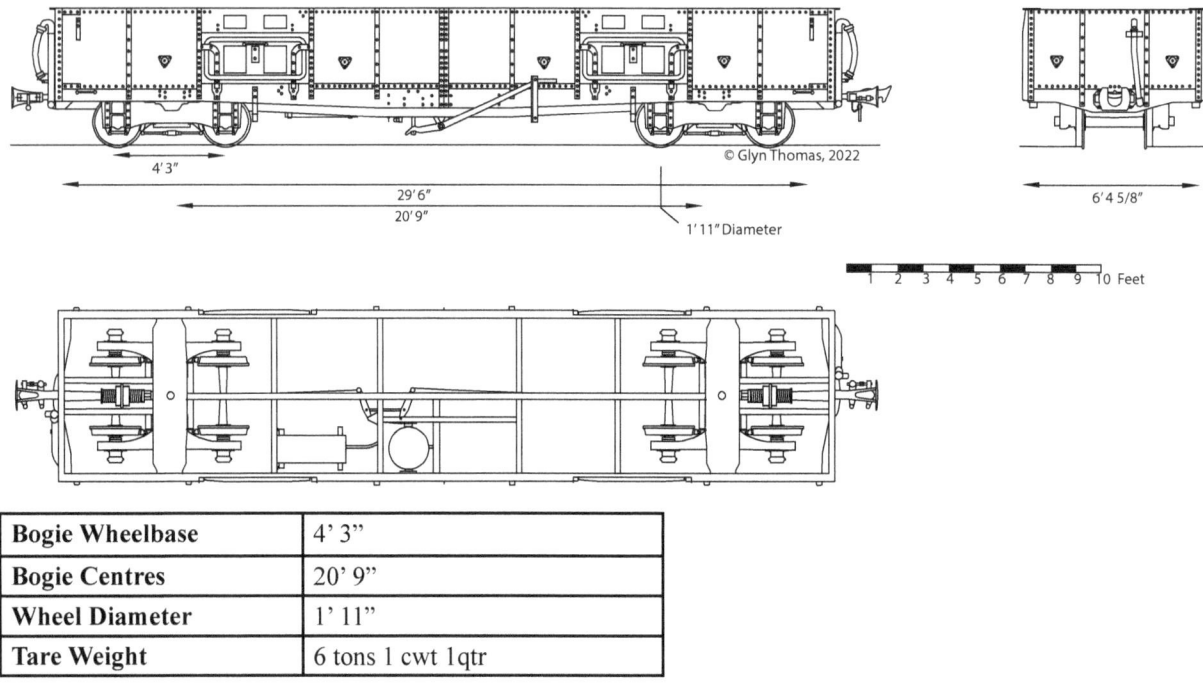

Bogie Wheelbase	4' 3"
Bogie Centres	20' 9"
Wheel Diameter	1' 11"
Tare Weight	6 tons 1 cwt 1qtr

[Reference: Indian Engineer, 1907]

Built for the Gondia-Chanda and Purilia-Ranchi lines, which opened in 1907.

Barsi Light Railway Bogie Open Wagon 1910

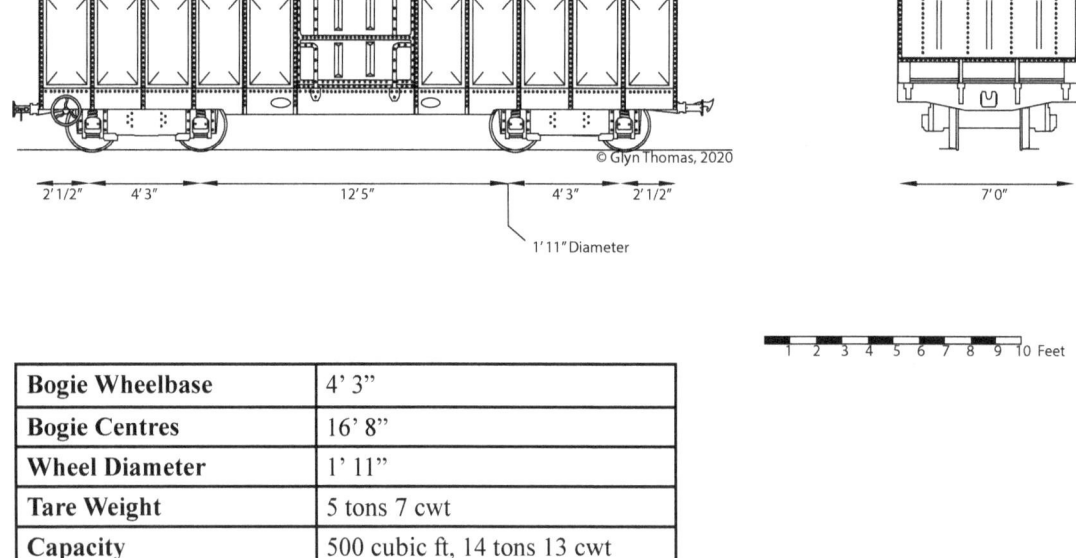

Bogie Wheelbase	4' 3"
Bogie Centres	16' 8"
Wheel Diameter	1' 11"
Tare Weight	5 tons 7 cwt
Capacity	500 cubic ft, 14 tons 13 cwt

The bogie open wagon was probably more common than its 4-wheel equivalent on the BLR. This design uses Pressed Steel bogies.

[Reference: Light Railways at Home and Abroad, WH Cole 1899; bogies, Railway Engineer, January 1897]

2' 6" Gauge Rolling Stock

Low-Sided Bogie Open Wagon with Doors

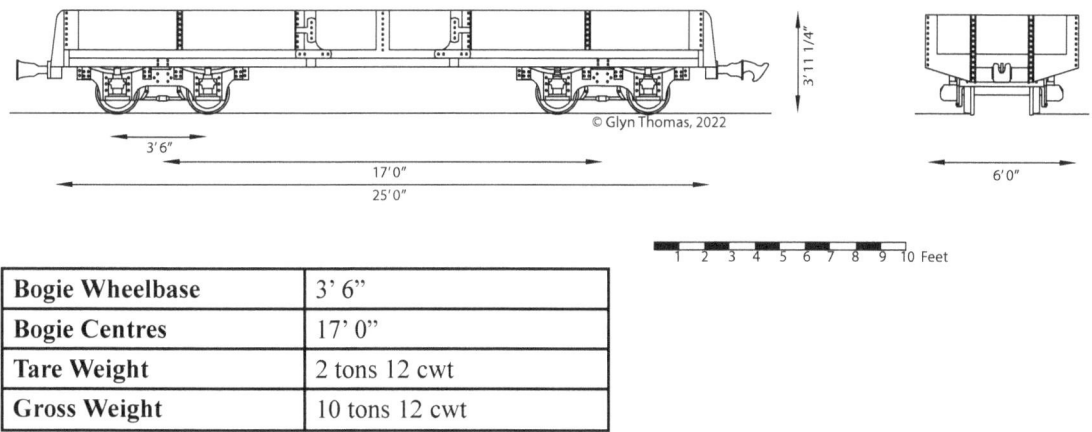

Bogie Wheelbase	3' 6"
Bogie Centres	17' 0"
Tare Weight	2 tons 12 cwt
Gross Weight	10 tons 12 cwt

[Reference: BBCIR Diagram Book via Kelvin White]

Low-Sided Bogie Open Wagon with Doors, 1911

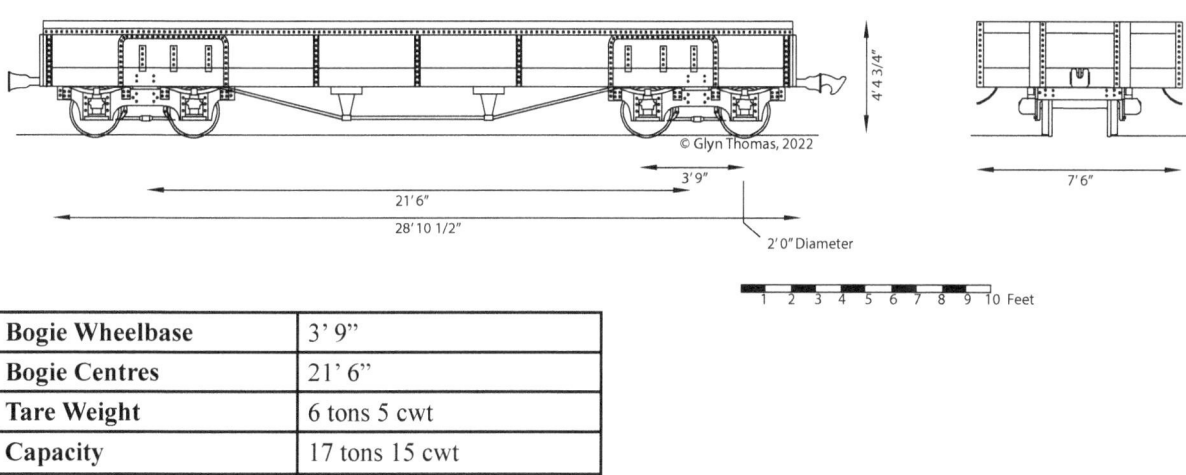

Bogie Wheelbase	3' 9"
Bogie Centres	21' 6"
Tare Weight	6 tons 5 cwt
Capacity	17 tons 15 cwt

[Reference: BBCIR Diagram Book via Kelvin White]

Type BKC on the GBSR, 8 built in each year from 1911 to 1913 and 2 provided in 1914. Manual braked. Some survived to be re-rated in metric tonnes. Loading guidance provided for bauxite and sand.

High-Sided Bogie Open Wagon without Doors, 1915

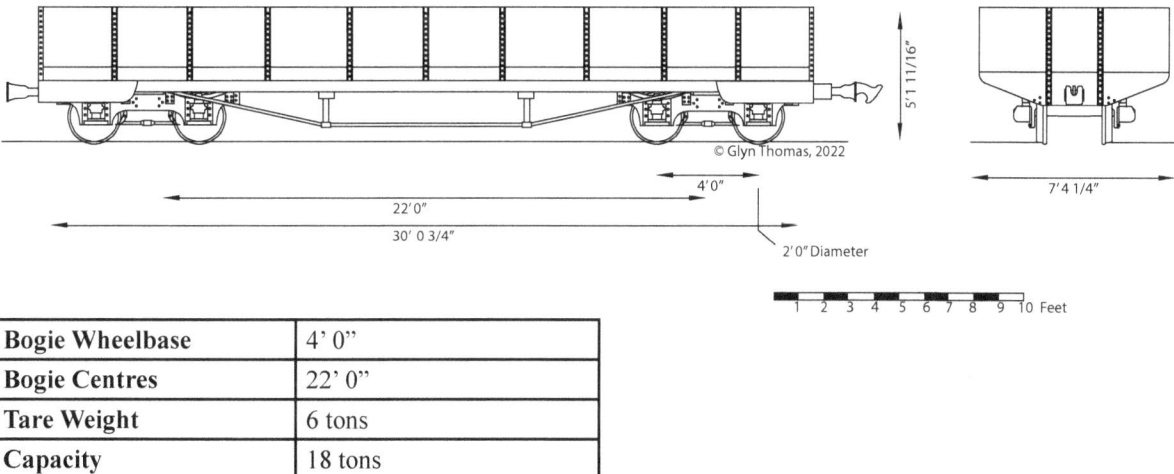

Bogie Wheelbase	4' 0"
Bogie Centres	22' 0"
Tare Weight	6 tons
Capacity	18 tons

[Reference: BBCIR Diagram Book via Kelvin White]

On the GBSR, 22 built in 1915 and another 22 in 1916. Manual braked. Some survived to be re-rated in metric tonnes. Loading guidance provided for bauxite and sand. Numbers included 0616 and 0660.

4-Wheel Covered Vans

Rendition of narrow gauge covered van, based on diagram in Indian Industries and Power

The BBCIR (GBSR) Diagram Book is very useful to fill-in details of the progressive development of 4-wheel vans on the railway. The earliest van designs were wooden with wood or corrugated iron roofs. These would have been built in the railway's own workshops, using underframe components from Britain. These designs are typical of light railway construction in the 19th Century.

By the 20th Century, steel designs were becoming much more common. These were usually built using components from Britain. It is interesting that GBSR bought a large batch of these from the domestic manufacturer, Burns and Co., in 1910.

The final development was a wagon-top design introduced in about 1921. These eventually became the predominant design on the railway.

Early GDR Wooden Van

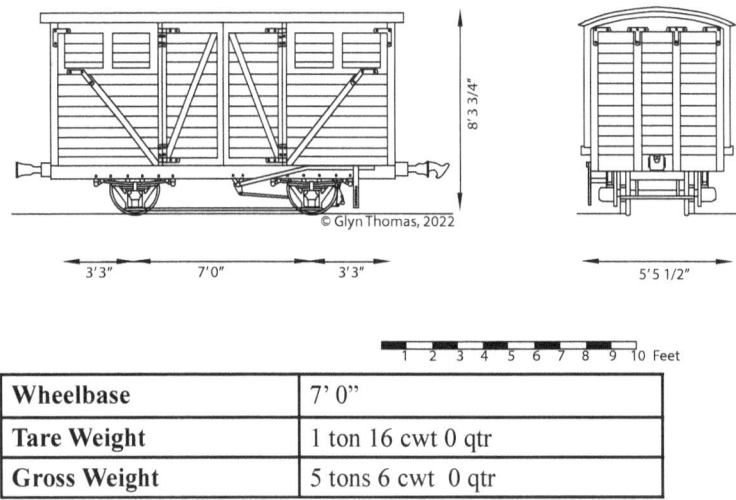

Wheelbase	7' 0"
Tare Weight	1 ton 16 cwt 0 qtr
Gross Weight	5 tons 6 cwt 0 qtr

[Reference: BBCIR Diagram Book via Kelvin White]

The diagram book provides two very similar diagrams of wooden covered vans. One has a higher floor and corresponding roof line.

2' 6" Gauge Rolling Stock

Early GDR Wooden Van with Iron Roof

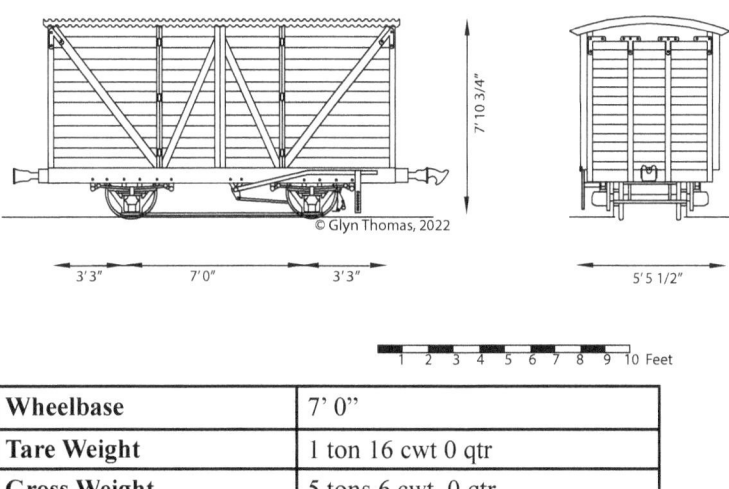

© Glyn Thomas, 2022

Wheelbase	7' 0"
Tare Weight	1 ton 16 cwt 0 qtr
Gross Weight	5 tons 6 cwt 0 qtr

[Reference: BBCIR Diagram Book via Kelvin White]

BSR Van, 1910

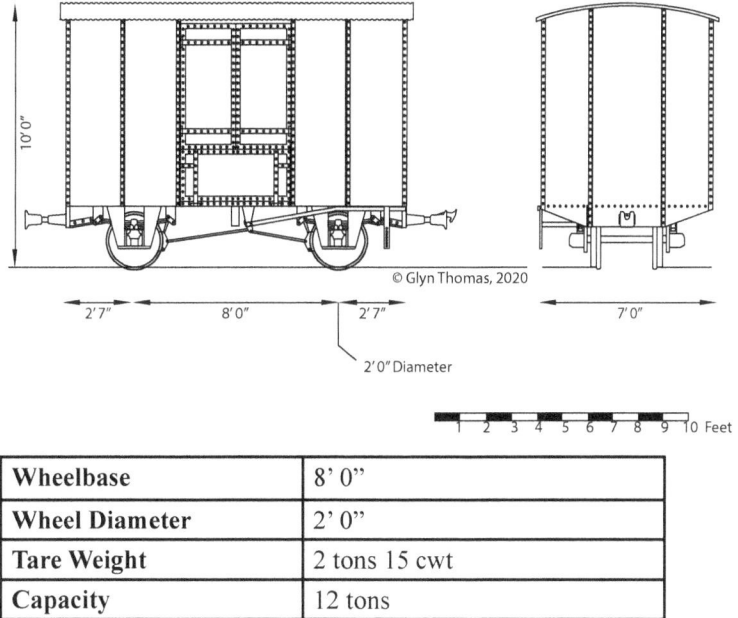

© Glyn Thomas, 2020

Wheelbase	8' 0"
Wheel Diameter	2' 0"
Tare Weight	2 tons 15 cwt
Capacity	12 tons

[Reference: Indian Industries and Power, 1910]

In 1910, the Baroda State Railways ordered 50 wagons from Burns and Co. for use on the Gaekwar's Dabhoi Railway. This was notable as an early order for wagons from a domestic private manufacturer.

By the 1980s, the corrugated roof vans had largely been superseded by wagon-top 4-wheel vans and bogie vans. At least one survived in use to be seen in the background of photos.

2' 6" Gauge Rolling Stock

Wagon-top Van, 1921

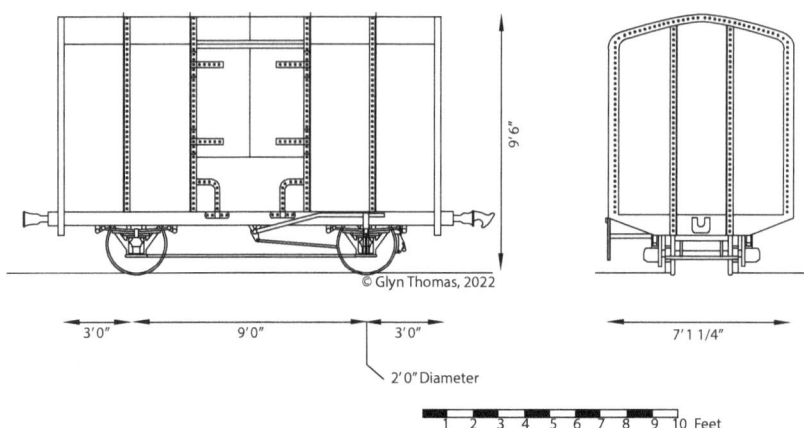

Wheelbase	9' 0"
Wheel Diameter	2' 0"
Tare Weight	3.14 tons
Capacity	12 tons

[Reference: BBCIR Diagram Book via Kelvin White]

Observer's note on the original diagram states that this is Western Railway diagram 6 and that several variations of the design were available with different roof shapes.

It appears that 36 of this specific design were provided in 1921, and a further 52 in 1925. These vans weren't vacuum fitted, but most had a train pipe. Notes were provided for maximum loading of either coal or firewood.

GBSR Horsebox

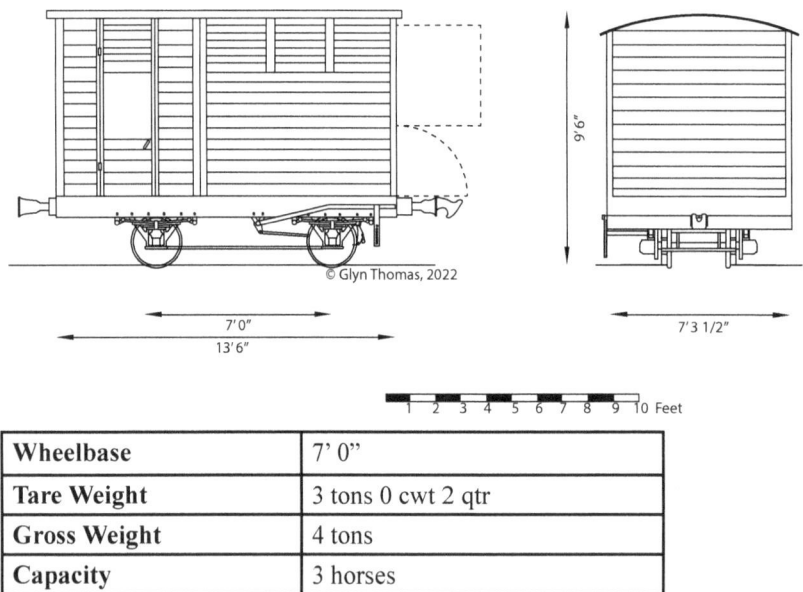

Wheelbase	7' 0"
Tare Weight	3 tons 0 cwt 2 qtr
Gross Weight	4 tons
Capacity	3 horses

Attendant's compartment at one end. Carries three horses.

Bogie Covered Vans

F Class 2-8-2 no. 713 banking a train at Ramling in 1977 [John Tolson, Transport Treasury, JMT2653]

Bogie covered vans were made popular on Indian narrow-gauge railways following Calthrope's work at the Barsi Light Railway. These rapidly became the most common type of freight rolling stock on narrow-gauge lines, and many survived until the end of freight on these lines. Vans with their doors open sometimes supplemented passenger trains as makeshift coaches during peak times.

This section starts with a couple of early examples. It is also interesting to see that Indian Railways continued to build new designs in the 1950's, including a very long variation.

Barsi Light Railway covered van at Pandharpur in 1981. These vans could be used to carry passengers if trains were overcrowded [David Churchill, DHRS]

2' 6" Gauge Rolling Stock

BNR Bogie Covered van 1908

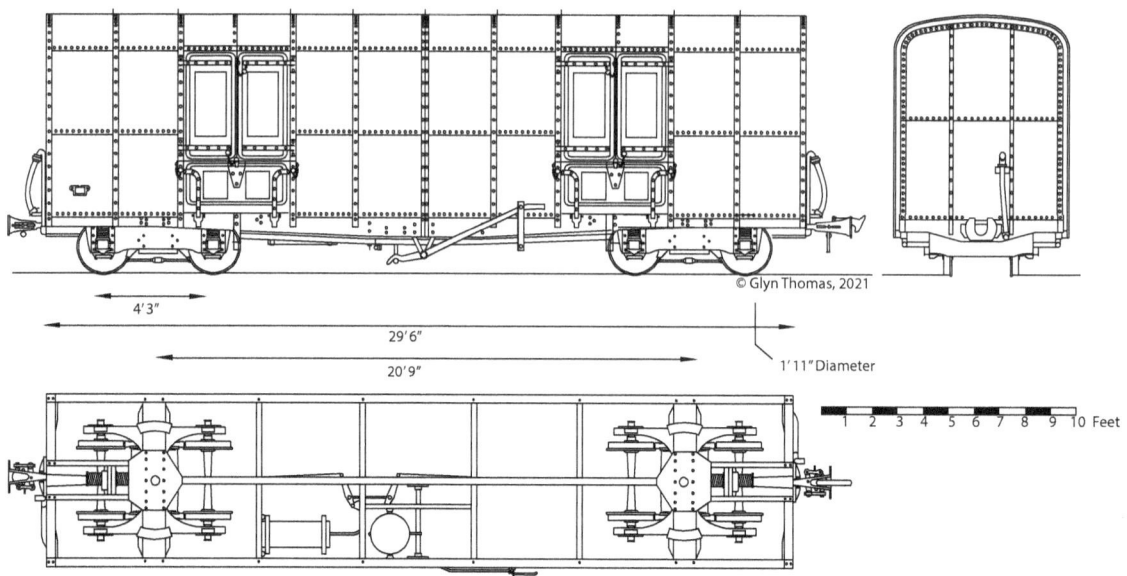

Bogie Wheelbase	4' 3"
Bogie Centres	20' 9"
Wheel Diameter	1' 11"
Tare Weight	6 tons 12 cwt

[Reference: Indian Engineering, 1908]

Built for the Gondia-Chanda and Purulia-Ranchi Extensions.

Barsi Light Railway Bogie Covered Van, 1910

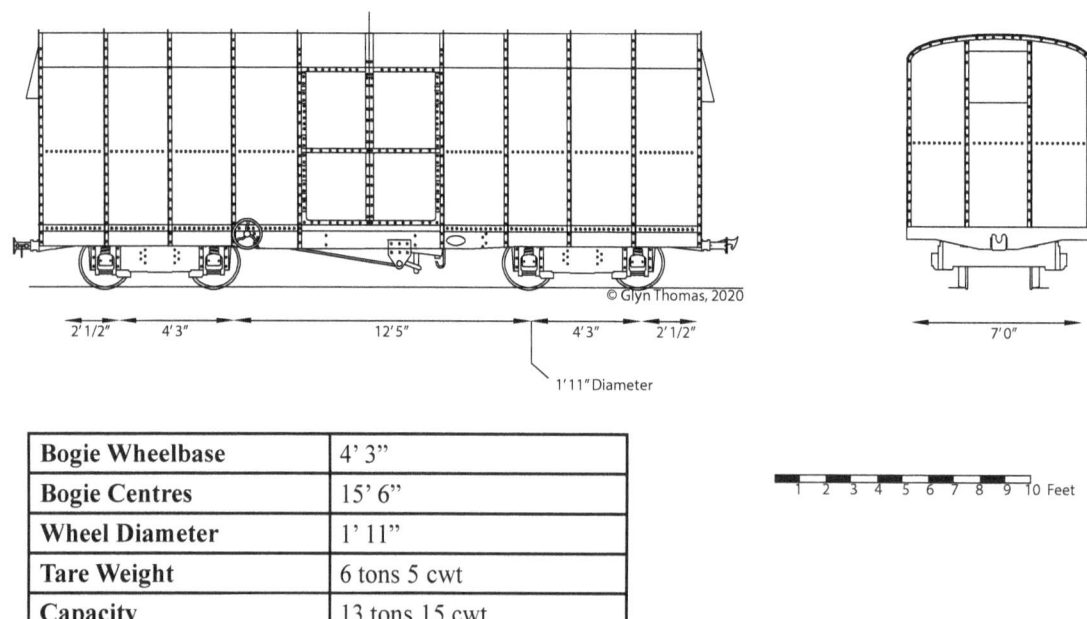

Bogie Wheelbase	4' 3"
Bogie Centres	15' 6"
Wheel Diameter	1' 11"
Tare Weight	6 tons 5 cwt
Capacity	13 tons 15 cwt

[Reference: Light Railways at Home and Abroad, WH Cole 1899, Railway Engineer, July 1910; bogies, Railway Engineer, January 1897]

2' 6" Gauge Rolling Stock

Indian Standard Covered Vans 1951

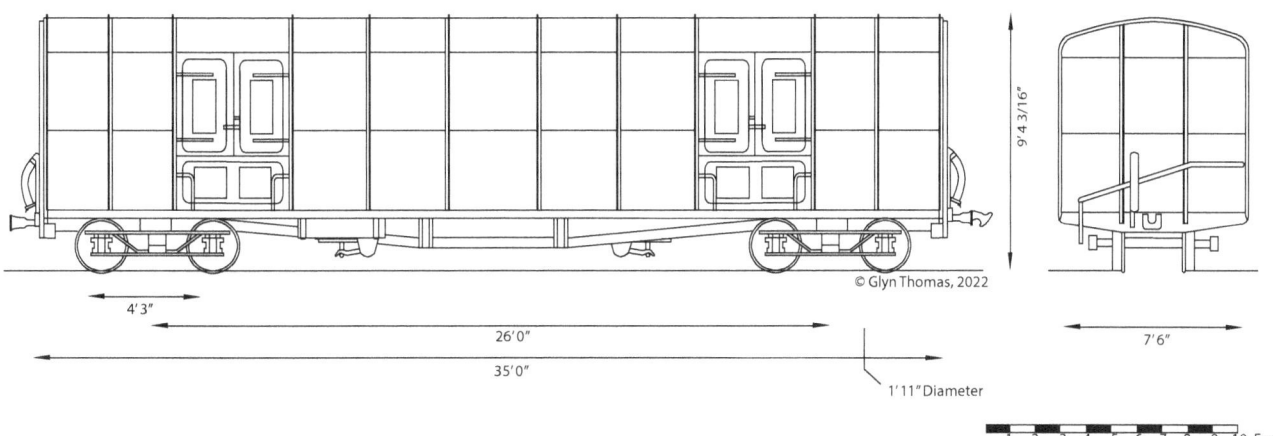

Bogie Wheelbase	4' 3"
Bogie Centres	26' 0"
Wheel Diameter	1' 11"
Tare Weight	9.19 tons
Axle Load	8 tons

[Reference: BBCIR Diagram book via Kelvin White]

RDSO Design, type NCL, 1951

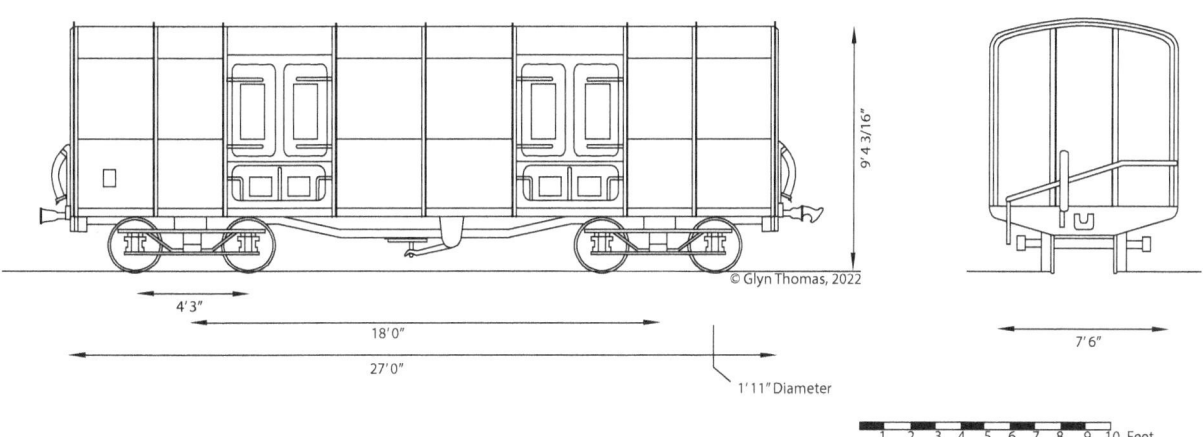

Bogie Wheelbase	4' 3"
Bogie Centres	18' 0"
Wheel Diameter	1' 11"
Tare Weight	7.45 tons
Capacity	24 tons

[Reference: BBCIR Diagram book via Kelvin White]

RDSO Design, 1951

Flat Cars

The flat cars shown here often shared common underframe designs to their contemporary bogie open wagons and vans. Some were adapted to specific types of traffic, such as the bolsters added to the timber wagon (a very common traffic on Indian narrow gauge lines).

BNR Timber Wagon 1908

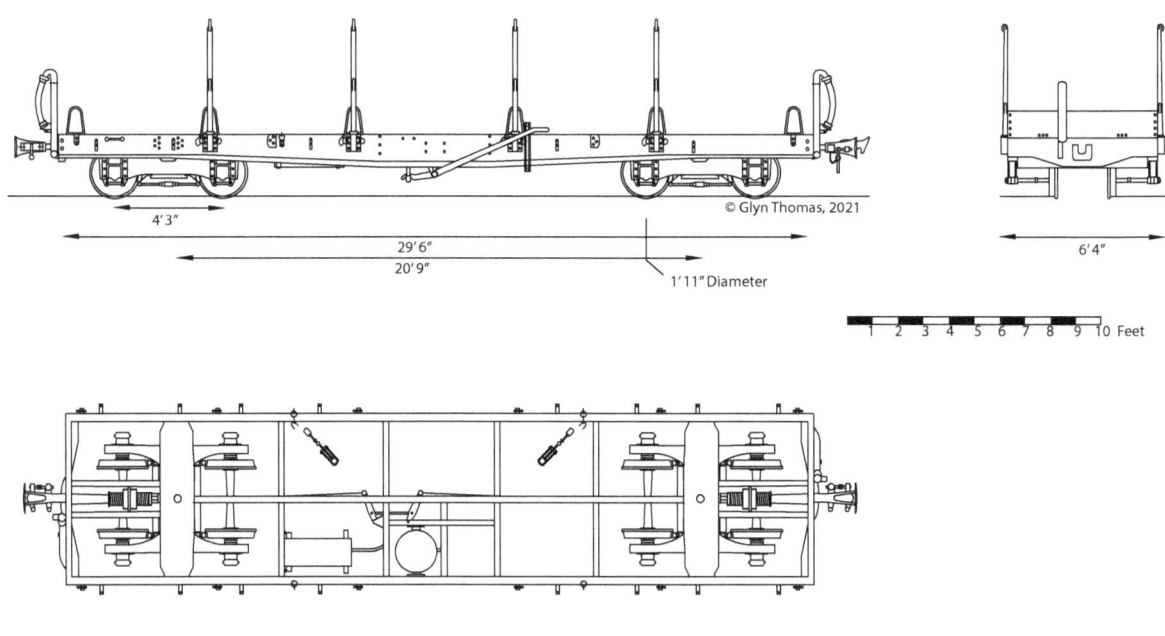

Bogie Wheelbase	4' 3"
Bogie Centres	20' 9"
Wheel Diameter	1' 11"
Tare Weight	5 tons 15 cwt

[Reference: Indian Engineering, 1908]

Barsi Light Railway Bogie Flatcar, 1910

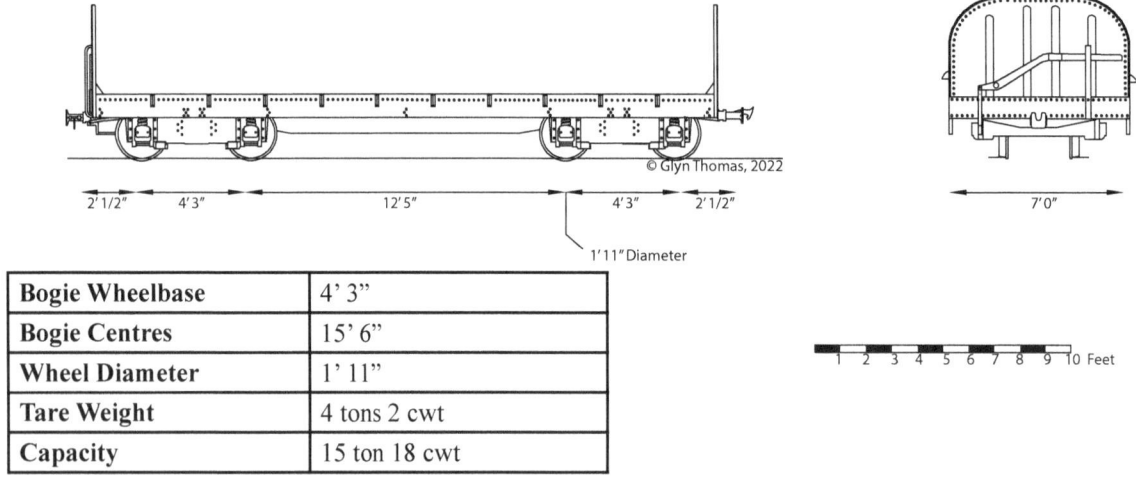

Bogie Wheelbase	4' 3"
Bogie Centres	15' 6"
Wheel Diameter	1' 11"
Tare Weight	4 tons 2 cwt
Capacity	15 ton 18 cwt

The bogie flat car shared the Pressed Steel bogie design with the covered wagon. The illustration is based on photos and known dimensions.

[Reference: Light Railways at Home and Abroad, WH Cole 1899, Railway Engineer, July 1910; bogies, Railway Engineer, January 1897]

GBSR Flatcar, 1915

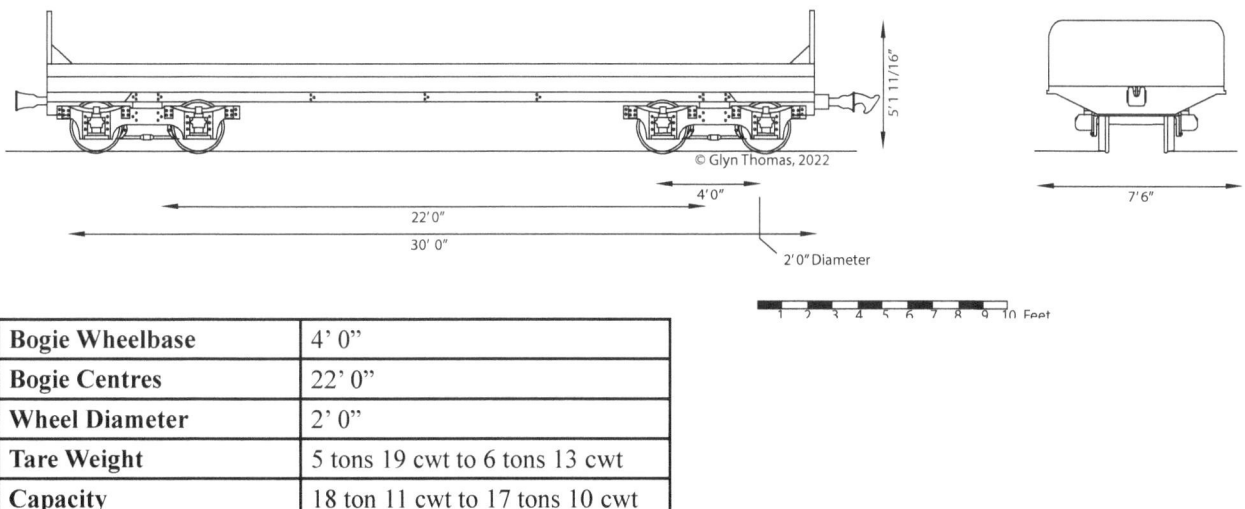

Bogie Wheelbase	4' 0"
Bogie Centres	22' 0"
Wheel Diameter	2' 0"
Tare Weight	5 tons 19 cwt to 6 tons 13 cwt
Capacity	18 ton 11 cwt to 17 tons 10 cwt

[Reference: BBCIR Diagram Book via Kelvin White]

Type BKU, 3 provided in 1915 and 2 provided in 1916. Manual brake. Some survived to be re-rated in metric tonnes. Loading guidance provided for ballast and sand. Running numbers included 01058, 01060, 01064, 01070, 01071.

Barsi Light Railway Flat Car [Author's Collection]

Brake Vans

Brake vans were vehicles that showed considerable variation of design on the narrow-gauge lines. Early examples for GBSR and the Barsi Light Railway are illustrated.

Eventually, Indian Railways introduced a standard design that resembled its broad- and metre-gauge equivalents.

BBCIR Brake Van

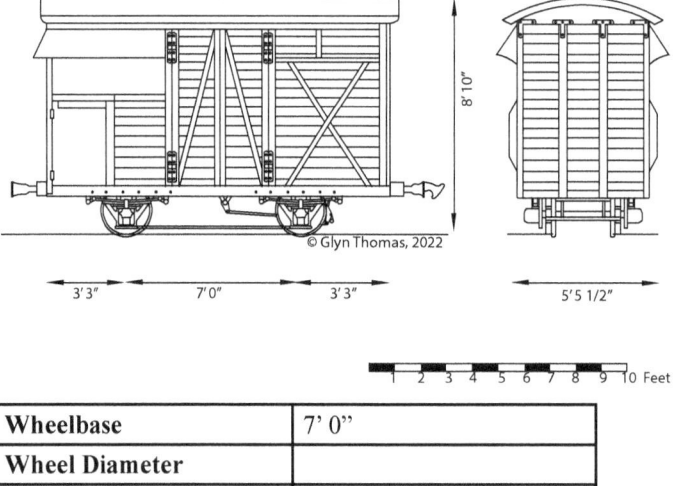

Wheelbase	7' 0"
Wheel Diameter	
Tare Weight	2 tons 2 cwt 0 qtr
Gross Weight	5 tons 17 cwt 0 qtr

[Reference: BBCIR Diagram Book via Kelvin White]

1924 BLR Brake Van

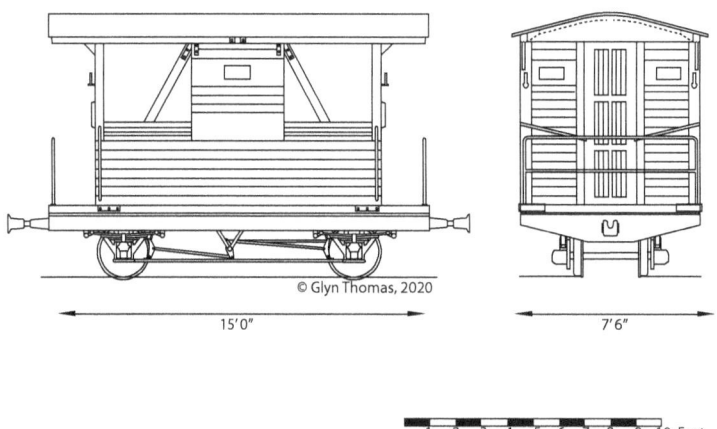

[Reference: Calthrop drawing in the Historical Model Railway Society archive]

2' 6" Gauge Rolling Stock

Indian Standard Brake Van

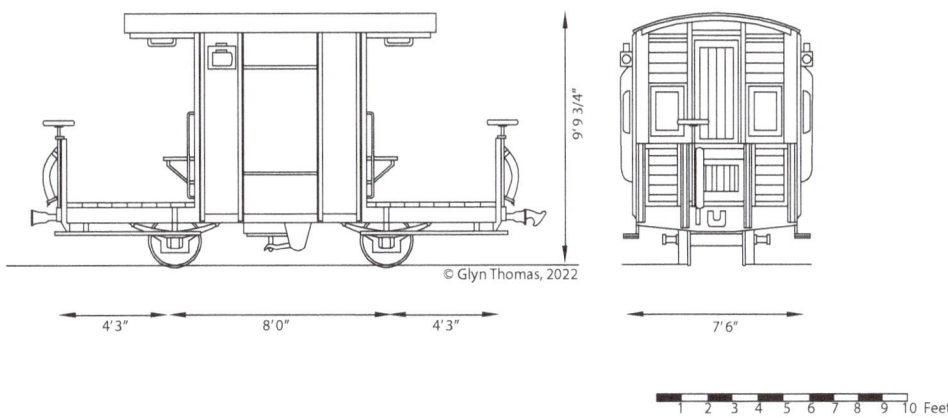

© Glyn Thomas, 2022

Wheelbase	8' 0"
Tare Weight	5.35 tons
Axle Load	6 tons

[Reference: BBCIR Diagram Book via Kelvin White]

Designed by RDSO, class NBVG, plan dated 1951

Wooden brake van at Ranchi in 1981 [David Churchill, DHRS]

EBR 4-Wheel Coaches

Old coaches at Mysore Iron and Steel on November 19th, 1977. The background coach is a 4-wheel saloon similar to the example illustrated here [John Tolson, Transport Treasury, JMT2814]

The Eastern Bengal Railway (EBR) was not ever a large operator of narrow-gauge lines. In 1899, when the illustrated coaches were built, they were only operating two sections: the 16-mile line from Kaunia to Kurigram (Dharla), which had been absorbed by the railway in 1887 (converted to metre gauge in 1901), and the eventually 53 mile Cooch Behar State Railway from Mogal Hat to Jainti (converted to metre-gauge in 1910). It is possible that the stock was later transferred elsewhere, because the EBR took over the Ranaghat-Krishnagar railway from Martin and Co in 1904, and constructed the Khulna-Bagerhat Railway in 1918.

Separately, in 1902, the Bengal Duars Railway was built to extend northwards from Kaunia towards Kuchbihar and transport tea from the Assam valley. The Bengal Duars Railway remained independent until 1941 when it was absorbed into the EBR.

Most of these narrow gauge lines went to East Pakistan (Bangladesh) at Partition and were eventually closed or converted to broad gauge.

The illustrations are based on plans that appeared in Railway Engineer in 1899. The show a 1st class salon, a 3rd-class "toast rack" coach, and a 1st-2nd class composite coach.

EBR 4-Wheel 1st Class Saloon

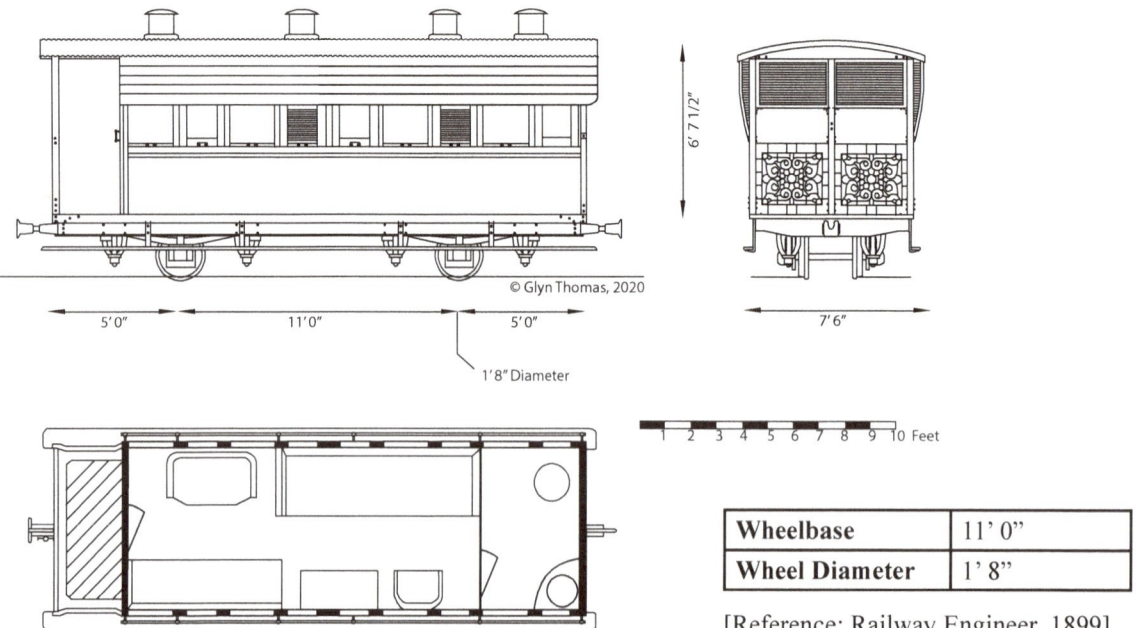

Wheelbase	11' 0"
Wheel Diameter	1' 8"

[Reference: Railway Engineer, 1899]

2' 6" Gauge Rolling Stock

EBR 4-Wheel 1st-2nd Class Composite

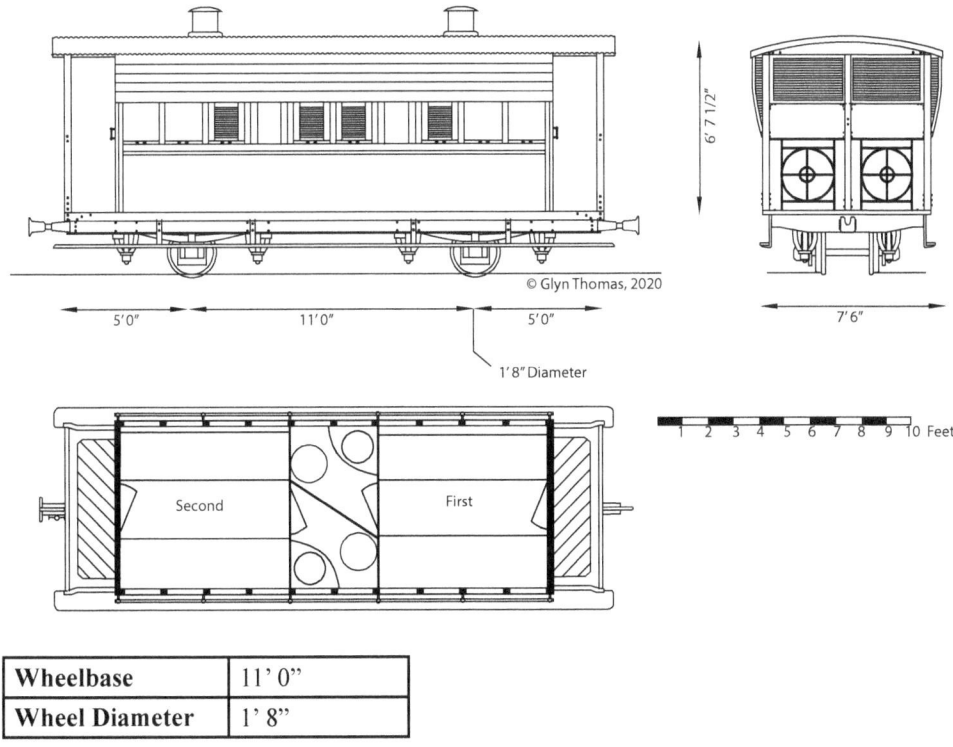

© Glyn Thomas, 2020

Wheelbase	11' 0"
Wheel Diameter	1' 8"

[Reference: Railway Engineer, 1899]

EBR 4-Wheel 3rd Class "Toast Rack" Coach

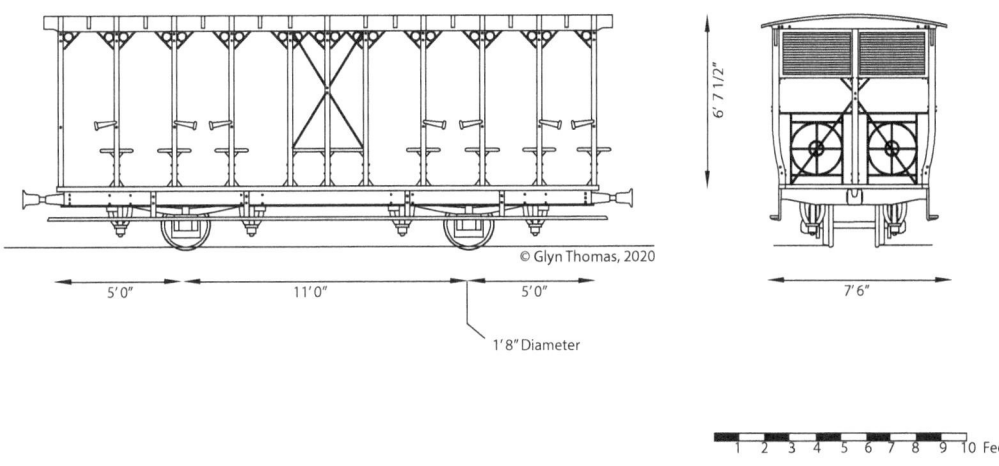

© Glyn Thomas, 2020

Wheelbase	11' 0"
Wheel Diameter	1' 8"

[Reference: Railway Engineer, 1899]

Kalighat-Falta Railway Coaches

Delta 2-6-2T KF10 with train at Canal and Diamond Harbor Road, Calcutta, 1944. This train is composed of coaches that have doors on every compartment, unlike the plans. [Author's Collection]

The Kalighat–Falta Railway (KFR) was one of the McLeod's group of privately-owned light railways, which were discussed in Indian Steam Locomotives in HO Scale. The illustrated coaches were built by Metro Cammell, probably for the opening in 1917.

The drawings are based on plans in the HMRS collection and show: a 3rd-class coach, 3rd-class with baggage and brake, 3rd-class with brake, and a 1st-2nd class composite.

The McLeod lines did not receive much investment in the 20th Century, so these coaches likely served on the line until it closed in 1957. It is possible that some stock was transferred to remaining McLeod's lines after that time.

Photos from the 1940's show that in later years, trains were more commonly composed of third-class coaches with doors on every compartment instead of the end-entry coaches shown here.

Martin and Co. used very similar coaches on their lines, although they had a turn-under on the sides. This photo shows a 0-6-2T 4H and train on the Futwah-Islampur Light Railway at Futwah on December 30th, 1985 [GH Taylor, Transport Treasury, GHT12888]

2' 6" Gauge Rolling Stock

KFR 3rd Class Coach

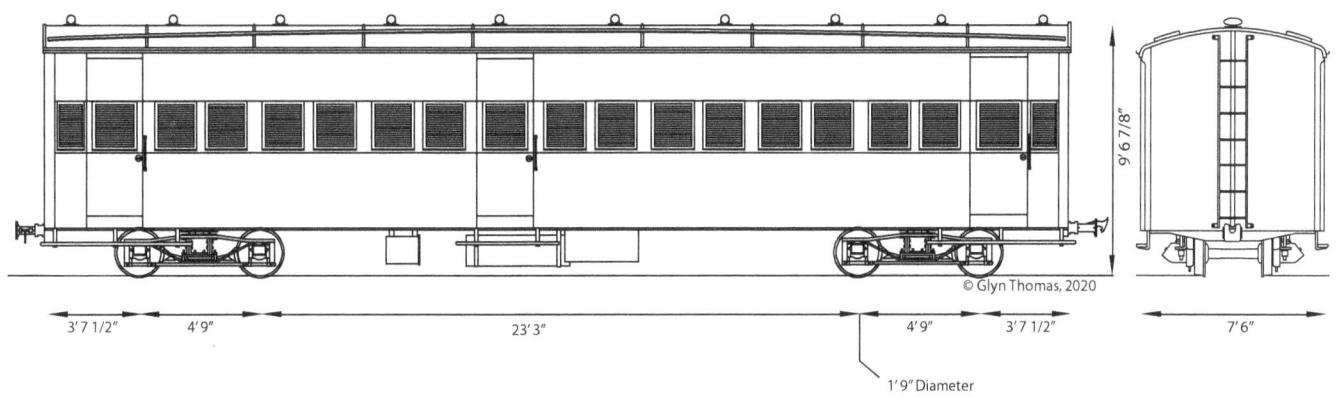

9' 6 7/8"

3' 7 1/2" 4' 9" 23' 3" 4' 9" 3' 7 1/2" 7' 6"

© Glyn Thomas, 2020

1' 9" Diameter

1 2 3 4 5 6 7 8 9 10 Feet

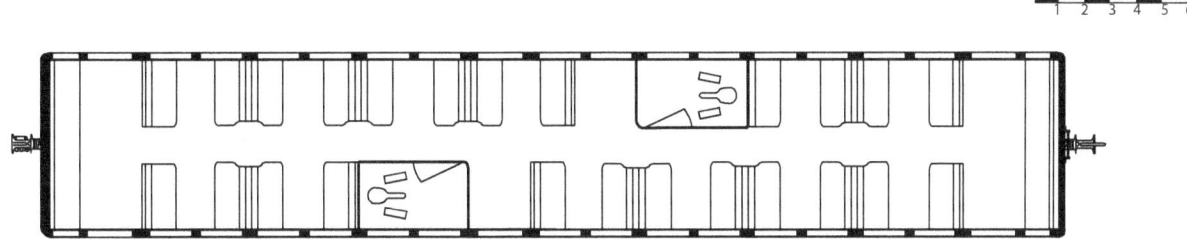

Bogie Wheelbase	4' 9"
Bogie Centres	28' 0"
Wheel Diameter	1' 9"
Capacity	58 passengers

[Reference: Metro Cammell drawing via Historical Model Railway Society]

KFR 3rd Class Brake Coach

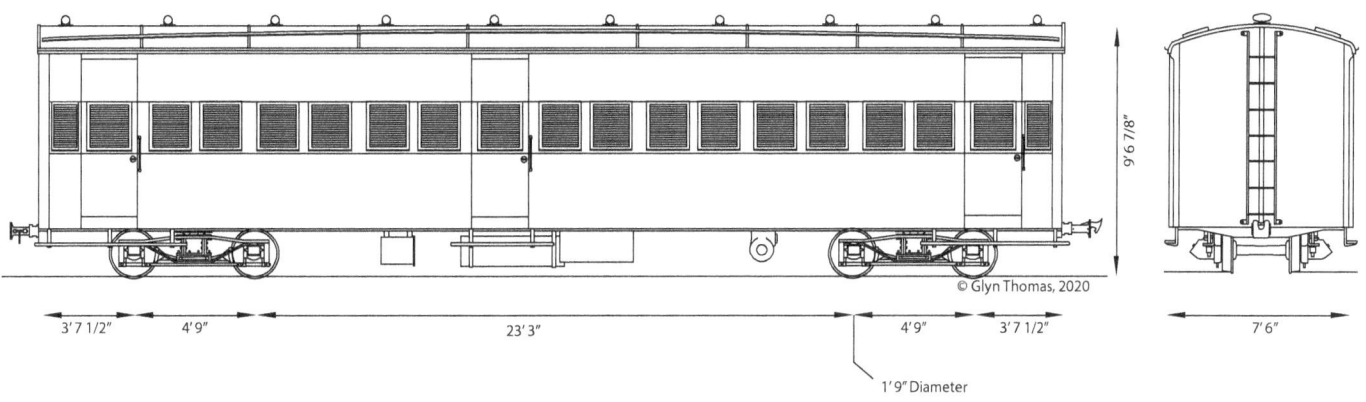

9' 6 7/8"

3' 7 1/2" 4' 9" 23' 3" 4' 9" 3' 7 1/2" 7' 6"

© Glyn Thomas, 2020

1' 9" Diameter

1 2 3 4 5 6 7 8 9 10 Feet

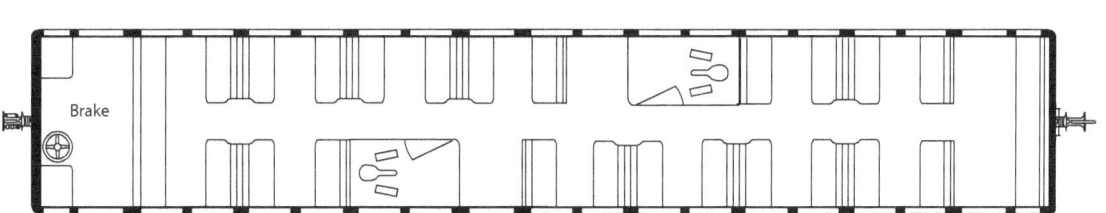

Brake

Bogie Wheelbase	4' 9"
Bogie Centres	28' 0"
Wheel Diameter	1' 9"
Capacity	54 passengers

[Reference: Metro Cammell drawing via Historical Model Railway Society]

2' 6" Gauge Rolling Stock

KFR 1st-2nd-Inter Composite Coach

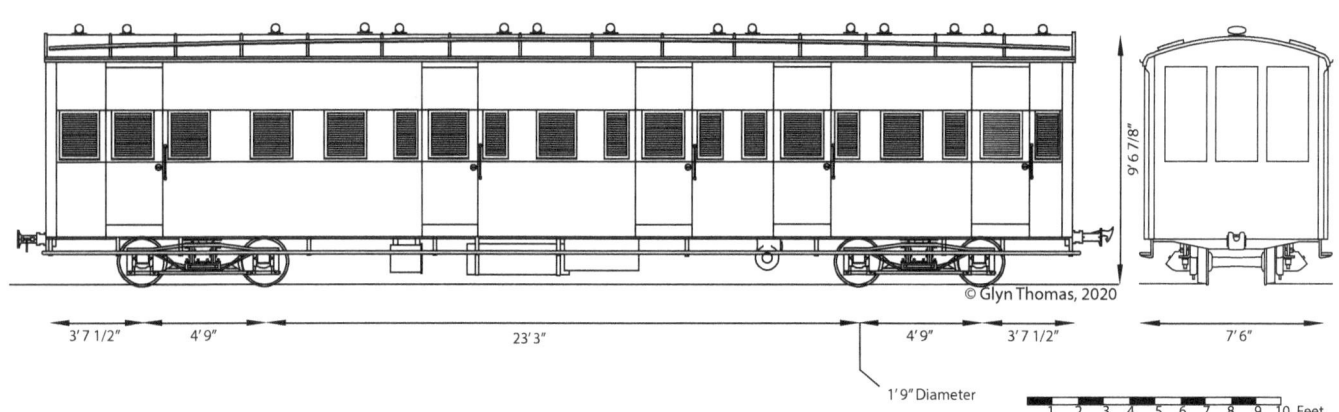

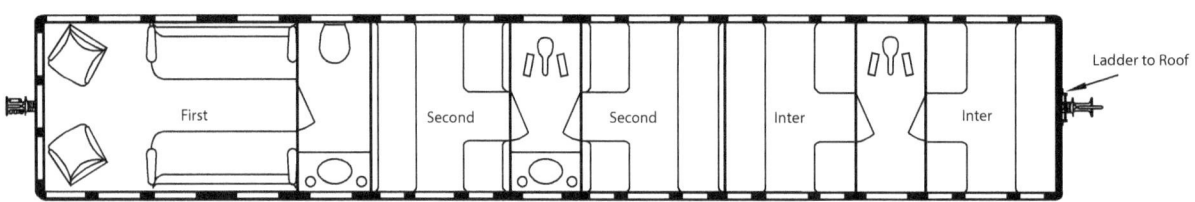

Bogie Wheelbase	4' 9"
Bogie Centres	28' 0"
Wheel Diameter	1' 9"
Capacity	8 1st class, 8 2nd class, 8 inter passengers

[Reference: Metro Cammell drawing via Historical Model Railway Society]

KFR 3rd Class Luggage Brake Coach

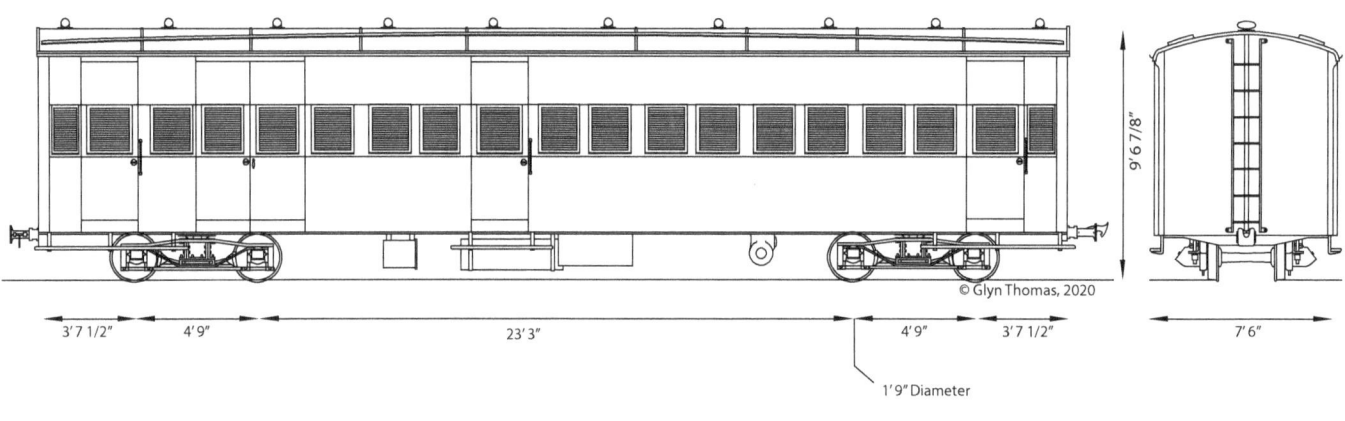

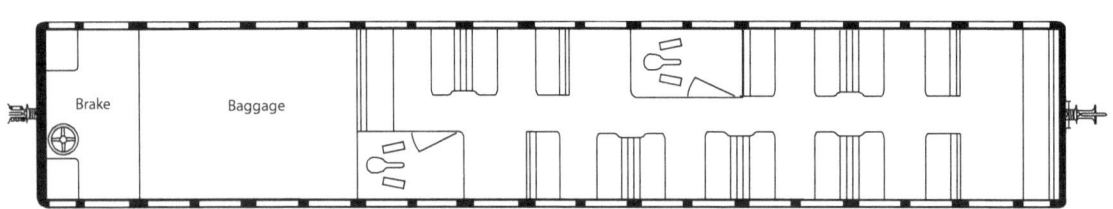

Bogie Wheelbase	4' 9"
Bogie Centres	28' 0"
Wheel Diameter	1' 9"
Capacity	39 passengers

[Reference: Metro Cammell drawing via Historical Model Railway Society]

North Western Railway Coaches

Kalka-Simla Train [Julian Rainbow Collection]

The Kalka-Simla Railway is a hill railway through the mountains to the former colonial summer capital of Simla in north-west India. Further details of the line, including a map and gradient profile can be found in "Indian Steam Locomotives in HO Scale".

The line was equipped with both 4-wheel and bogie carriages at the outset (the line opened in 1903). These were initially built of wood on steel underframes. Starting in 1908, the bogie coaching stock was rebuilt at the North Western Railways workshop at Lahore with the aim of increasing capacity while reducing tare weight. The coaches were enlarged and fitted with longer wheel-base diamond framed bogies from Leeds Forge. Steel framing was used for the bodies, with aluminium panels to reduce weight. Following the introduction of these modified coaches, train lengths could be extended from four to six coaches. Designs were provided for 3rd class coaches, composite coaches, first class coaches, and an exclusive salon coach for the use of the Viceroy. At the same time, the line introduced petrol-engined rail-motors for transporting first-class passengers on an accelerated schedule. It is likely that many first-class passengers preferred these to riding on the regular service train.

Observed numbers from the 1918 Engineer article are 170 for a composite coach, and 133 for a 3rd class coach. 1958 photos show 3rd class coaches 172, 191, 196, 213, and 224 - by that time, the ventilators over the windows had been plated over. These coaches were gradually replaced by more modern designs starting in the 1960s.

The diagram is based on one for a composite coach in the Mike Satow collection at the British Library. Other configurations are extrapolated from photographs.

Similar coaches to this design were also provided across the NWR. The Kangra Valley Railway used similar stock as evidenced by early photos.

Three lines that went to Pakistan after Partition also used the design: Khushalgarh-Thal, Kalabagh-Bannu, and Bostan Junction to Zhob. These three lines were eventually closed in the early 1990's. One or two of the Pakistan Railway coaches have been preserved at Golra Sharif Railway Museum.

2' 6" Gauge Rolling Stock

Viceroy Saloon

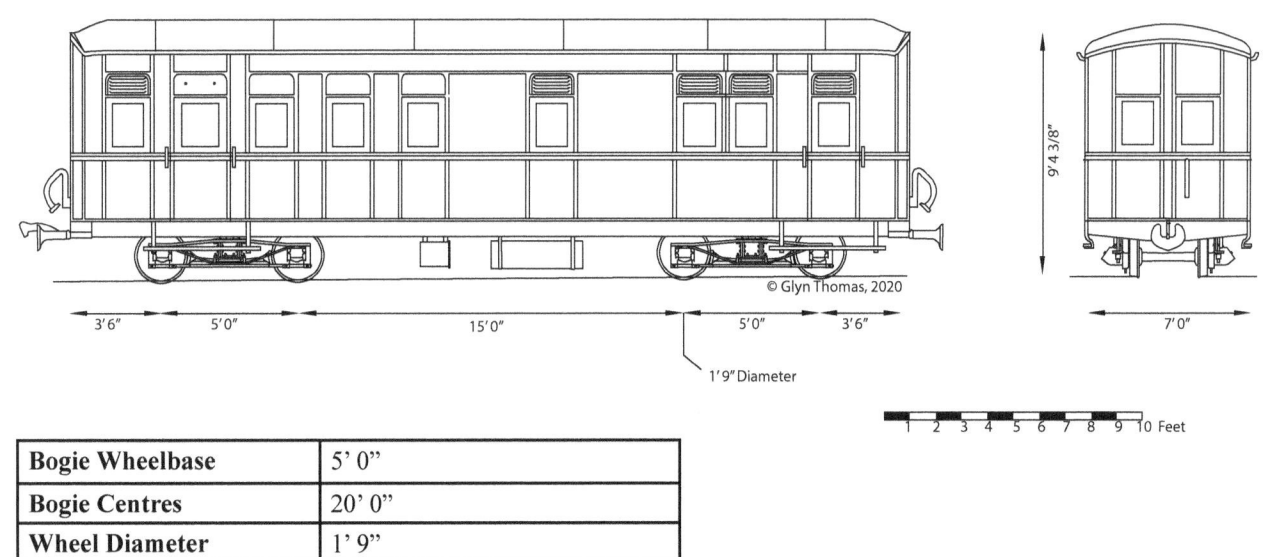

© Glyn Thomas, 2020

Bogie Wheelbase	5' 0"
Bogie Centres	20' 0"
Wheel Diameter	1' 9"

[Reference: Mike Satow Collection, British Library]

1st-2nd Composite

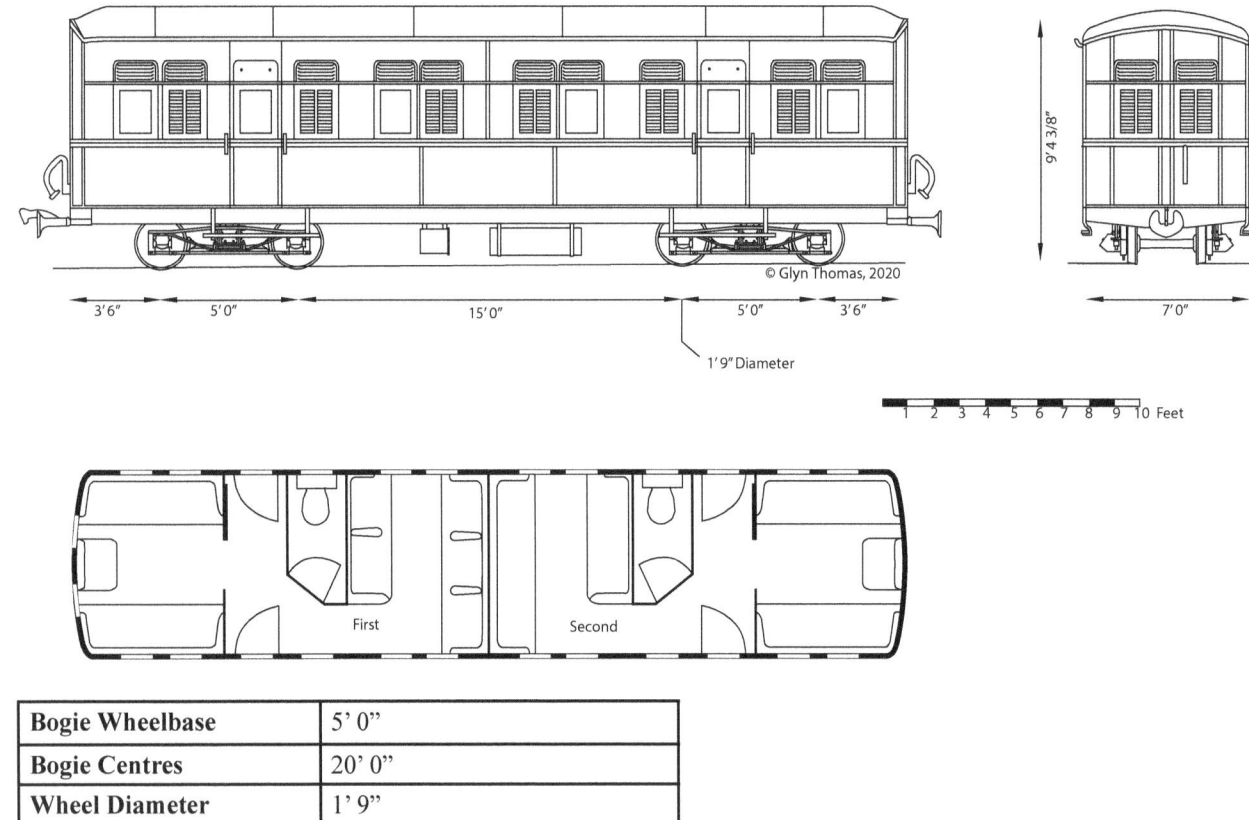

© Glyn Thomas, 2020

Bogie Wheelbase	5' 0"
Bogie Centres	20' 0"
Wheel Diameter	1' 9"

[Reference: Mike Satow Collection, British Library]

2' 6" Gauge Rolling Stock

3rd Class Coach

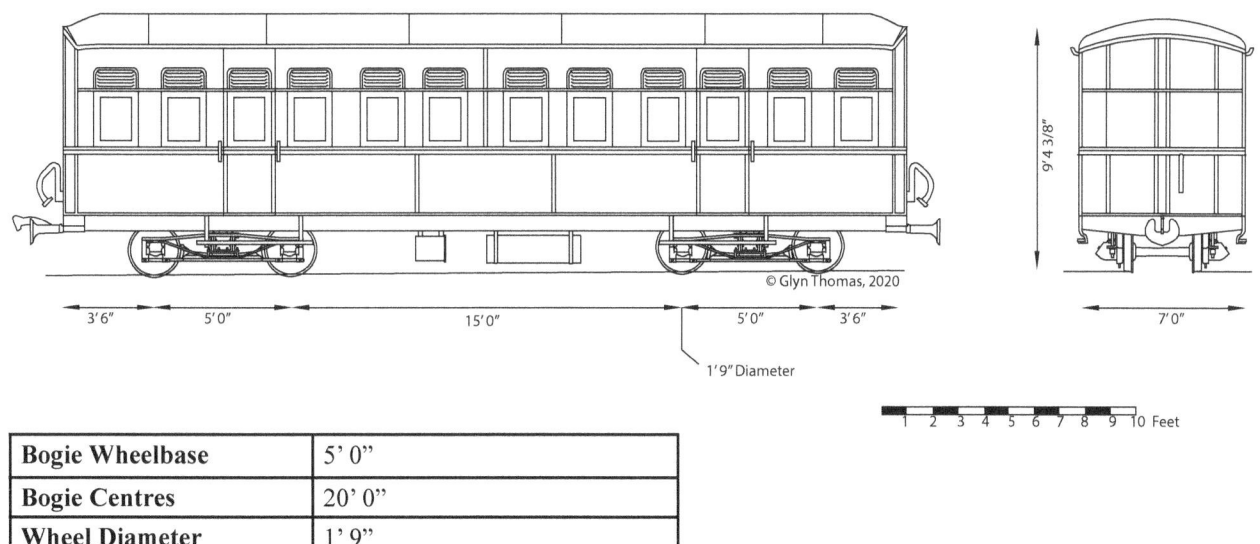

© Glyn Thomas, 2020

3'6"   5'0"   15'0"   5'0"   3'6"

1'9" Diameter

9' 4 3/8"

7'0"

1 2 3 4 5 6 7 8 9 10 Feet

Bogie Wheelbase	5' 0"
Bogie Centres	20' 0"
Wheel Diameter	1' 9"

[Reference: Mike Satow Collection, British Library]

Baggage Van

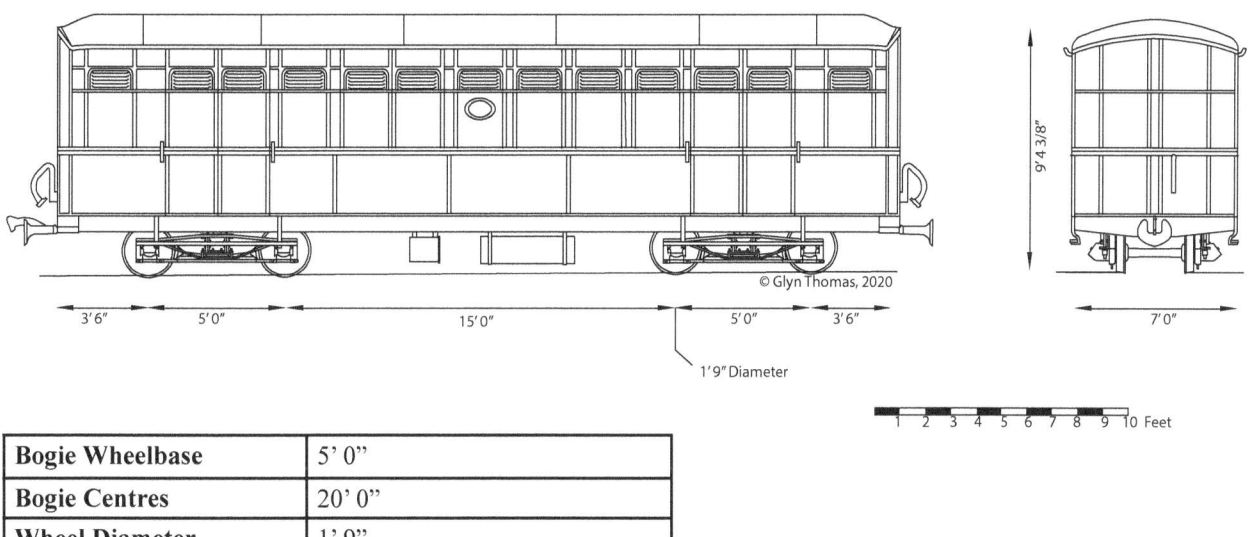

© Glyn Thomas, 2020

3'6"   5'0"   15'0"   5'0"   3'6"

1'9" Diameter

9' 4 3/8"

7'0"

1 2 3 4 5 6 7 8 9 10 Feet

Bogie Wheelbase	5' 0"
Bogie Centres	20' 0"
Wheel Diameter	1' 9"

[Reference: Mike Satow Collection, British Library]

Barsi Light Railway Coaches

Barsi Light Railway train in the 1930's [Author's Collection]

The Barsi Light Railway was one of the best-known Indian narrow-gauge lines due to it's association with its Consulting Engineer, E.R. Calthrop, and his influential designs. The overall line ran from Miraj, through Kurdavadi to LaturTown - a distance of 202 miles - the longest continuous narrow gauge route in India. The line was originally owned by the Barsi Light Railway company of London. It was taken into Indian Railways ownership in 1954.

The BLR survived into the 21st Century as a narrow-gauge branch on the Central Railway. It was converted to broad-gauge in sections between 2002 and 2008.

A demonstration train of the line's original wagons and coaches was displayed at the Newlay Exhibition in England before shipping to India. The demonstration train included two brake-1st-3rd composite coaches. The coaches had steel underframes and wooden bodies by Lancaster Railway Carriage and Wagon Company. It is likely that these used the same bogie style as the wagons for the first batch. These were fitted with sunshades above the passenger windows. The initial shipment to Bombay included a salon, brake-composite, and third-class variations of this design, although the numbers supplied are unknown.

In 1906 several third and brake-third coaches were supplied for pilgrim service. These had longitudinal seats with end platforms and diamond bogies. The full third coach could seat 67 passengers, but they usually carried many more during pilgrim service. These were designed to run in 'sets' of four coaches, and a train often comprised of four sets (16 coaches). This design had turn-unders on the side profiles, and a different roof profile. Very similar coaches (without the sunshades) were used on the British Leak and Manifold Valley Light Railway, built 1902-4, for which Calthrop was also Consulting Engineer. Remarkably, a brake-third from this batch has survived to become part of the Delhi National railway Museum collection.

The 1926-7 coaches illustrated here were built by Leeds Forge and are more conventional than the line's original stock. The third class coaches were numbered 97-100. The mail-baggage cars were numbered 264-267.

2' 6" Gauge Rolling Stock

Brake 1st-3rd Composite Coach, 1896

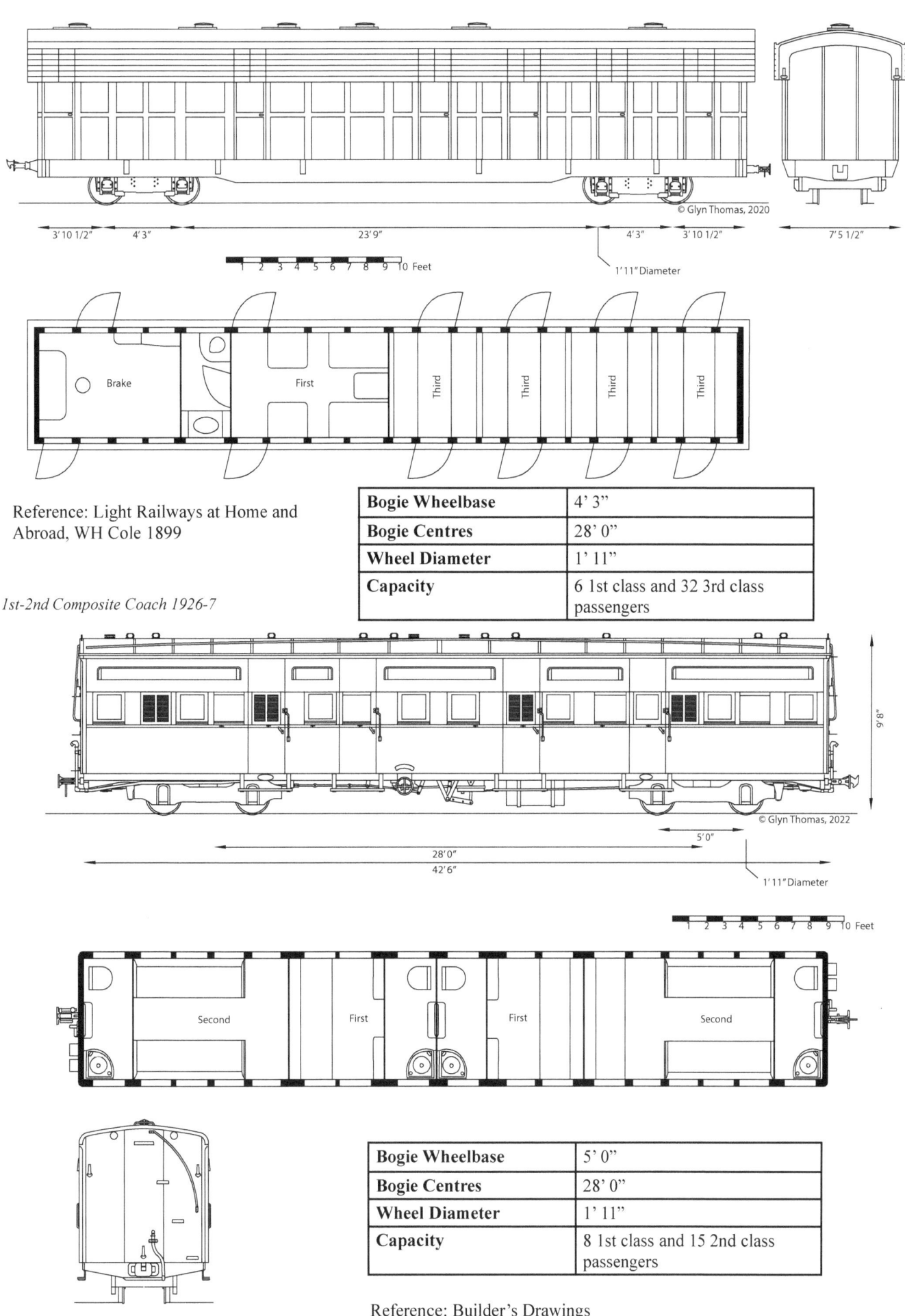

© Glyn Thomas, 2020

3' 10 1/2"   4' 3"   23' 9"   4' 3"   3' 10 1/2"   7' 5 1/2"

1' 11" Diameter

1 2 3 4 5 6 7 8 9 10 Feet

Brake   First   Third   Third   Third   Third

Reference: Light Railways at Home and Abroad, WH Cole 1899

Bogie Wheelbase	4' 3"
Bogie Centres	28' 0"
Wheel Diameter	1' 11"
Capacity	6 1st class and 32 3rd class passengers

1st-2nd Composite Coach 1926-7

© Glyn Thomas, 2022

9' 8"

28' 0"
42' 6"

5' 0"

1' 11" Diameter

1 2 3 4 5 6 7 8 9 10 Feet

Second   First   First   Second

Bogie Wheelbase	5' 0"
Bogie Centres	28' 0"
Wheel Diameter	1' 11"
Capacity	8 1st class and 15 2nd class passengers

Reference: Builder's Drawings

7' 6"

2' 6" Gauge Rolling Stock

3rd Class Coach 1926-7

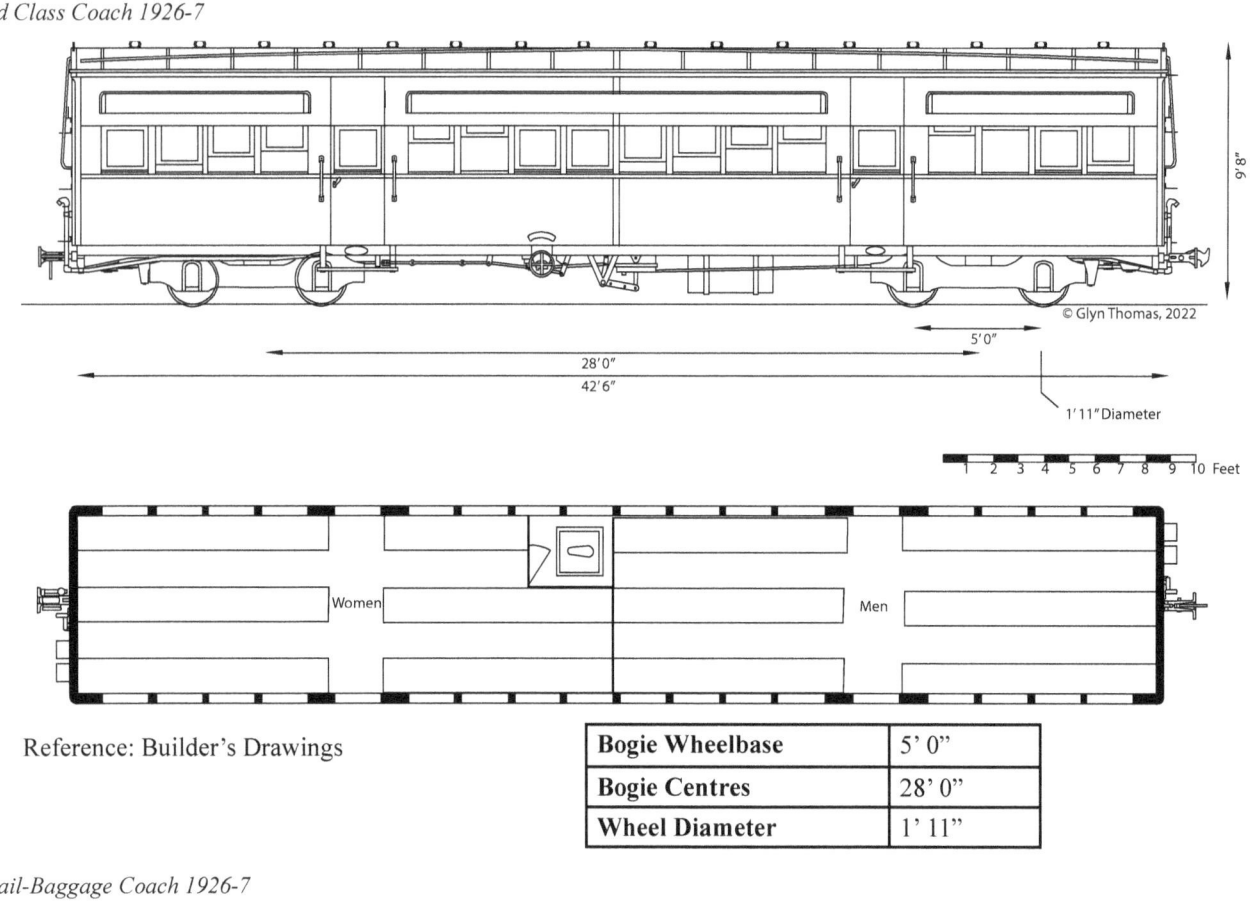

© Glyn Thomas, 2022

5' 0"

28' 0"

42' 6"

1' 11" Diameter

9' 8"

1 2 3 4 5 6 7 8 9 10 Feet

Women   Men

Reference: Builder's Drawings

Bogie Wheelbase	5' 0"
Bogie Centres	28' 0"
Wheel Diameter	1' 11"

Mail-Baggage Coach 1926-7

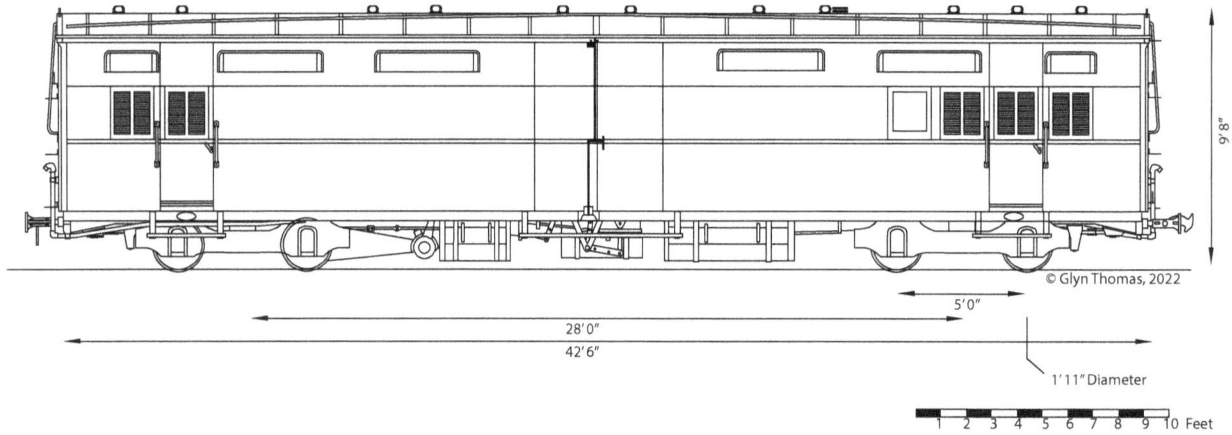

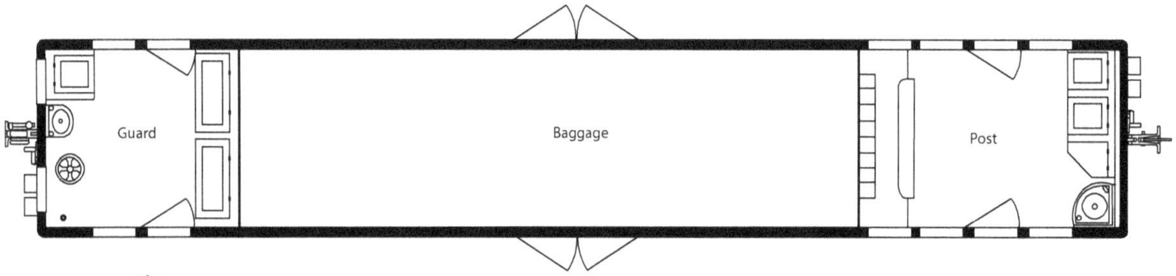

© Glyn Thomas, 2022

5' 0"

28' 0"

42' 6"

1' 11" Diameter

9' 8"

1 2 3 4 5 6 7 8 9 10 Feet

Guard   Baggage   Post

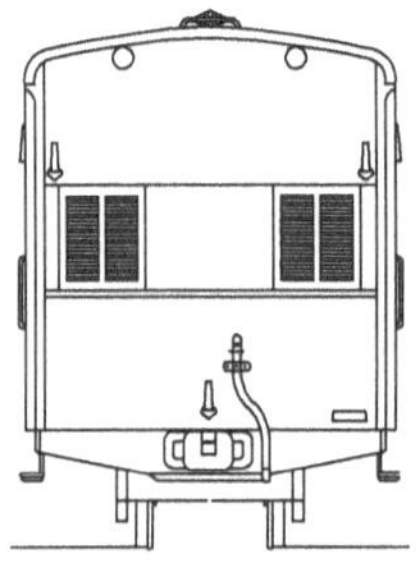

Bogie Wheelbase	5' 0"
Bogie Centres	28' 0"
Wheel Diameter	1' 11"

Reference: Builder's Drawings

2' Gauge Rolling Stock

Jorhat (Provincial) State Railway

The Jorhat (Provincial) Railway was built to link Gosaigaon on the Brahmaputra River to the city of Jorhat and onwards to the Assam Bengal Railway at Mariani Junction, with the intention of expanding tea production in the area. It was surveyed in 1882, as the Assam Kokilamukh Railway, and 2' gauge was selected due to the influence of the DHR. It opened in 1885 as the Kokila Mookh Tramway, owned by the province of Assam. In 1886 it became the Kokilamukh State Railway when passenger services commenced, and in 1889 it became the Jorhat Provincial State Railway (JPR) when the link to the ABR was completed. The ultimate length of the line and branches was 32.5 miles. The line was worked by the state until 1927, after which it was operated by Messrs Macneil and Co. and Messrs Kilburn and Co. The line was nationalised in 1937, and it was merged into the Bengal and Assam Railway in 1943. Narrow gauge operations finished around the time of the BAR merger and some of the alignment was converted to metre-gauge (this was subsequently converted to broad-gauge in the 2010s).

The Railway Gazette illustrated the line's rolling stock in their 1913 Indian Railways Special Edition. This would appear to have been an odd choice, since by that time most of India had already standardised on 2' 6" for narrow gauge feeder lines instead of 2' gauge. Even so, the coaches are similar to the EBR's 2' 6" gauge coaches illustrated in the previous section.

The freight rolling stock poses an enigma because they have different couplings to the coaches and are probably older designs. The first two locomotives on the line were 0-4-2Ts built by John Fowler and Co. in 1883-1884. John Fowler and Co. was a licensee of the French Decauville lightweight portable railway system for industrial and agricultural uses, and had also introduced their own version of portable track in 1879. The wagons' short wheelbase bogies and low couplings pivoted at the bogie bolster are very characteristic of Fowler products. It is probable that the wagons were either fully constructed by Fowler, or built using parts sent from Britain. The covered van is interesting for not using the full extent of the loading gauge, and this may have been intended to keep the centre of balance low on the small bogies. These wagons may have been primary used on lightweight track within the plantations, instead of on the main line.

No photographs have emerged for the JPR, so some major assumptions are made in the appearance of the wagons. It isn't even clear whether the wagon bodies were steel or wood. Most Fowler open wagons were steel, but many of their covered vans used slatted wooden bodies. The modeller can adjust as they feel fit.

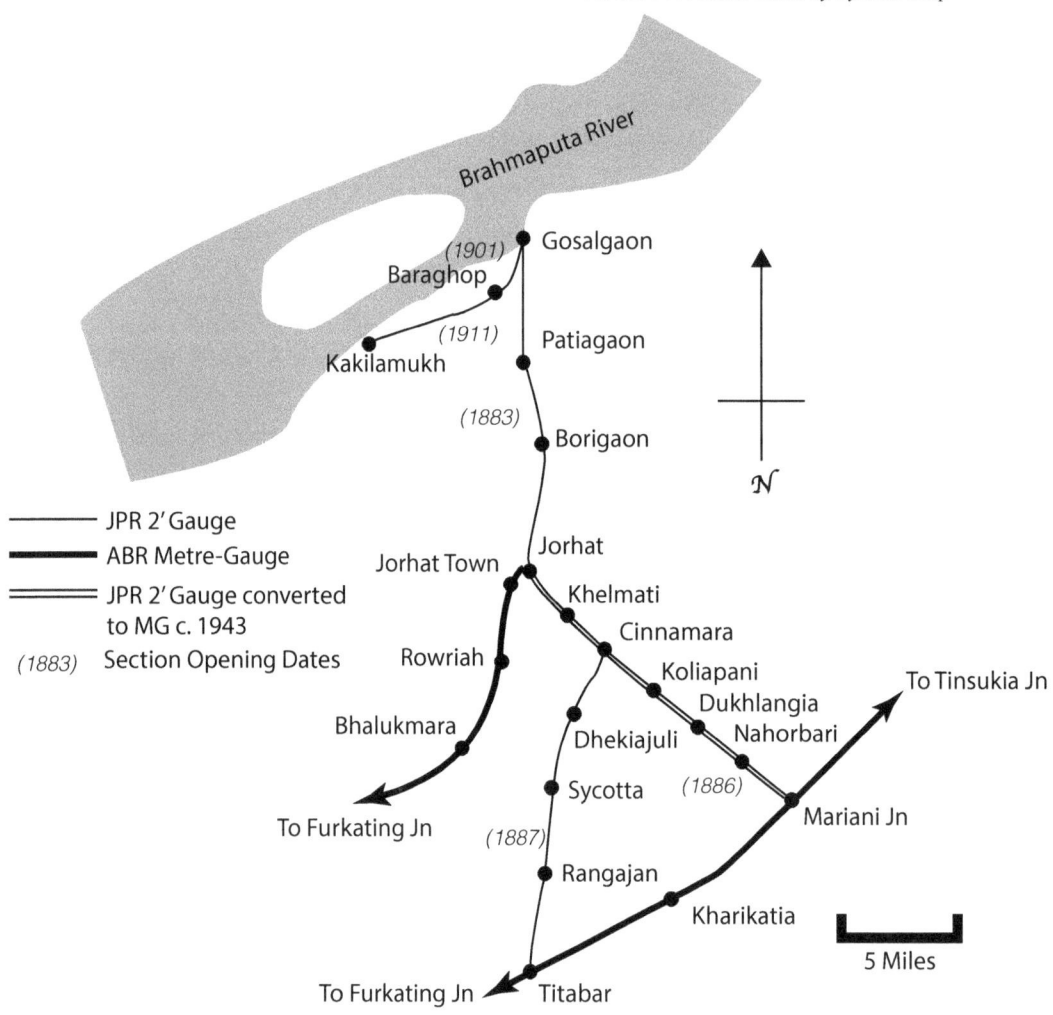

Jorhat Provincial Railway System Map

JPR 2' Gauge
ABR Metre-Gauge
JPR 2' Gauge converted to MG c. 1943
(1883) Section Opening Dates

1st-2nd Class Coach

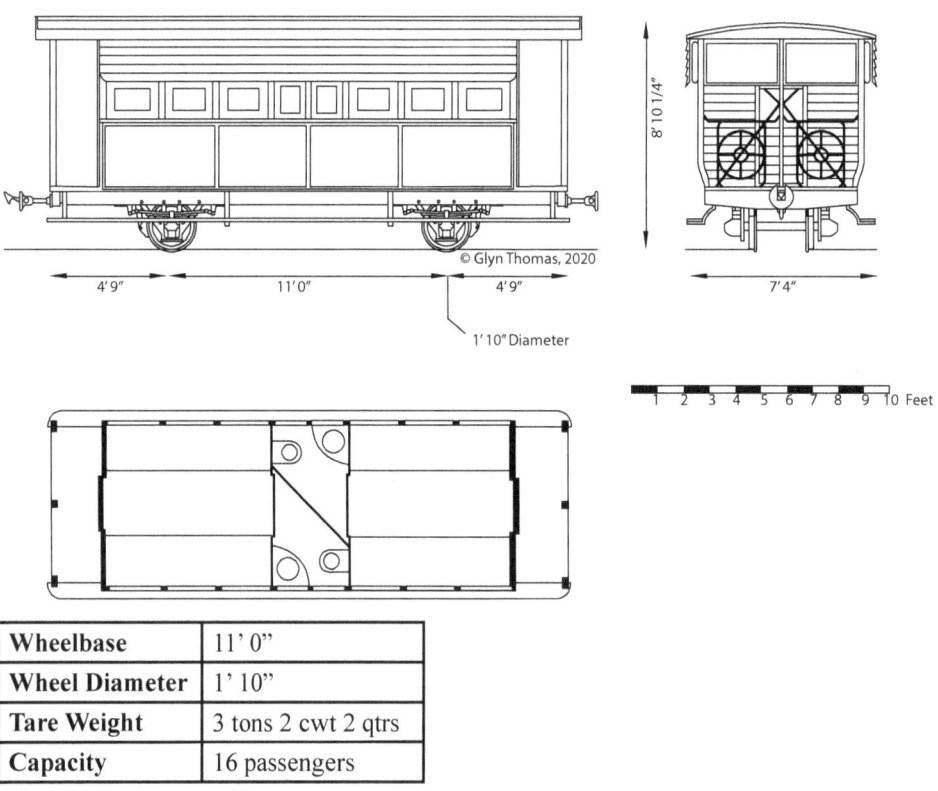

© Glyn Thomas, 2020

Wheelbase	11' 0"
Wheel Diameter	1' 10"
Tare Weight	3 tons 2 cwt 2 qtrs
Capacity	16 passengers

[Reference: Railway Gazette Indian Railways Special Edition, 1913]

2' Gauge Rolling Stock

3rd Class Coach

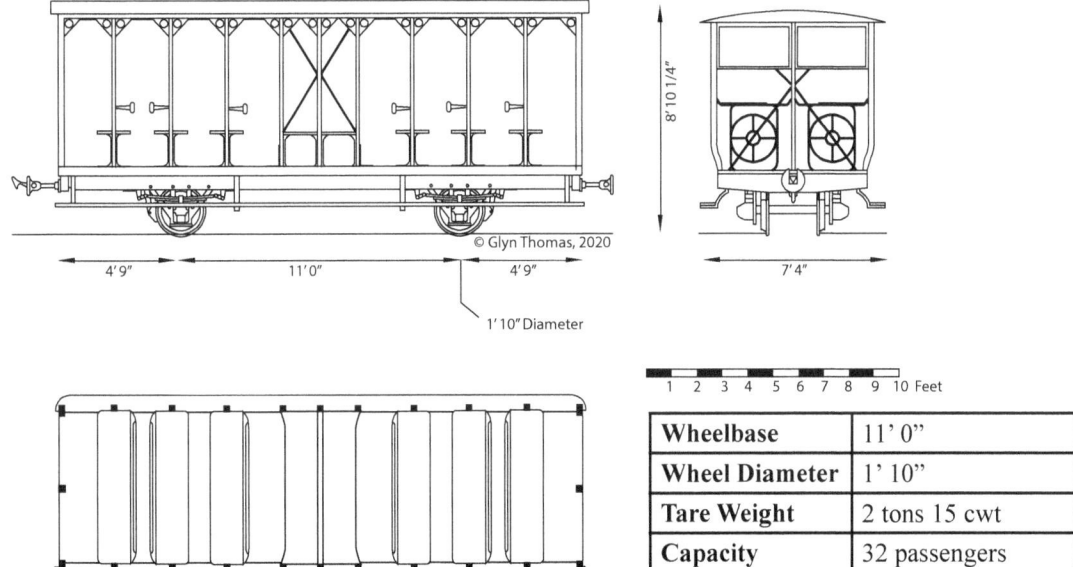

Wheelbase	11' 0"
Wheel Diameter	1' 10"
Tare Weight	2 tons 15 cwt
Capacity	32 passengers

[Reference: Railway Gazette Indian Railways Special Edition, 1913]

Bogie Open Wagon

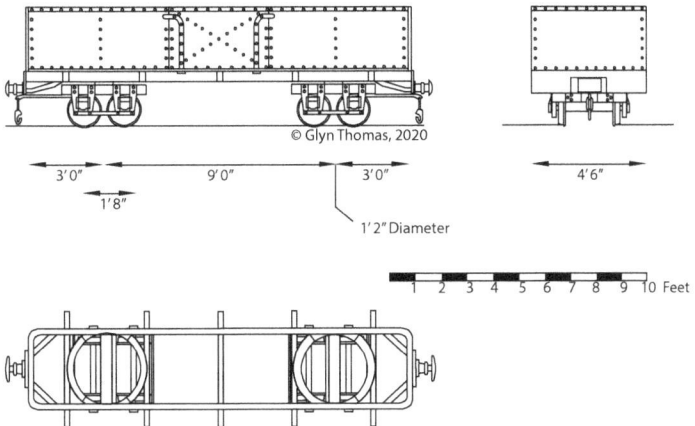

[Reference: Railway Gazette Indian Railways Special Edition, 1913]

Bogie Covered Van

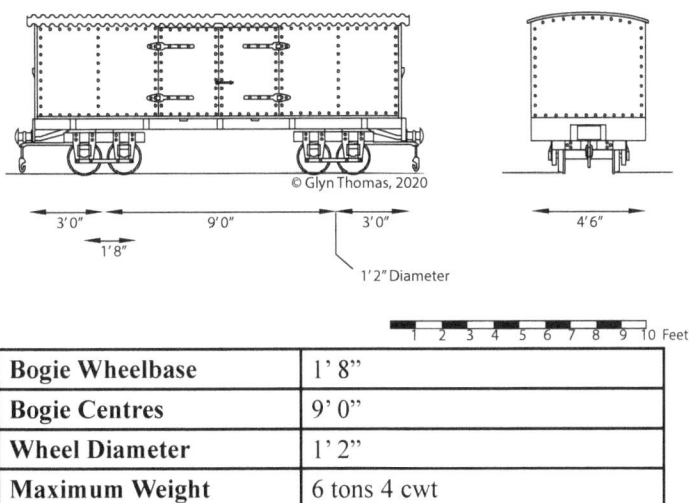

Bogie Wheelbase	1' 8"
Bogie Centres	9' 0"
Wheel Diameter	1' 2"
Maximum Weight	6 tons 4 cwt

[Reference: Railway Gazette Indian Railways Special Edition, 1913]

BRCW Photographs

Julian Rainbow has collected works photographs of Indian railway rolling stock built by Birmingham Railway Carriage and Wagon. Collectively, they show many variations on the standard designs illustrated in this volume, and are a useful supplement to the diagrams. Modellers can use these photos to add variation into their wagon fleets.

Indian State Railways 4-Wheel Covered Van, 1904 [BRCW Photo, Julian Rainbow Collection]

Indian State Railways EBR 4-Wheel Covered Van, 1904 [BRCW Photo, Julian Rainbow Collection]

BBCIR 4-Wheel Covered Van, 1908 [BRCW Photo, Julian Rainbow Collection]

Madras Railway 4-Wheel Covered Van, 1904 [BRCW Photo, Julian Rainbow Collection]

EIRR 4-Wheel Covered Van, 1913 [BRCW Photo, Julian Rainbow Collection]

GIPR 4-Wheel Covered Van, 1912 [BRCW Photo, Julian Rainbow Collection]

SIR 4-Wheel Covered Van [BRCW Photo, Julian Rainbow Collection]

GIPR 4-Wheel Covered Van, 1928 [BRCW Photo, Julian Rainbow Collection]

GIPR 4-Wheel Covered Van [BRCW Photo, Julian Rainbow Collection]

Indian Railway CR 4-Wheel Covered Van, 1944 [BRCW Photo, Julian Rainbow Collection]

BBCIR 4-Wheel Open Wagon, 1908 [BRCW Photo, Julian Rainbow Collection]

NWR 4-Wheel Open Wagon, 1908 [BRCW Photo, Julian Rainbow Collection]

GIPR 4-Wheel Open Wagon, 1922 [BRCW Photo, Julian Rainbow Collection]

BBCIR Low Sided 4-Wheel Open Wagon, 1908 [BRCW Photo, Julian Rainbow Collection]

GIPR 4-Wheel Tank Wagon, 1922 [BRCW Photo, Julian Rainbow Collection]

MSMR 4-Wheel Tank Wagon, 1923 [BRCW Photo, Julian Rainbow Collection]

SIR 4-Wheel Tank Wagon, 1929 [BRCW Photo, Julian Rainbow Collection]

SIR 4-Wheel Tank Wagon, 1929 [BRCW Photo, Julian Rainbow Collection]

NWR Bogie Covered Van, 1923 [BRCW Photo, Julian Rainbow Collection]

GIPR Bogie Covered Van, 1910 [BRCW Photo, Julian Rainbow Collection]

GIPR Bogie Open Wagon, 1915 [BRCW Photo, Julian Rainbow Collection]

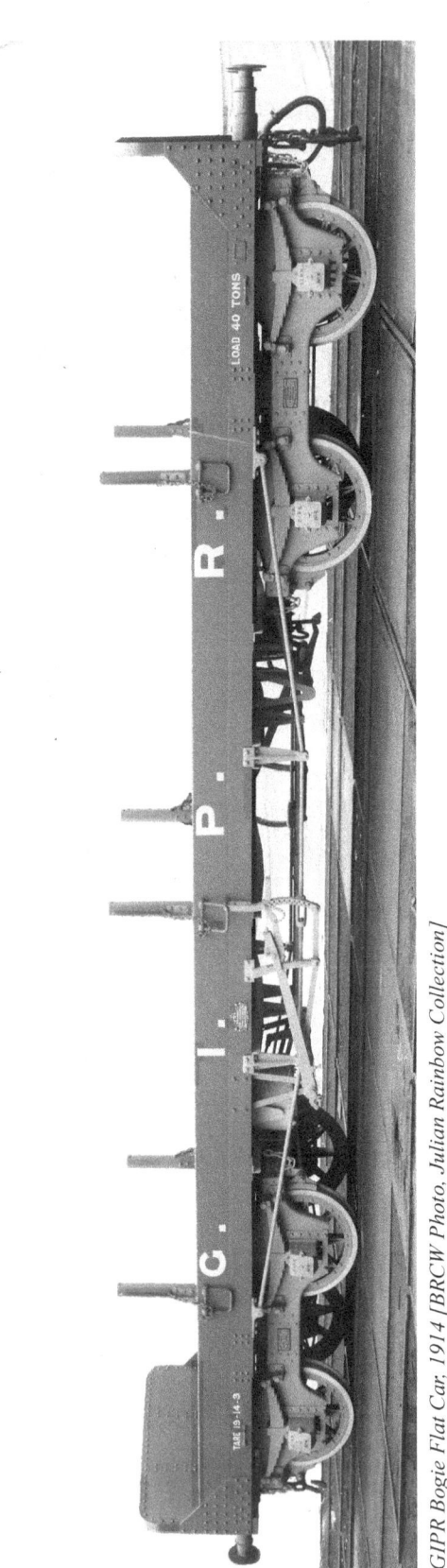

GIPR Bogie Flat Car, 1914 [BRCW Photo, Julian Rainbow Collection]

GIPR Bogie Flat Car, 1921 [BRCW Photo, Julian Rainbow Collection]

BNR Bogie Coal Hopper, 1915 [BRCW Photo, Julian Rainbow Collection]

TISC Bogie Coke Hopper, 1930 [BRCW Photo, Julian Rainbow Collection]

Acknowledgements and References

Thanks

Particular thanks are due to the following people:

- Julian Rainbow at the BORHT for editing the book and provision of many historic photos

- Derek Turner for early reviews and advice

- Gerald Futej for publishing advice

- Ashish Kuvelkar, Shashanka Nanda, and various members of the Indian Railways Fan Club for providing photos; photographers include: Jimmy Jose, Abhijit Lokre, Apurva Bahadur, Ramdev Gowda, Prakash Tendulkar, Naveen Jain, and Lalam

- Alon Siton, who maintains the Historical Railway Images collection on Flickr - probably the best source of British colonial photos and documents on the Internet

- David Churchill, modelling coordinator at the Darjeeling Himalayan Railway Society for photos and assistance

- Paul Garratt, Drawing Archivist at HMRS

- Kelvin White, founder of the Indian Railway Study Group

- Ken Walker

- Jay Balakrishna for video stills of MG rolling stock

- Donald Kerr, Special Collections Librarian at the University of Otago, New Zealand

- The staff of the Asian Collection at the British Library

- The staff at the library of Amherst College

- Tony Bowles at the Restoration and Archiving Trust

- Hayley Anne & Jeremiah Bunya of Pegasus designs/ Precision Model Works (makers of 3D printed Indian rolling stock models) for copies of their diagrams

- John Tolson, GH Taylor, and Brian Walker at the Transport Trust for permission to use their photos.

My wife, Annie, and sons, Gavin and Duncan, have provided unwavering support through this and my previous book - thanks.

Sources

A comprehensive bibliography of Indian railway books was provided in "Indian Seam Locomotives in HO Scale" and will not be reproduced here.

The sources of material for a book on rolling stock differ from locomotives and are summarised here:

- The largest single set of source material came from the Historical Model Railway Society's collection of plans, which covers Metropolitan Cammell and it's constituents during the colonial era

- The remarkable Ernie Webber collection at the University of Otago is a rare collection of many Indian diagram books, and I'm very indebted to Donald Kerr and John Hughes for assistance with access to the archive

- Ken Walker from Australia provided scans of coach diagrams from a Western Railway Metre Gauge Diagram book

- Kelvin White, founder of the Indian Railway Study Group, provided copies of the BBCIR narrow gauge diagram book.

- Indian Railways has published some technical material on-line, including maintenance manuals for wagons, ICF, and LHB coaches, which have diagrams and other useful information; some coach diagrams can also be found on-line separately; there are also some technical slide decks with plans, but these should be used with care because the authors sometimes distort plans to fit the PowerPoint format

- Amherst College has a complete set of "Locomotive, Carriage, and Wagon Review", which is a good source of diagrams

- A number of engineering journals up to about 1920 are now available on-line via Google Play and were a good source for high-quality plans - these include some issues of "Locomotive, Carriage, and Wagon Review" (sometimes called "The Locomotive"), "Railway Engineer", and "Engineer"

- Grace's Guide on-line has the complete set of "Engineer" available to download including the period after 1920, but it is necessary to pay for downloads

- Some modern Indian wagon leasing companies provide on-line diagrams of the wagons they lease; for example, Touax (touaxtexmaco.com) provides tank and other wagon diagrams

Acknowledgements and References

- The Mike Satow collection at the British Library is useful for locomotive and railcar diagrams, but unfortunately only includes one coach diagram, of the Kalka-Simla coach
- The online Chris Walker Collection at the Restoration and Archiving Trust (gwrarchive.org) has a good collection of historic Indian railway photographs.

General books used:

- Private Investment in India 1900-1939, Amiya Kumar Bagchi, Cambridge University Press, 1972

A number of photographic sources are also used:

- IRFCA
- Historical Railway Images collection on Flickr
- Julian Rainbow Collection

Diagrams from Other Sources

The following table lists plans that are available from publications that are readily available at the time of writing.

Gauge	Subject	Railway	Source	Author
2' 6"	Western Railway Narrow Gauge Coaches on IRS Underframes	Indian Railways	Continental Modeller, Jan 00	Ken Walker
Broad	Old 4-Wheel Coach	GIPR	Indian Railway Study Group, Jul 91	
2'	Early coach, trolley, tea van, and open wagon	Darjeeling Himalayan Railway	Indian Railway Study Group, Jul 92	Ken Walker
Broad, Meter	Tourist Cars	Various, colonial era	Indian Railway Study Group, Oct 92	Hugh Hughes
2' 6"	Western Railway Narrow Gauge Coaches on IRS Underframes	Indian Railways	Indian Railway Study Group, Apr 93	Ken Walker
2' 6"	4-Wheel and Bogie Coaches, Brake Van	Morvi Railway	Indian Railway Study Group, Jul 93	Geoff Wilkins
Metre	Tourist Cars	SIR	Indian Railway Study Group, Jul 93	
2'	Covered Vans	Darjeeling Himalayan Railway	Continental Modeller, March 02	Ken Walker, D. Churchill
2'	Various Wagons	Darjeeling Himalayan Railway	Darjeeling Railway Wagons (book)	DHRS
2' 6"	Brake-3rd Coach	Central Provinces (GIPR)	Continental Modeller, Jan 96	Ken Walker
2'	4-wheel coach, 4-wheel brake van, 4-wheel covered van, 4-wheel open wagon	Matheran Railway	Darjeeling and Matheran 1969 - Steam on 2ft Lines	Kemuri Pro
2'	Bogie coaches, 4-wheel covered van, 4-wheel open wagon, 4-wheel flatcar, bogie covered van, bogie open wagon, bogie flat car	Darjeeling Himalayan Railway	Darjeeling and Matheran 1969 - Steam on 2ft Lines	Kemuri Pro
2' 6"	RA-6 Bogie Coach (1925)	Predecessor of Western Railway	Western Railway Narrow Gauge System	R.R. Bhandari
2'	4-wheel Coaches, 4-wheel open wagon, bogie salon interior plan	Darjeeling Himalayan Railway	Exotic Indian Mountain Railways	R.R. Bhandari
2' 6"	3rd class coach, 1st-3rd-luggage coach	Central Provinces (GIPR)	Indian Locomotives, Part 3 (Narrow Gauge)	Hugh Hughes

Gauge	Subject	Railway	Source	Author
2' 6"	1st-3rd composite coach	Tezpore-Balipara Railway	Indian Locomotives, Part 3 (Narrow Gauge)	Hugh Hughes
2'	3rd class coach, covered van	Howrah-Amta Light Railway	Indian Locomotives, Part 3 (Narrow Gauge)	Hugh Hughes
Broad	Early double-deck 3rd class coach	BBCIR	Railways of Asia and the Far East	OS Nock
Broad	Early double-deck 3rd class coach (same as above)	BBCIR	Railways of the Raj	Michael Satow and Ray Desmond

Abbreviations

The following table defines abbreviations used in this book.

Abbreviation	Description
ABR	Assam Bengal Railway
BBCIR	Bombay, Baroda and Central India Railway
BDR	Bengal-Dooars Railway
BNR	Bengal Nagpur Railway
BNWR	Bengal North Western Railway
DHR	Darjeeling Himalayan Railway
EBR	East Bengal Railway
EIR	East India Railway
GIPR	Great Indian Peninsula Railway
HMRS	Historic Model Railway Society
ICF	Integrated Coach Factory
IR	Indian Railways
IRCA	Indian Railways Conference Association
IRFCA	Indian Railways Fan Club (enthusiast's group)
IRS	Indian Railway Standards
ISR	Indian State Railways
KFR	Kalighat–Falta Railway
KSR	Kalka-Simla Railway
LHB	Linke-Hoffmann-Busch
MAN	Maschinenfabrik Augsburg-Nürnberg AG
MR	Madras Railway
MSMR	Madras and Southern Maharatta Railway
NSR	Nizam's State Railway
NWR	North Western Railway
ORR	Oudh and Rohilkhand Railway
SIR	South Indian Railway
UIC	Union Internationale des Chemins de Fer/ International Union of Railways

www.ingramcontent.com/pod-product-compliance
Lightning Source LLC
Chambersburg PA
CBHW041645120626

46547CB00017B/2621